STO

3-9-76

# BROADCAST NEWS
# HANDBOOK

Donald W. White Miles

A HUDSON GROUP BOOK

HOWARD W. SAMS & CO., INC.

INDIANAPOLIS · KANSAS CITY · NEW YORK

FIRST EDITION

FIRST PRINTING—1975

International Standard Book Number: 0-672-21183-1
Library of Congress Catalog Card Number: 75-2550

## Acknowledgments

Special thanks for ideas, inspirations, and various contributions to: Clark Andrews, Joe Barbarette, Bob Brady, J. Michael Brooks, Gorton Carruth, Phil Cutting, Walt Dibble, Steve Feica, Curt Hahn, Dr. Donald Hastings, Bob Kalomeer, Harold Kneller, Shelton Lewis, Bob Michaels, Cynthia Morani, Abe Najamy, Andrea Plukas, Dick Shermer, John Swope, and to countless others who helped out along the way.

Back Cover: *Courtesy of ABC Radio News*

*To Mini, Julie, and Rich*

# Preface

This book was written to help fill a gap. In recent years, studies have shown a rather large gap between the real world of broadcasting and the academic world of the classroom. Colleges have been blamed for turning out naive, idealistic graduates who want to be well paid for exercising all of their creativity and who often believe that they have most of the answers. One study done at the University of Michigan found that, out of 869 station managers surveyed, *about half* expresed an unfavorable attitude toward college students.*

This book should do more than just help you pass a course. Instead of giving you just "the answers," it will give you more than 750 *questions* to ask as you look for a broadcast news job, begin work in a newsroom, and start to cover stories. It should give you a sense of what effect personality hangups, equipment failures, poor planning, strained relationships, and other weaknesses may have in preventing good news coverage and in damaging careers, regardless of what degrees or other credentials you may hold.

Radio is used primarily as the model or "vehicle" for most of the text, and for the discussions, projects, and assignments in this book for several reasons:

(1) Radio is the most practical and economical from a teaching standpoint. Cassette tape recorders are easy to own and easy to use, and a school need not own video or film equipment in order to use this book for a beginning course in broadcast news. Individual instructors or schools may easily add whatever TV production techniques may fit their curriculum.

(2) Radio is the most convenient medium in which to learn as a beginner in broadcast news. The basic concepts and

---

*"The Tough World Out There in Radio Careers," **Broadcastng**, December 2, 1974, p. 28.

skills are not only easily taught, easily learned, and easily applied, but almost all of them are applicable in TV news, which is taught in subsequent courses at many schools.

(3) We are living in an age of not just all-news radio stations, but of all-news networks and audio services. Without even counting individual radio newsrooms, these networks feed news to more than 5000 affiliates throughout the United States, and a CBS survey recently found that 57% of American adults (61% if you count only those with incomes of over $15,000 per year) list *radio* as their primary source of news in the morning.*

Clearly this proliferation of radio-oriented facilities and services means that job opportunities for beginning broadcast journalists are far more abundant in radio. As the reader will notice in beginning the first chapter, this book is written as though the author were a News Director addressing a new employee. The purpose of this approach is not just to help the reader pass a certain course, but to serve as a handy guide on the job. It would not be surprising to find that a beginning broadcast news student who has read this book and who has completed a number of the assignments and projects will find himself more qualified to do the news than some of the relatively inexperienced and poorly trained individuals sometimes hired by stations in towns near a school where this book is being used in a course. For this reason, this book should be helpful in qualifying the student for a news job at a small market station even while still attending school.

If you are reading this book as a student, the author hopes you *will* take this book with you into the newsroom when you do get a job in broadcast news. The investigative projects at the ends of the chapters, the guidelines, the glossary and bibliography, and much of the other material were written specifically as a handy reference guide and belong right there, at your fingertips, on the desk of a broadcast newsroom.

Good luck!

Donald W. Miles

---

* "Radio Credo for the 70's: Journalism Spoken Here," **Broadcasting**, January 6, 1975, p. 27. (The 61% figure for higher incomes most likely accounts for greater automobile ownership and therefore more listening on car radios.)

# Contents

# Chapter 1

# The Basics

Welcome to our news department! We are going to assume that you are just "breaking in" for your first day on the job. (Maybe you are!) The following are some of the things your News Director would like to say to you if he had the time. We will outline a few of the obligations and warn you of a few of the pitfalls you may encounter.

## BEING FIRST IS NOT AS IMPORTANT AS BEING RIGHT

That title is worth memorizing! It is a fairly profound statement, and there is hardly a veteran newscaster who cannot tell you of several instances where he has been "burned" by the repercussions from a story that turned out to be less than the whole truth. What often appears to be the truth as you sit down to the typewriter becomes warped into falsehood by the time it is delivered in a newscast, and much of the blame for this can be placed on *false assumptions.* Here are some typical situations to watch out for:

▶ A person calls and says that a fire is "out of control" or that it is "very large." Do not believe it. First of all, check with the fire department and get *them* to admit there is a fire.

Photo by Chip Hires.

Even then, you do not say how big it is until you have an official statement from a fire official or other qualified person at the scene. Even qualified observers will differ, depending on the situation. Another newsman or perhaps a policeman may be able to tell you that a fire is large, but an excited neighbor or bystander is no judge of such matters. Not even your policeman, newsman, or other qualified judge of size has the credentials to tell you whether or not the blaze is under control—*only* fire officials themselves should make such a statement.

The fire officials, on the other hand, are not qualified to comment on whether someone injured at the scene is in "good," "fair," or "critical" condition. That comes from authorized hospital sources, who will be discussed later. The point is: always be sure you are quoting a *qualified* and *authorized* individual.

The person who called the station may be a good friend who is trying to be helpful. He may be sincere, but that does not make him an expert. Always thank your caller for the information (he could be right) but never use it on the air without checking its accuracy. Your caller is not responsible for how accurate the story is, but *you* are!

► A caller claims there is a riot, demonstration, or disturbance going on. You say *nothing* on the air about this! First of all, to tell your audience that there is a riot in progress and to give the location is just like yelling "Charge!" to every troublemaker for miles around. In fact, it may have been just such an agitator who called, hoping to use you as his starting gun. Check with police to see if there is any truth to the claim. If there is, contact the News Director and other station authorities to check on policies for this kind of situation.

Since the U.S. went through some big-city riots a number of years ago, radio and TV stations have learned how to handle incidents of this type, whether or not the events themselves actually turn into large-scale disorders. In fact, the stations tend now to avoid reporting trivial matters that have the surface appearance of being something larger. They have found that such reports only tend to "fan the flames" and to heighten public tension and fear. If you are new at this kind of work, you will find that most stations will want to send someone with more

experience than you have to the scene. Do not take it personally. If the events turn out to be more than trivial, a station's
policy will most likely be to say nothing on the air while police
get into the troubled area and try to control it, and to weigh
every word carefully even after trained newsmen have arrived
to cover it. More on this is given in Chapter 3, on civil disorders.

▶ The lady you have called at the hospital tells you that the
accident or shooting victim died. Get *her* name as well as that
of the victim. Repeat to her the victim's name and the fact that
he died, and say that you are just making sure that you have it
correct. Imagine the plight of a family hearing the name of a
relative mistakenly listed as "dead" over the air. In any case,
always get the name of the hospital spokesman. There have
been people at hospitals who tell us that a dead person is in
"good" condition, and somehow these people tend to disappear when the radio station calls back to account for the error.
No one at the hospital is likely to admit ever having given out
such information. To know more about what you are permitted
to ask at hospitals and what kind of information is restricted,
read Chapter 6, on relationships with hospitals.

▶ A good friend gives you a "tip" and asks you not to use
his name in the story and not to tell anyone he told you. This
clearly leaves *you* holding the bag if the story is not true. The
"tip" may be useful for purposes of making an inquiry so you
can find out if the story is actually true, but if you cannot get
someone to stand up for it *by name,* do not use it on the air.
Stories that start with phrases like "informed sources tell us
that . . ." are only for top-flight, seasoned newscasters. Beginners who use them are skating on very thin ice. Remember that
if you promise somebody you will not use his name, and then
you put the story on the air, *you* are 100-percent responsible
for its being true. This type of story comes up most often in
political circles or where "office politics" situations exist. You
will find this kind of story within the ranks of police, fire, and
city hall employees locally, but it is not entirely missing in other
walks of life. Thank your informant so he does not go away
angry, but keep the story off the air until you have checked
it thoroughly and have a *source you can name.*

▶ The police radio crackles with word that something has just happened—anything from a bank holdup to a riot, rape, plane crash, or hotel fire. Never put anything on the air based on what you hear from a police monitor. In the first place, it is against the rules of the FCC (Federal Communications Commission). That information is *not* for public distribution. It could very well be a false alarm, and it could be that police themselves are only checking the *possibility* that such an incident may have occurred. If you intend to use the information for a story, you must call the police and not only "verify" it but get them to "release" it for broadcast. Be sure to give the cruiser assigned to the job enough time to get to the scene and report back to headquarters. Nothing irritates a desk sergeant more than to have a "cub reporter" phone for details when the squad car itself has not even arrived at the scene. More on this is given in Chapter 5, "The Police Beat and the Courtroom."

▶ An authoritative or perhaps sincere voice (male or female) tells you on the phone that a school or industrial plant is closed due to the weather. If you have not been briefed by the station management on procedures for such calls and how to verify them, tell the person you will make a note of it but that you are not authorized to have it broadcast until someone who *can* verify it is able to do so. Most stations use a list of authorized callers, a code or password, an unlisted phone number, or even a combination of these things to screen out hoax calls. If another station has a closing announcement that you do not have, do not steal it. The writer has seen hoax callers get free publicity on two stations for just one phone call this way. If you expect to handle such calls, ask the News Director and other station authorities how it is done.

## DON'T PANIC THE TROOPS

News should always be broadcast in a manner that will avoid panic and unnecessary alarm. When you go on the air with something that is going to cause concern, you are taking on more than just the normal responsibility. In most cases, such stories will have further developments that will affect the emotions of your listeners just as much as the original version. Because of this, you have some "follow-up" obligations which *must* be taken care of.

▶ Interrupting a program causes excitement to begin with. Never do it as a promotional stunt to gather listeners for your next newscast, nor as proof that you are faster than the competition. As former White House Press Secretary and ABC News Vice President James Haggerty once told a broadcasters' gathering, "Bulletinitis is the evil of the day." Haggerty said that interrupting programs with sensational-sounding hodgepodge comes close to the story of the boy who cried "wolf," and he hinted that the public and the FCC were getting tired of it. Since his comments several years ago, most stations have taken a serious second look at the matter of bulletins and the trend has been to avoid interrupting programs. (If you are not sure what the policy is at your station before you start to work, be sure to ask.)

▶ The fact that the wire service (usually AP or UPI) rings bells on the teletypewriter machine and labels something a "bulletin" does not automatically make it a bulletin at every station that receives it. For example, the censure of Senator Dodd in the U.S. Senate some years ago might have been a bulletin in his home state of Connecticut, but not necessarily in Idaho, where it could easily wait for the next newscast. Likewise, a bank holdup may be a bulletin for the stations near the town where it happens, but not 'way across the state where listeners from the holdup area rarely travel (unless somebody was shot or a very large amount of money was taken.)

▶ If you have called out the engines, you had better call them back when the fire is over. A small station, with just one newsman, broadcast word of a "major fire." The newsman went to the scene, leaving his fellow employees with all the phone calls asking about the fire. Several newscasts went by, with disc jockeys simply "ripping and reading" from the wire service machine. The other employees at the station knew nothing about the fire, the newsman was at the scene without a dime for a phone booth and no other way of getting word back to the station, and some alarmed listeners wondered what was going on. As it turned out, nothing of any consequence had really happened! Someone had tripped an alarm at a local industrial plant. There was no fire. The fault for such unnecessary public alarm was with both the newsman and the people at the station. The latter made no attempt to keep the public informed in the interim, or at least to assure listeners that they were trying to get more information. The newsman had already violated rule No. 1 of this chapter by falsely assuming there was a fire and saying so on the air without checking it.

▶ Know what the procedures are for disasters and emergencies at your station. The writer has known of several stations where there is no "disaster plan" at all. Invariably, confusion reigns in the wake of a local train derailment or plane crash. Employees of the station who do not normally handle news will tend to react in any number of ways that can be particularly damaging. Some will not want anything to do with it, especially if it is not during their regular working hours. Others will try to play the "hero" role and race to the scene, annoy police and firemen, and give unqualified "panic" reports that will distort the whole picture. You may find that those who happen to be on duty at the station as disc jockeys, engineers, etc., when the incident occurs will be the first to tell you "It's not my job." You may find yourself acting as a "one-man band," and the boss will expect you to be on the air, on the phone, at the crash scene, and at the hospital all at once. Frequently, management has given no thought to who is going to relieve you after umpteen hours or how you are going to be paid for all this. If you do not have a clear policy in mind, be sure to read Chapter 7, "Searches, Rescues, and Disasters," and then ask both your News Director and Station Manager the questions about such emergencies in Chapter 11 on personnel policies so they spell it out for you *before* it comes up.

▶ An individual brings a news release or statement to the station and asks you: "When will it be broadcast?" *Never* make commitment under such circumstances to broadcast anything in advance. The person may be a politician, an extremist, a PR man putting on a disguised commercial pitch for his company, or an inciter or agitator of any number of breeds. He may be interested in pushing just *one* side of an issue or controversy or in starting some kind of trouble. Typical subjects range from defeat or passage of a school bond issue or city budget to busing, sex education, fluoridation of public water supplies, and the like. Frequently the topic centers on the Board of Education or City Hall, and often it involves an attack on some public official or other prominent person. Any responsible individual can wait until the News Director or someone in the station management rules on the "news worthiness" of the statement. If he seems a bit too anxious to get his statement on the air, that is your danger signal right there. There is probably something wrong with it. Take it, thank him, and explain that you have no authority to put it on the air. (Even if you normally *do* have such authority, this is a legitimate situation in which you can hold this person off until you get some backing from your boss.) More on this is dealt with in Chapter 4, "Fairness To Minorities," and in Chapter 8, "Government and Politics."

## LET SLEEPING DOGS LIE

There are some parties that react more sensitively than others when they hear the news. Regardless of how people may react by calling the newscaster, writing to the management, spreading gossip about your allegedly poor reporting, or by not doing anything at all, it is the newsman's obligation to respect the dignity, the privacy, and the well-being of every person and group with whom the news deals. Here are just a few examples of how to "play it safely" and to take care of this obligation.

▶ Unless you have the Fire Chief *on tape* saying it was an oil burner that started the fire, never blame a fire on an oil burner. Do not take the word of neighbors or spectators, and do not even make such a conclusion by yourself. Call it "defective heating equipment" if such is the case, without saying *what kind* of heating equipment it was. If you do not, the oil-heat people may have their lawyers bother you for days, even if you were right! If a fire is caused by gas or a gas stove, the bottled-gas people and the piped-gas people will approach you from both sides to try to get the blame pinned on their competitors. This is another case where it is better to leave details out, because the trouble they can give you is not worth it.

▶ Husband-and-wife squabbles are touchy, and unless someone really gets shot or knifed, avoid reporting them. Their emotions are already out of balance, and what they might view as an uncomplimentary news story could touch off threats of suing the station, punching the newsman in the mouth, or almost anything from an enraged spouse. On stories involving teenagers in trouble, always write it as though the kid's father were listening. In fact, do not say the youngster is "in trouble" or "ran afoul of the law" or "got caught," because right there you are violating his constitutional right to be presumed innocent until proved guilty. Play it *very* straight, with no clever lines or adjectives that imply anything more than police have told you.

▶ "Police brutality" is a sensitive term. Unless those are the actual words used and you can quote the person who said them, do not use such a term. There have been cases where an attorney files for damages against the city and describes injuries to his client, linking the injuries to an arrest or some kind of police activity, but *not* saying "police brutality." The lawyer, you see, does not want the policeman fired. He just wants money for his client. If you rewrite the story and insert the term "police brutality" on your own to describe the situation, you are implying departmental charges against the policeman—and that is something else.

▶ Bomb scares should be *left off the air* entirely. It is okay to turn the matter over to police and to authorities in the building involved, but going on the air does not help. For one thing, the people who like to phone these things in anonymously are weirdos who get their kicks out of seeing everybody scramble, and if you broadcast one such story you will bring a whole bunch of others out of the woodwork for the next few days. Stations in most large cities will tell you that even after a legitimate story about an actual bomb explosion, they have to endure a rash of these "kook calls" for days. For another thing, you are frightening friends and relatives of those who may be in the building where the alleged "bomb" is said to be hidden, and both your station and the building concerned are likely to be swamped with phone calls wondering if everything is all right. Even a real bomb of the size discussed here is not going to topple a whole building, and if authorities feel they can contain the search to one floor or a few rooms they would not appreciate a stampede of evacuation touched off by a story on the radio.

▶ Other stories best left off the air—*"fender-benders,"* or accidents where no one was seriously injured. Beginners and small-town radio stations like to give complete details about the drivers and all the passengers involved, including middle names, ages, complete street addresses, etc., along with the names of policemen investigating, how many fence posts were knocked down, make, color, and year of the car, how long the skid marks were, etc., and then wind up by saying there were no injuries! Leave this to the newspapers. *City Hall trivia*— beginners and small stations are also famous for telling about the mayor's cold, how many feet of 2-inch hose were unravelled at the rubbish fire by Volunteer Engine Company No. 6 and Truck Company No. 10. Forget these. *Minor fires*—just like minor accidents, unless there is an unusual angle (arson, death, heroic rescue, etc.), do not use them.

▶ Certain details and adjectives are best omitted from any story: Morbid, sensational, or alarming details not essential to the factual report should be left out. If the apartment was ransacked and the apparent motive was robbery, there is no need to comment that the woman victim was not sexually assaulted; just do not bring it up. If the wire service does, cross it out. Never describe an accident as "spectacular," because in recent years the word has come to bear the connotation of "exciting wonder and admiration." The word is inappropriate.

▶ Civil disorders are a whole arena unto themselves since the Los Angeles "Watts" riots of 1963, the Detroit rioting of 1967, and a host of others during the past decade or so. It has already been mentioned what to do about calls claiming such activity earlier in this chapter, and we will be dealing with how to write such stories and what follow-up procedures to use in detail later on in this book. Also, be sure to read Chapter 4 on the question of fairness to minority groups in the news and how to deal with them whether the news is violent or not.

▶ In *any* case, you are always reporting what *someone else* said when it comes to accusations or charges of any kind. You never say that someone has committed a crime; the *police* do. Your story had better read that way or you will be in trouble. It is *never:* "John Jones held up a grocery store . . ." It is *always:* "John Jones is *suspected* of . . ." or *"Police say* John Jones was apprehended . . ." or *"According to police,"* . . . or *"Police have charged* John Jones with . . ." One way or the other, it has to be the police who are making the accusation, not the radio station. Even words like "allegedly" or "reportedly" skillfully worked into the story will do the job as long as the radio station never comes out pointing the finger of guilt. If the suspect is later found innocent and you have left out the part about the police, you can be sued for defamation of character and a few other things.

## KNOW WHAT YOU'RE TALKING ABOUT

Are you from out of town? Nothing will tell your audience that fact faster than hearing you trip over unusual local names of prominent people and familiar locations. Ask your fellow employees at the station what the most common ones are before you speak them on the air. Also, ask what the station's "area policy" is. It depends on their signal strength, the size of city they are in, what the competitors are doing, etc. Do not go by the wire service to decide which stories are important in your area. Remember that wire services must cover a much wider area. Congressmen in other districts announcing federal grants to cities in some faraway part of the state will be of no interest to your local listeners. The same goes for accidents, holdups, fires, and other stories in distant cities.

How is your vocabulary? Do you stumble over three and four syllable words and the names of certain people and places? If so, that is a problem which will need constant attention. This is covered in more detail in Chapter 9, "The Style of the Newscast," but for now you can read the newspapers, magazines, and wire services every day (not just when you are on duty in the newsroom) and pin down those tough words on your own time before they pin you down on the air!

# A CODE OF ETHICS

The Radio Television News Directors Association (RTNDA) adopted the following code nationally in 1966 (revised in 1973) and resolved to encourage *all* newsmen to observe it, whether members or not.

The members of the Radio Television News Directors Association agree that their prime responsibility as journalists, and that of the broadcasting industry as the collective sponsor of news broadcasting, is to provide to the public they serve a news service as accurate, full and prompt as human integrity and devotion can devise. To that end, they declare their acceptance of the standards of practice here set forth, and their solemn intent to honor them to the limits of their ability.

### Article One
The primary purpose of broadcast journalists—to inform the public of events of importance and appropriate interest in a manner that is accurate and comprehensive—shall override all other purposes.

### Article Two
Broadcast news presentations shall be designed not only to offer timely and accurate information, but also to present it in the light of relevant circumstances that give it meaning and perspective. (This standard means that news reports, when clarity demands it, will be laid against pertinent factual background; that factors such as race, creed, nationality or prior status will be reported only when they are relevant; that comment or subjective content will be properly identified; and that errors in fact will be promptly acknowledged and corrected.)

### Article Three
Broadcast journalists shall seek to select material solely on their evaluation of its merits as news. (This standard means that news shall be selected on the criteria of significance, community and regional relevance, appropriate human interest, and service to defined audiences. It excludes sensationalism or misleading emphasis in any form, and subservience to external or "interested" efforts to influence news selection and presentation, whether from within the

broadcasting industry or from without. It requires that such terms as "bulletin" and "flash" be used only when the character of the news justifies them; that bombastic or misleading descriptions of newsroom facilities and personnel be rejected, along with undue use of sound and visual effects; and that promotional or publicity material be sharply scrutinized before use and identified by source or otherwise when broadcast.)

### Article Four

Broadcast journalists shall at all times display humane respect for the dignity, privacy, and the well-being of persons with whom the news deals.

### Article Five

Broadcast journalists shall govern their personal lives and such non-professional associations as may impinge on their professional activities in a manner that will protect them from conflict of interest, real or apparent.

### Article Six

Broadcast journalists shall seek actively to present all the news the knowledge of which would serve the public interest, no matter what selfish, uninformed, or corrupt efforts to color it, withhold it or prevent its presentation. They shall make constant effort to open doors closed to the reporting of public proceedings with tools appropriate to broadcasting (including cameras and recorders), consistent with the public interest. They acknowledge the journalist's ethic of protection of confidential information and sources, and urge unswerving observation of it except in instances in which it would clearly and unmistakably defy the public interest.

### Article Seven

Broadcast journalists recognize the responsibility borne by broadcasting for informed analysis, comment and editorial opinion on public events and issues. They accept the obligation of broadcasters for the presentation of such matters by individuals whose competence, experience, and judgment qualify them for it.

### Article Eight

In court, broadcast journalists shall conduct themselves with dignity whether the court is in or out of session. Where court facilities are inadequate, pool broadcasts should be arranged.

### Article Nine

In reporting matters that are or may be litigated, the journalists shall avoid practices which would tend to interfere with the right of an individual to a fair trial.

### Article Ten

Broadcast journalists shall not misrepresent the source of any broadcast news material.

**Article Eleven**

Broadcast journalists shall actively censure and seek to prevent violations of these standards, and shall actively encourage their observance by all journalists, whether of the Radio Television News Directors Association or not.

# IN-CLASS AND HOMEWORK ASSIGNMENTS

1. Pretend that you are on the newsroom phone with Charlie Fowler, the guy who drops by with coffee for the gang at the station every now and then on his way to work:

   "I'm over here at Al's Service Station, and you should see this fire. I thought I'd call you guys. It's a big one. Looks like it's out of control."

   "Gee, thanks, Charlie."

   "Oh, you're welcome. Anytime I see a story—you know me. I'll always give you a call. They've got three engines here now and I think they just issued a general alarm. One of the guys is hurt pretty bad. His name is Sam Gerard. He's a mechanic here. He looks in rough shape. Looks like the flames caught on to his clothing, you know? I'd say he's in critical condition. They saw some kids running from the place just before the thing started. Jim Hasbro—he's a friend of mine from the fire department—he says he thinks they threw something in the bays where the guy was working on a fuel pump and it blew up."

   a. What are some things you want to ask Charlie?

   b. Who else must you call, and what must you ask them?

   c. Assuming that everyone you have just named in your answer to the previous question confirms that Charlie's statements are true, write a story about the fire that will last no more than 30 seconds of reading time, as though you were going to use it on the next newscast. (You may add names and titles of the "officials" you contacted to round the story out a bit, if needed.)

2. How do some of the smaller local stations check their sources for news stories? Have any of them caused you to doubt their accuracy? (Tell how or why.)

3. Evaluate the performance of the stations in your area with regard to the things you have learned in this chapter. Do they seem to skate on thin ice when it comes to "sensitive"

news stories? Do any of them make assertions for which they might be held liable for not having quoted authoritative sources?

4. Do you think the larger stations and networks are less vulnerable to the errors mentioned in this chapter? Tell why or why not, comparing larger stations with smaller ones and giving the advantages and disadvantages you think each may have.

Photo by Chip Hires.

# Chapter 2

# On the Scene

If you have ever read the ads in *Broadcasting* magazine and other trade journals where people want to hire newsmen, you have most likely seen the comments to the effect that they do not want someone who just sits at a desk. Granted, there are network and large-station operations where people are hired to just write and edit, but most of these people have had years of on-the-scene experience before getting such jobs. Generally, the newsman who can *bring back* good stories just as well as he can read or write them will advance much faster in the industry.

## STRINGER ASSIGNMENTS

There are reporters who can go to the scene, size up the story, and phone back a few advance reports while they cover the event. While those reports are put on the air at the station, the reporters at the scene are busy picking up the actual sounds of the story in progress, asking questions, taking notes, and getting reactions. They can feed great eyewitness reports to the station from the nearest phone booth, or they can come back to the station and put together prize-winning actualities, concise stories, "wraparounds," and a host of goodies that can keep the newsroom running for hours.

There are also people who can disappear for hours and come back empty-handed. Sometimes the whole day slips by and one cannot tell whether they are dead or alive. They never phone the station, and major newscasts go by without a word on the progress or the outcome of the event they are supposed to be covering. What they *do* come back with, more often than not, is an excuse:

"The batteries went dead."

"I couldn't find the place."

"The telephone speaker caps wouldn't unscrew in the phone booths."

"I didn't have a dime for the phone."

"I got there too late and it was already breaking up."

"There wasn't much going on, so I decided it wouldn't be worth filing a story.

"Nobody wanted to talk about it."

. . . and a complete repertoire of alibis that you would never believe were given if you had not heard them!

In fact, the writer's station once tried sending two reporters to cover the same event. It was a parade. One fellow went to where the bands would be stepping off and got interviews, background sounds, narration over background, etc. He stopped by the studio and briefed us on what was on the first tape, then took a fresh tape and went along the line of march doing sidewalk interviews with spectators, getting more band sounds, and gathering enough material to keep an all-news station going for 24 hours! The other fellow stood somewhere along the line of march and watched the whole parade. At one point, he turned on his tape recorder and did a "voicer" report with some rum-ta-tumming in the background and a hefty grammatical error right in the middle of his *one* report. If you were the News Director, who would you send to cover a story the next time? You know!

If you are about to go out and cover a story outside the station—anything from a parade to a press conference—here is a checklist to help you to assure yourself of not coming back empty-handed:

## Know the Station's Phone Number

You may laugh, but there has been coverage fall-through for precisely this reason more than once. If there is an unlisted number for the newsroom and/or control room, be sure you jot this down as well as the main switchboard number. Later, you may find the main number tied up, or that the office may be closed for the night or the weekend, just when you want to phone in your story. Also, make sure that the people who will be answering the phone will know who you are if you plan to call collect.

## Know Where You Are Going

Get a map of the town or towns where you will be travelling. If it is a city of any significant size, the newspaper stands should have maps for reasonable prices. In most towns, some office at City Hall has a municipal map that is usually free or sold for a nominal price. Mass transit systems usually have maps available at their change booths or depots, and time-tables are usually free at these places. Do not try to get on something like the New York City subway system without a map if you do not really know your way around. "Faking it" like that can cost both you and the station some valuable time and some lost opportunities.

## Know the Layout at the Scene

If you have never been to where the event is taking place, ask someone who *has.* Determine whether you need an extension cord or a patch cord; whether or not you can use plug-in equipment at all, as opposed to batteries; whether you will need some dimes for phone calls; whether or not the speaker caps on the telephones will unscrew for alligator-clip or induction-coil feeds; whether there are regular press facilities or whether you will have to be jostled around with the crowd and play it by ear; and whether there are any friendly contacts in the neighborhood whose offices or stores you might be able to use for filing your story with the station, especially if it loks like you might have to compete with other newsmen for the use of the telephones.

## Check All Equipment Before Leaving

Plug in all the things that have to be plugged in, and count to "ten" on that tape. Then play it back. Has the tape been bulk-erased so that it will play back on a single-track, double-track, or any other kind of tape recorder? If you are recording at a certain speed at the scene, does the studio tape recorder have the same speed for playback purposes? Do you have the right patch cords? Do you have spare tape, splicing materials, and take-up reels? If you can "tap" their P.A. system when you get there, do you need any special connectors or other equipment to do that? If it is a portable tape recorder, do you have fresh batteries inside and some spare batteries "just in case"? If cassettes are involved, is the one in the machine bulk-erased and rewound to the beginning, and do you have some spares? (In some stations, a union contract may require that an engineer do all or part of the equipment handling. If you want to be sure that everything goes smoothly, get in touch with the engineers who are setting this equipment up and those who will be going to the scene with you, and go over the checklist with them.)

## Know Who Will Be Receiving Your Material

In smaller stations, it may just be the newsman on duty back at the station. In larger and more complicated operations, you may be dealing with assignment editors, producers, engineers, and a host of people who are involved in processing your story. In these larger operations, just filing your story with an engineer and not telling the right person in the newsroom about it can mean that your story will just sit there and die on the engineer's tape recorder. (The writer has actually had union engineers tell him with a straight face that it is only their job to *record* the stories filed by reporters in the field, not to advise the newsroom that such stories have arrived!) These larger stations where all the jobs are highly specialized frequently have problems with the right hand not knowing what the left hand is doing. Even in a smaller station, find out what happens when the *one* newsman on duty suddenly is not there. Do you give your story to a disc jockey, an engineer, or to whom?

Have these people been advised that you might be calling with some material, and are their tape recorders ready to receive it —or will you have to spend a while in the phone booth while they play records with one hand and try to find some tape and take-up reels with the other?

## Keep In Touch

There is nothing more frustrating back in the newsroom than to have a big story break and not be able to locate your man in the field to get him to the scene. When you are out on the road, always remember that the fellow back at the studio may have come upon a story that would be better than the one you had planned to cover. You and he will have to work out whether it would be better to switch to "his" story or whether you might risk losing both stories in the process.

## Know When NOT to Call

Some otherwise very excellent newsmen manage to make themselves very unpopular by placing their calls just when everybody is likely to be "tied up" at the station. Somehow, these "superstars" always seem to insist that the people at the studio drop what they are doing immediately to receive the story. Be sure to check the station's programming schedule and see where the sensitive spots are. (Obviously, during or just before a newscast would be one of the worst times to call if there is only one newsman back at the station.) Engineers are likely to have some transmitter duties that must legally come before any recording of news stories. Get to know what routines may be going on back at the station during a typical broadcast day. By being careful not to interfere with them, you will appear to be more considerate. This way, you are more likely to get that extra ounce of cooperation when a big story or an emergency does arise.

## Have Some Alternatives Ready

The chances for human or mechanical error are great in situations like this. Your tape recorder or the one at the station could break down, or something could go haywire with the people or facilities at the scene of the story. The first thing you should have ready is a very short story in your own words, ready to *dictate* to someone who will write it if they are unable to record it over the phone. Do not start by doing all the elaborate things first (interviews, actualities, etc.) and then finding when you call that for some reason (at your end or at the station's end) that you cannot file any of it. Get the *story* first; then embellish it. At least this way when you call, you can be assured of getting *something* onto the air.

### Know What Is Wanted

Bob Brady, who does some field work for New York City's WOR, tells about how he once covered a parade. He managed to get by police and climb into the reviewing stand, gathering interviews from the governor, the mayor, an archbishop, two senators, and an astronaut. He took his prize to a phone booth, called up the newsroom, and the producer yawned and said, "Naw, I don't want any of that. Just gimme some of the band music." Be sure to check with those who will be putting the story on the air about the kind of material they will be looking for.

## GETTING THE STORY TOGETHER

All this time was spent getting you to the scene, without a word about what goes into your story. This is because the world's best stories are of no value at all if you cannot *deliver* them! It is like owning the world's most prestigious newspaper with a staff of Pulitzer-Prize winning writers and suddenly encountering a printers' or delivery truckers' strike. Where does it all leave you?

Now that you have arrived with all your equipment in order and there is a reasonable chance that you will be able to file something with the station that is likely to get on the air, you must know what you will put into your on-the-scene coverage.

### Know Your Topic

Get all the "advance" material that has been written about the story you are about to cover. Look through those boxes of stories or stacks of newscasts in the newsroom. Look through the file drawers for past coverage. Check the newspaper and the wire-service stories. Look in the "futures" file or the day-book to see if there are any brochures, advance releases, or other material that might help you. Get the names straight. Line up the agenda, the pro-and-con issues if any, and some of the questions you plan to ask.

## Stake Out the Basic Story

As soon as you arrive—before the event gets underway—have that little report ready that was mentioned in the previous checklist (where it says "Have Some Alternatives Ready.") Confirm for the newsroom that you have arrived and that the event will (or will not) take place as scheduled. Deliver that little advance story with the "Five W's" somewhere in it (who, what, when, where, why). Make it short enough to dictate if necessary, and word it as though everything is still "planned" but not yet happening. Do not "fake" anything in your story about the progress or outcome of the event, because if things do not happen as you said they would, you have painted yourself into a very embarrassing corner!

## Pull Out All the Stops

Now that you have come this far, make the trip worthwhile. There is nothing more disappointing than to see a reporter who asks the Mayor just one question and then shuts his tape recorder off with a meek "thank you," or one who files a bland voice-only story that could have been done on a typewriter back at the station without going to the scene at all. Here are some of the many things that you can do with a story that will give the newsroom enough material for several newscasts without having it sound the same every hour. Some of them apply best to news conferences where there is a podium and news releases are handed out, while others apply better to parades, rallies, and demonstrations. See how many of these techniques you can use in preparing your story:

*Voice Report*—without actualities, based on notes you have taken, phrases you have marked out in someone's speech or release, and your up-to-the-minute eyewitness observation, delivered in your voice as a correspondent.

*Actualities*—straight tape-recorded excerpts from the speech or whatever is taking place, which can be inserted into a story back at the station.

*Wraparound*—your voice report with an actuality inserted into it. This is something you will have to learn how to do with a portable tape recorder before you try it at the scene of a story, but it is a very effective technique. It leaves little or no work to be done back at the station other than to introduce it and play it back. You have done all the "writing" and editing for the fellows in the newsroom, and the chances of their using this on the air are usually much greater than with other versions.

*Interview*—between yourself and one of the:

(1) leaders involved, especially the principal speaker,

(2) members of the audience, or supporters of the program,

(3) opponents,

(4) bystanders or neutral observers.

(There is a difference between just plain bystanders and neutral observers. Neutral observers may range from a referee to another newsman, as long as they have some knowledge of what is going on. Their comments may add interpretive insight to your story. Bystanders, on the other hand, may sometimes be the *least* valuable sources for an interview. Walking up to one of them and asking things like "how do you feel about this" or "what do you think of all this" will get you a worthless answer much of the time. Occasionally, by accident, you may get one who is very colorful, but you are better off looking for someone who is actually participating pro or con and who has something to say.)

*Raw Sound*—a good 60 seconds of something like band music, demonstrators chanting, crowds cheering, etc. Make sure it is long enough to use as a background under some story they will be reading back at the station, and be sure to tell both the newsman and the person recording it that this is what you are sending it for. If you do not identify it, an engineer may just think you were checking microphone levels or something and will just throw it away.

*Narration*—several short versions (or "cuts") of your own ad-lib interpretation in the foreground, with the raw sound of the event (music, chanting, cheering, etc.) in the background. Be sure to *number* these cuts as you make them, so that you can tell the newsmen and engineers back at the station which ones not to use because of errors or false starts.

Here are some additional hints about on-the-scene narrations:

▶ Stand at various distances from the sound that you will be using as a background. Stop and play some of the material back to yourself to see if you are far enough away from the background sound or if it is drowning you out. If the event you are covering is moving too fast to allow this, mention that fact between the cuts so the people at the station can hunt through the tape for the cuts which have the best sound levels.

▶ Make one or two of your cuts deliberately brief (under 30 seconds) so that if some of the other cuts turn out to be too long-winded, the newsman will at least have a choice of using these as opposed to throwing them all away.

▶ Make one or two of your cuts deliberately *past tense* so that the station may use them as much as five or six hours later without their sounding too "dated." If you are filing this material late at night, make one or two cuts that are worded for broadcast the next day.

## SOME DAMAGING FLAWS

You may think that by following all the steps outlined so far you would be able to get some pretty good on-the-scene reports back to the station, right? Well, almost, but there are some "don'ts" to watch out for:

**Don't "Fake" It If You Don't Know the Topic**

A great many beginners stumble right at this point. They are so concerned with how to turn on the tape recorder that they have no specific questions in mind as they arrive at the scene. Instead, they just start asking inappropriate questions right off the tops of their heads. One asked a U.S. Congressman what he would do about state taxes and received the reply that in Washington the Congressmen handle *federal,* not state, taxes. Another asked Igor Sikorsky, father of the helicopter, how many more helicopters the American military forces might buy during the Southeast Asian War. (Mr. Sikorsky was in his late 70's at the time, had only come out of retirement to attend the event as an honorary guest, and probably could not have cared less.)

If your knowledge of the topic is skimpy, it is safer to stick to the "Five W's" (who, what, where, where, why) and run them through a past-present-future pattern of questioning:

*Past:*      What led to this? How did it start?
            Who started it? Why was it started?

*Present:*   Who is in charge of the project? What is your role, your reaction, your position in this matter? How do you plan to bring this about? Tell us what is happening right now. (The last one is the easiest!)

*Future:*    What is the next step? Who will take it? What reactions do you expect? Will there be any opposition? What problems do you hope to solve? What outcome do you expect?

**Don't Make a "Documentary" Unless You Were Asked for One**

Think of the newscasts for which your material may be used back at the station. How long are they? How long should tapes on these newscasts be? Several versions of your story are fine, as was pointed out in the previous checklist on techniques, because it gives the fellows in the newsroom a wide selection to choose from and allows them to use different versions of the story on successive newscasts. One great big "term paper," though, is strictly out. Listen to the tapes used on the networks: They are rarely more than 40 seconds long, and sometimes run as short as 10 seconds. Whole stories with introductions and taped portions combined rarely run as long as 50 seconds.

## Don't Just "Dump" Reels of Unedited Audio on the Desk

On the early morning news shift at one station, the writer would occasionally find a reel of tape on the desk as he arrived, with a note attached to it saying that this was "last night's meeting." It was a whole reel of anonymous voices, and no scorecard from which to tell the players. The *least* you can do if you are just recording a whole meeting is to leave a list of the speakers and the order in which they appeared, plus some indication of where the high points were. If you were not assigned to do any interviewing, writing, or editing, at least this "table of contents" will help those who will have to attempt to break the reel down for newscasts.

## Don't Use a Chronological Approach

If you are doing a story about a meeting or similar event, leave chronological order for the recording secretary. Back at the newsroom, they will not care who called it to order, gave the invocation, or seconded the motions. Leave out routine committee reports and motions, and pick out only the *major* actions and statements that are of interest to the general public. (For example, what will the newspaper run as a headline: that the school board *met* last night, or that they plan to raise taxes?) If several major items were acted on during the meeting, make two or three short stories, with each version emphasizing a different item rather than one big, rambling, detailed account that will bore the audience for one newscast and leave your newscaster with no alternate version of the story for his *next* newscast.

## Don't Try too Hard for Clever Lines and Flowery Phrases

The fellows back in the newsroom can embellish the story as needed while making up the newscasts. To do it at the scene might not fit the mood they need to put your story next to others. If you are looking for creativity, let the sounds and the people in the story do it for you. *These* are the ingredients of a story you can get on tape at the scene, while the people back in the newsroom cannot.

## Don't File too Many Items Without Some Kind of Index

When the fellows in the newsroom get quite busy, they are not listening to everything you are sending in. If there is no one on duty in the newsroom and you have filed your stories with a disc jockey or an engineer, the next newsman will probably just get a reel of tape with a note saying that you phoned it in. You may have gone to a lot of trouble to gather all this material, but the newsman does not have time to listen to the whole thing, so it just "dies" there on the desk. The first thing you should do, then, as you call the station with a number of items and they turn on their tape recorder for you, is to address yourself to the newsman on duty and give him a list of what is going to follow on the tape. This list, in the growing industry of audio services to radio stations, is called a "billboard." It helps a busy newsman who is "on the desk" to select the items

Photo by George Kochaniec, Jr.

he needs for his next newscast without having to sit and listen to the whole tape. It could make the difference between whether your work gets on the air or not. In fact, besides telling whether each item is a voice report, an actuality, a "wrap-around," or whatever, it would help tremendously if you had some kind of watch with you and could *time* each report. Knowing the duration of each cut also helps the newsman at the desk to decide which ones he wants to use.

## NEWS CONFERENCES

There is a story that has been going around for several years now about a "cub reporter" who loused up one of the few news conferences ever to be held by a U.S. President in one particular state. It seems that then-President Lyndon B. Johnson was making a swing through part of the country and that his itinerary was so packed that he could only "touch base" in this state by stopping for an hour at the airport outside the capital. The President's party set aside 15 minutes of that hour for a news conference, and they probably regretted it for months afterward. It was during this session that a young man with a tiny, inexpensive, portable tape recorder stood up in the tenth row, and, holding his microphone high in the air (blocking the view of the TV cameras), asked the President of the United States whatever happened to the sewer grant for his town. LBJ hinted that as President he did not have time to keep up with all the local sewer grants and that the young man might check with his Congressman. Apparently the questioner thought the President was being evasive or something, so he really went after him verbally while the men from the newspapers stared in shocked disbelief and the network cameramen pounded their heads against the wall in the back of the room.

Of course you recall the anecdote from the list of "damaging flaws" about the stringer who asked the Congressman what he would do about state taxes. The answer about Congressmen just handling federal rather than state matters should have been sufficient, but the reporter also thought the Congressman was being evasive and pursued the point while the other members of the press gathered to watch the fun. The Congressman probably went around with his teeth clenched for the rest of the evening!

A most damaging incident of this sort once occurred when the New York Stock Exchange was thinking about moving away from Wall Street and across the state line into Greenwich, Connecticut, to avoid a proposed tax hike. Asked what steps he might take to help bring about such a move, the Governor of Connecticut at the time told reporters that: "First I'd have to be sure that—ah—the Stock Market is definitely *coming* to Connecticut." This was later played back on at least one station starting with the words: "The Stock Market is definitely *coming* to Connecticut" A slight difference! That Governor never allowed tape recorders near him for the rest of his term in office, unless he was making a prepared statement about something like Girl Scout cookies.

Newspaper reporters share some of the hostility that politicians often feel toward radio and TV newsmen. The newspaper people do not like to be cast as "actors" for cameras and tape recorders, asking all the questions while we broadcasters just turn our machines on and off. Too often, they feel that broadcasters do not do their homework. Not only do the radio-TV people fail to help with the questions most of the time, but they put whoever is giving the answers on the defensive by seeking spectacular "one-liner" responses. Broadcast news coverage on the air tends to be quite superficial, lacking the depth and insight provided by our colleagues from the print media. By the time they can publish it, we have already had it on the air a few times and many of their readers feel they have already heard all there is to tell about the matter.

How can you be *sure* of successful news conference coverage? Well, it is something that does not come overnight. Aside from following the basic checklists already given in this chapter, there are some techniques that can start you on your way. The biggest factor working for all the "pros" who ask the best questions and who come back with the best stories from news conferences is *experience*. The writer cannot give you that here, but he can give you a few ideas to start with:

## Do Your Homework

As mentioned in the previous checklists during this chapter, *know your topic* and *do not fake questions* if you are not sure of what you are talking about. Sure, your fellow newsmen would appreciate it if you would help out with the questions, but nothing will mark you as a beginner more quickly than a scandal-seeking "go-for-the-kill" question that is somehow not appropriate (like the examples involving the President and the sewer grant or the Congressman and state taxes). Leave the so-called heavy questions to the veteran news reporters if this is one of your first press conferences. If you get yourself out on a limb with questions that *embarrass the press* more than they embarrass the individual being questioned, you may find that they will try to avoid calling on you in future news conferences.

## Treat Your Colleagues With Respect

You will find that you will be running into the same reporters from other stations and other news media quite often. You could find them saving a seat for you, saving extra copies of news releases for you, helping you to find the phone, and doing a number of other considerate things if you win their friendship early in the game. Think of ways to reciprocate. The place to compete with these people is at your typewriter and on the air, not in elbowing each other out of the way whenever you are covering stories together. Otherwise, it could get to be a really cutthroat affair every time you go out to a news conference, and it would not improve your journalism one iota.

As a rule, you will find that many of the newspaper people assigned to cover these news conferences are a little older and have been covering the beat a good deal longer than you have. They can be especially helpful in the long run, providing additional insight, background, and reference tips. Be sure to nurture their respect. They may hold their cards close to their chests for the first few months, until they have determined whether or not you are a mature and responsible colleague, but then they will admit you to their circle and swap confidential tips with you if you have earned your place among them.

**Learn the Ground Rules for Your Area**

There are some places, like certain courtrooms, governors' and mayors' offices, etc., where you cannot just walk in with a tape recorder. This is unfortunate, and of course the broadcast industry frowns upon it, but in many cases some previous abuse or fear of possible abuses has forced newsmen to attend with just pad and pencil. The RTNDA code does mention trying to "open doors" that are closed to cameras and tape recorders, but it is best to find out what is behind such a policy wherever it exists and to cooperate with your colleagues in getting it modified or reversed. If you just decide to mount your own campaign, you may "freeze up" the whole news conference and earn the hostility of other newsmen who will have to report back to their bosses empty-handed.

Other ground rules may concern such areas as facilities or local union contracts. In New York City, for example, a prominent figure was about to start speaking at the Overseas Press Club when someone yelled from the back of the room: "There's a non-union camera crew here!" Everything ground to a halt. Apparently, the people holding the conference were forced to exclude the non-union crew before they could resume. There have been other situations where competing stations all but "came to blows" over the right to use the wall plug for electricity. Still other disagreements break out over whose call letters will be displayed most prominently from the podium. Failure to anticipate these hassles (as childish as some of them may be) can seriously damage your efforts to come back with a good story.

**Watch Your Personal Behavior**

Many organizations holding press conferences like to serve drinks and/or food at these occasions. That is very considerate of them, but somehow there are always a few newsmen who cannot hold their liquor. There is nothing more ludicrous than the sight of a young newsman with his "umpteenth" drink in his hand, slapping the Majority Leader of the State Senate on the back and laughing uproariously as though they were old buddies. They are not, and drinking will not make them so.

Manner of dress can also work against you—and your colleagues—if you flaunt the extremes. Sure, longer hair and beards, more flamboyant clothing, etc., are "in" for many occasions, but not for *all* of them. The writer can recall a hot afternoon session in the New Jersey House of Representatives when a sweaty young man with uncombed shoulder-length hair, dressed in a blue denim shirt which was opened a bit to show his masculine chest, and wearing shorts and sandals with no socks, went around parking his rear end on the desks of conservatively dressed legislators to get good camera angles during an important debate. It did not take long for a member of this rather august body to question the credentials of all members of the press, and they were all excluded for a good portion of the debate. Those who were readmitted were assigned to less desirable seats. Actions like these are inappropriate for members of the press, whether from the print or broadcast media. It is very much like kicking over the beehive while trying to gather honey, and could very well jeopardize not only your own coverage but that of your colleagues for the event you are working on and for future occasions.

### Don't Be Easily Taken In

There are many hard-working beginners in the news field who are tied to the radio station for most or all of their paid working hours. What first appeared to be a glamorous job turns into the day-after-day drudgery of phoning and typing, ripping and reading, etc. Along comes a nice invitation from someone who wants this newsman to attend a dinner at a plush hotel ballroom and to bring along his tape recorder. The newsman attends, on his own time, and thoroughly enjoys himself. The next day, audiences tuning in for "news" hear stories about which local building contractors won the Gold Medallion for all-electric homes and taped interviews with the president of the local utility company on the advantages of electric heat. The newsman has fallen into a very common trap.

Another very common trap is that of allowing your personal preferences to color your reporting. Either you accept some ideas too easily or you question others too severely. This happens even to the most seasoned reporters. In the 1972 Presidential election campaign, New York *Times* columnist Tom Wicker, an admirer of George McGovern, wrote a very sympathetic article about the McGovern proposals to change the country's welfare system and to redistribute personal income. When experts began to question the controversial plan, Wicker admitted that he should have checked the figures with disinterested parties *before* accepting the proposals so uncritically. It took a lot of courage, but Wicker apologized for having been misled, and said that the moral was ". . . that everything said and done by politicians seeking or holding power has to be constantly challenged." It might be added that this same rule applies to commercial interests or to anyone else who is *seeking* attention. They may have a perfectly legitimate story, but it is *your* job to stop and question it. (More on this is given in the chapter on Government and Politics.)

The kinds of cases illustrated here are classics in the annals of journalism. Volumes are filled with case after case in which the so-called objectivity of newsmen is compromised. The RTNDA Code in the previous chapter addresses itself to the problem by saying that broadcast newsmen ". . . shall seek to select material for newscast solely on their evaluation of its merits as news, . . ." and that ". . . subservience to external or 'interested' efforts to influence news selection and presentation . . ." shall be excluded. This does not mean that you should refuse all invitations or that you should be hostile toward all politicians and public relations men, but it *does* mean that you should be sure that circumstances surrounding these invitations, friendly contacts, etc., do not color your stories about them.

## INVESTIGATIVE PROJECTS

*Note:* Many on-the-scene stories are "event-oriented," or tied to a particular event as opposed to a situation in which you are simply asking questions. Event-oriented stories range from parades, press conferences, and picket lines to fires, civil disorders, and disasters. The following story ideas are *not* necessarily tied to an event, which is why for the moment they are called "investigative." The projects for this chapter are chosen for the *background sounds* which may be present as you do your narration or interview, using a tape recorder.

1. Is tipping still a good old American habit? Try asking barbers, beauticians, taxi drivers, bellhops, waiters, newspaper boys, etc., how things are in your area lately.

2. Do an investigative report on "noise pollution" in your area and on what is being done to alleviate it. Use some of the noises as your background.

3. What about the four-day work week? There may be some good background sounds as you interview workers in various occupations about their views on this.

4. Survey a number of housewives, asking under what conditions should a wife go to work. Use things like children playing, dogs barking, dishwashers, etc., as background noises if they are actually present, but do not "stage" the interviews by shouting over the noise of vacuum cleaners or the like.

5. On-the-street interviews are easy to do, but the noise of crowds, downtown traffic, etc., may not necessarily be relevant to the question, other than to simply indicate that you did your survey downtown. The questions can range from things like the voting age to permissiveness in the raising of today's children, or from today's laws to the traffic situation.

6. What is the status of mass transportation in your area? Survey bus or train commuters on whether or not passenger service should be partly or completely subsidized. Ask passengers and railroad officials alike about the performance of the Amtrak system since its inception.

7. See if the management of a supermarket will let you stand around in their store and get opinions on needed consumer laws, like ones requiring that meat be wrapped in see-through containers so that you can examine all sides, enforced unit-pricing, price controls, etc.

8. Ask Motor Vehicle personnel, people getting licenses, police, and others about the proper age for driving: whether the state's minimum age requirement for driving is too high or too low, whether there ought to be a maximum age for drivers' licenses, periodic reexamination of drivers, etc.

## IN-CLASS AND HOMEWORK ASSIGNMENTS

1. Write a story that lasts no more than 30 seconds of reading time, based on these notes of a school board meeting:

   "The Clarksville Board of Education meeting was called to order at 8:06 p.m. last night by Michael J. Grossi, the President of the Board. The invocation was given by the Board Chaplain, Rev. Wiliam P. McGuiness of St. Theresa's Church. The minutes of the last meeting were read by Mrs. Frances Mitchell, Board Recording Secretary. Motion for approval was offered by Board Member Harold Weinstein and seconded by Board Member Arthur Monroe.

   Dr. Alan Stokes, district superintendent, announced that fourteen teachers had indicated they would not be teaching in the Clarksville system in the fall. Six of them were elementary teachers, including two from kindergarten, one first-grade teacher, two fifth-grade teachers, and Mrs. Worthington, the speech specialist. The others include Mr. Duane Evans, the high-school football coach who has led the local team through two successive unbeaten seasons, three junior-high English teachers, two math teachers, two social studies teachers, and one Spanish teacher, all from the high school.

   The Board also ratified the contract recently approved by the Clarksville Teachers' Association. It grants beginning teachers $400 more than last year's figure and raises salaries of other teachers $400 as well in each step of the seniority scale, plus an additional $600 for each six credits earned toward the Masters' Degree. Board Member Stephen Parks warned that they would have to seek additional revenues to meet the contract in next year's budget, perhaps by as much as another 2 mils in property taxes.

The Activities Vice President of the P.T.A., Mrs. Erich Turner, gave a report on the successful cake sale held last week outside Central Supermarket, saying that they had raised $212.65 for the Scholarship Fund. The motion to adjourn was made by Board Member Earl Johnson and seconded by Board Member Dolores Grimes. The Board adjourned at 10:57 p.m."

2. Pretend that you have just been covering that meeting reported above. The Superintendent says he will be glad to answer a few questions for you before he leaves. What would be some good questions to ask him? List about six.

3. Write a short story about the board meeting above, including a tape-recorded insert with Board Member Stephen Parks answering a question for you after the meeting. The whole story, including his answer, should take no more than about 45 to 50 seconds of reading time.

4. If you could break the long "Board Meeting" story into several smaller ones, what would the smaller ones be about? How would you rotate these topics for subsequent newscasts?

Photo by United Press International.

# Chapter 3

# Civil Disorders

A rumor going around in one of the major cities hit by riots in the past few years was this: A not-too-well–trained substitute disc jockey was holding down the control room on a hot weekend afternoon in midsummer. A call came in, telling him that there was a "riot" going on at a certain intersection. He broke into his program and repeated what his caller had told him (including the word "riot") and touched off several days of burning, looting, sniping, and rioting the town will never forget. True? Some will swear to it, others will say "no." Possible? It certainly is, and you can believe many a News Director and Station Manager has lain awake at night thinking about it.

You would not want to be that "not-too-well-trained" fellow, would you? The writer would not want you to be him, either! The whole broadcast industry knows by now that a civil disorder, particularly one involving racial strife, is different from any other kind of story for one major reason—*what we say will affect the outcome of the story!* Your very first words will affect the development, the intensity, and the duration of what is happening. This kind of story demands, and gets, special, exceptional treatment.

The following suggestions will help you to avoid the most serious of blunders:

# DON'T BE TAKEN IN

△ Don't *ever* believe an unchecked or unauthorized source. Do not even believe the police radio. (They may be just checking out a rumor.) Contact the proper authorities for verification.

△ At the first indication that a civil disorder may be developing, call the News Director and other station personnel whose decisions may be needed to handle such a situation. (Both your station and the local police should have some procedures established by now. Ask what they are at your earliest opportunity. You will be reminded again in Chapter 11 of this book when it comes to your employment interview with the boss.)

△ *Nothing* is to be broadcast about the first moments of a developing civil disorder. This is not to say that you shall never mention it at all, but those first few moments are critical. The rule-of-thumb agreement with most police departments is to give them at least half an hour to quell the trouble. It would be better for all concerned if you could later report that an incident had been quieted than if you were to invite more troublemakers to the scene while it is still in progress. (You may get a few heckling calls from listeners, asking things like: "What's the matter with you guys, are you asleep?" or "You people have a duty to warn the public." Be ready to tell them exactly why you are holding back, but do it in a calm, responsible way and thank them for the call. They might be good for another news tip later on.)

△ Once clearance has been granted by proper station authorities, only calm, objective, verified information should be presented, emphasizing the steps being taken to restore order.

△ Never assume that a shooting, a fire, or a large gathering is racially caused. Never say any such incidents are connected with a general civil disorder unless you can quote the city official, by name, who said so. A "friend" on the police force or even the wire service when it does not name its source is not good enough in this case. Anything from them is a "tip" which must be cleared with proper authorities.

For example, a wire service once reported that "Violence . . ." had broken out ". . . in the same neighborhood where racial disorders occurred last summer." A check with police revealed that they had arrested a drunk for making trouble in a tenement hallway. Learn to be suspicious of the stories you tear off that machine.

△ Do not use terms that are stronger than those used by official spokesmen:

▶ An "incident" is not a "disturbance."

▶ A "disturbance" is not an "outbreak of violence."

▶ An "outbreak of violence" is not a "riot."

▶ A crowd is not always "large."

▶ Shots being fired do *not* mean "snipers."

▶ Fires are never listed as "set" or "out of control" or even "large" in these cases unless proper authorities can be quoted.

▶ A "set" fire does not mean "arson." It could just be hobos trying to keep warm or kids playing with matches.

△ Exact locations of intersections, addresses, housing projects, etc., should not be broadcast unless authorities have announced one of the following: that order has been established; that some kind of control is being applied to the area; or that a seal-off or curfew order has been issued and that you are to tell your listeners to stay away from that part of town. Take great care to be in close contact with police on this, so that you do not jeopardize their efforts to control the situation.

## SOME RELATIONSHIPS CHANGE

△ Suddenly, you are not "competing" with other stations nearby as you normally do. In fact, you should be maintaining contact with them throughout the disorder with top priority on ways to "cool it." Your primary goal is to give authorities, and the public, maximum assistance in re-establishing control. Your emphasis should be to reassure the listener in times of great peril or volatility that everything that can be done is being done to meet and solve the problem.

△ Don't ever appoint yourself as a "committee of one" to go to the scene of a potential trouble spot without proper authorization from station management. The writer can remember one newsman who drove his brand-new car through a tense ghetto area after work one summer evening just to see what was going on. Nothing had been going on—until he got there. They took one look at his big whip antenna and his "press" license plates and greeted him with a shower of rocks and bottles. The station management refused to cover the damage to his car with their insurance policy because no one had told him to go there.

Even if you are not worried about possible damage or injury to yourself or your belongings, it is simply a rule throughout the industry now that no one should go to the scene of a civil disorder or potential trouble spot without the specific permission of the News Director, the Station Manager, or other authorized station official in charge. Properly trained and identified newsmen should be sent to the police command post (not to the scene of the disorder) to communicate with officially designated police staff members for pertinent information concerning the disorder.

△ If your station has no one they can call within the affected area, it may be a sign that you have been out of touch with this segment of the community. Do not just clutch at statements from self-appointed "spokesmen" who pop up suddenly when things are chaotic. For example, if the disorder involves a ghetto area, you should have kept your contacts warm over many months and should know responsible community leaders, heads of antipoverty groups, Model Cities programs, tenent and housing groups, etc. (See Chapter 4, on "Fairness to Minorities," for more hints on this.) A similar rule would apply to keeping college contacts warm in anticipation of any campus unrest, and to such areas as labor trouble, antiwar efforts or other situations that may be accompanied by disorders.

△ Beware of staged events. Richard Townley once wrote in a series for *TV Guide* about the time the militant Jewish Defense League called up the assignment editor at a New York City television station and asked when it would be convenient for them to come over and film the burning of a Soviet flag in front of the U.N. building. "This blatant offer was refused," says Townley, but he does quote one of the city's News Directors as saying that ". . . those who would manipulate us are getting smarter." If you have a group in your area that has been in contact with the station often and has been a good news source, do not let your guard down. Never feel that you have any obligation to buy their continued friendship by giving them coverage they do not deserve.

△ On the other hand, just because you have been in contact with a group or with certain individuals over a period of time, do not suddenly expect them to identify themselves with the violence. Calling the NAACP and asking them to "explain" a civil disorder or to issue a statement in connection with it is downright insulting to them. It means *you* are implying racial causes (or assuming them) and implying some kind of connection between their organization and the disorders. They did not *start* the trouble, they do not want to be identified with it, and they will wonder where you have been all this time when they have had some positive things to say.

Photo by United Press International.

△ This is no time for station promotion. Conspicuous display of station call letters, equipment, mobile units, and so on is inappropriate. It tends to further inflame the situation and leads to the familiar comments later on that the news media are hungry for violence. Instead of just reporting a story, you are becoming part of it by your conspicuous presence. This is especially true with TV coverage, because as soon as those lights go on and those cameras are aimed, everybody at the scene turns into an actor.

One station, arriving just after a demonstration had broken up, realized that the competitors had filmed the whole thing. The newsmen went up to the leaders of the group and asked if they would not mind doing it all over again. This is about as disgusting a display of irresponsibility and news fakery as one can imagine. Police were lucky enough to have prevented violence during the first round, and the station's asking for an instant replay certainly did not help. Serious trouble might have erupted, provoked by the media and not by the demonstrators.

## SOME MISLEADING IMPRESSIONS

△ A civil disorder is no occasion in which to try for creativity with your tape recorder. Tapes or other reports with sounds of fighting, shooting, screaming, raging, or violence— or interviews with obvious lawbreakers and inciters—should never be used while a disorder is in progress. Even if things are calm, reports from the scene should never be considered as "the overall picture" but simply as one reporter's viewpoint from where he stands. Things could be much different a block away. No such single reports are to be overemphasized or presented out of context.

△ Avoid implicating minorities. Seeing a few members of one ethnic group involved in some kind of misbehavior and then reporting that a particular "community" is involved is like saying "If you've seen one, you've seen 'em all." It is not that simple, but there are enough bigoted minds in any large audience who believe it is. Do not help to reinforce these generalizations that some people hold as prejudiced beliefs. (More on this is covered in the next chapter, "Fairness to Minorities.")

△ Advisory information and tips for those who are back at the station (if you are at the scene) should clearly be identified as such. Otherwise, someone could accidentally just take it and put it on the air. If what you are saying to the newsroom is not for public consumption, be sure to say so. Never tell a radio audience where your reporters are stationed during a civil disorder, and never broadcast the precise locations of command posts, public officials, firefighting units, military units, police staging areas, or any other such information on the air. Any information of this type sent back to the newsroom from the scene should be labeled "confidential" before you start talking about it.

Many volumes of material on the subject of civil disorders have been published in recent years. The writer recommends in particular that you read Chapter 15 about the news media in *Report of the National Advisory Commission on Civil Disorders.* It is published by Bantam Books, and the paperback edition sells for $1.25.

## INVESTIGATIVE PROJECTS

Lacking an actual violent outbreak itself, your role while investigating such a topic is not to stir one up! In all of the following projects, thank the people who contribute but do not feel obligated to use what they have said. Stick to the more responsible statements and avoid such things as a prediction that ". . . this town could erupt at any time." On the other hand, you don't want to be "Pollyannish" and pretend that everything is sunlight and flowers. It is all right to acknowledge that there are some problems, but for broadcast presentation it is best to emphasize what *can* be done or what *is* being done to solve them.

1. Arrange to interview officers or members of the area National Guard unit, perhaps at one of their meetings. Find out if there were any changes in their training following

nationwide campus disorders and antiwar demonstrations, in addition to the training of earlier years which presumably focused more on ghetto unrest. Have they managed to shake off any of the "Kent State" image? How?

2. With the same National Guard unit, you might even do a documentary on the men themselves. Get permission from the commanding officer to put together the sounds of Guard activities plus close-up interviews on the men's daily family and business lives, their educational or occupational goals, and their thoughts about the possibility of being called to handle a disturbance. (Have they been called up before? What was it like?)

3. Arrange to sit with a group of local police officers and to have a chat about their efforts to keep things peaceful lately. Has their community ever had disorders? If so, what changes have been made in the department since then? If not, what steps have they taken as a result of the so-called Koerner Commission Report and the experiences of other cities?

4. Do a report with police officials on what the average citizen can do to help restore order or to prevent outbreaks when there is community unrest. If you are in a small town where disorders are unlikely, maybe State Troopers have spokesmen who are especially trained to discuss this topic with you.

5. What is the role of the fire department when there is the threat of civil disobedience? Have local firemen been given any special training for such an eventuality? What cooperation would they like to see from the community?

6. Do policemen or firemen make appearances at area schools to talk to the children? Can you arrange to attend such a presentation and record the program itself, the children's reactions, and the policemen's or firemen's reactions to it afterward? What about junior-high and high-school levels? How do presentations to these age groups differ, and how effective are they?

7. Ask newsmen and management personnel from several area radio and television stations what they have learned

from civil disorders over recent years. (Yes, including your competitors!) Put together a report on what the broadcast industry has done in order to play a more responsible role in view of this topic.

## IN-CLASS AND HOMEWORK ASSIGNMENTS

1. In the following imaginary transcript of a radio broadcast, there are at least 20 serious errors involving the coverage of civil disorders. Identify them, tell why they are wrong, and tell what changes you would make at each point:

*In the middle of a record, WIZZ Newsflash Sounder:* "Whoop—Whoop—Whoop."

*Disc Jockey:* "We interrupt this program to bring you a special bulletin from the "WIZZ" Newsroom. There are reports of a riot breaking out at the Fulton School Playground on South Eleventh Avenue. The Puerto Rican community is said to be angry about insults made by several white youths to one of their girls. Some shooting has been reported in the area. W-I-Z-Z reporters are en route to the scene, and we'll have firsthand reports for you as soon as they become available."

*Tape, with echo-chamber effect:* "Remember, when you see news happening, call seven-seven-seven, four-six-eleven. It pays! And keep tuned to "WIZZ" Radio, where news breaks *first!*"

*(Record Continues)*

*(Commercial)*

*(Weather Check)*

*News Sounder:* "Whoop—Whoop—Whoop."

*Disk Jockey:* "And now we take you directly to "WIZZ" news-man John Ellis, reporting from the Police Command Post at South Tenth Avenue and West 3rd Street."

*John Ellis:* "Thank you, Dick. Actually, I've left the Command Post and I'm headed west along 3rd Street right now for a better look. In the background you may be able to hear fire engines arriving. I think those are the two trucks from Company D over on Birch Street, and there'll probably be more before the night's over. There appears to be some fighting still going on. I can still see quite a crowd in the street, but it's hard to make out who's who. As far as I can tell, "WIZZ" Radio is first on the scene. There are no other reporters anywhere around. One or two were back at the Police Command Post, but "WIZZ" Radio is bringing you a closer look. We're in the first moments of what's going to be a long, hot night for the south side. By the way, Dick, if you're listening at the station, you may want to have someone check on a "Signal 73" that I heard before I left the Police Command Post. If I remember correctly, that's arson, and we could possibly have some snipers up there; I don't know. Also, Dick, you might call the South Side Puerto Rican Club and see if they have a statement on all this violence that's erupting here tonight. This is John Ellis on West 3rd Street near South Eleventh Avenue, where an all-out riot appears to be taking place. Dick?"

2. Assume for the moment that you are a member of a college group planning a demonstration. Your manner of dress, hair style, use of slang expressions, and other behavior is quite similar to that of your friends in this group. You happen to own a portable tape recorder and you have been earning some extra money on the side by working part-time for the local radio station. The boss at the radio station would like you to cover this demonstration for them, and you can use the money; so you have accepted. You hear that extra police are being brought in on standby, and that there is likely to be some violence. Outline your preparations for such coverage, listing at least ten things that you would be sure to *do*, at least ten things that you would be sure *not* to do, and give your reasons for each.

3. The following is an imaginary phone call to the newsroom from one of your listeners:

"What the hell kind of newsmen are you people, anyway? Don't you know a whole busload of niggers was just turned back at the exit from the Interstate Highway?"

(You tell your caller that you had not heard this.)

"Well, you guys better get on the stick. How's the public supposed to protect itself from this kinda stuff when even the radio station doesn't know what's going on? Hell, the whole town could be burnin' down by now. Did you know they all had baseball bats? That's right, and maybe even rifles, too, who knows? My God, I don't know what this place is comin' to. You know Lieutenant Shelton on the police force? Well, he turned 'em around. He told 'em to get right back where they came from, but they might get off somewhere else, who knows? You guys better *warn* people!"

a) What are some things you want to *ask* your listener?

b) What are some responsible things you can *tell* your caller?

c) What are some other actions you will take and why? (List at least three.)

4. You are at the scene for one of the following incidents, and as an eyewitness you are describing it for your audience. (It can be live or taped; it does not matter.) Write a transcript of your imaginary description for one of the two situations below, lasting no more than 35 seconds of reading time. Then list at least six things you were careful *not* to say.

a) "Peace" demonstrators are on one side of the street; flag-waving "hardhat" construction workers are on the other side. You, the police, and the traffic are in the middle.

b) It is St. Patrick's Day, and angry demonstrators are picketing the Irish Airlines office. The demonstrators wear orange, indicating they are *Northern* Irish and have anti-Catholic sentiments, and are harrassing those who attempt to enter or leave the airline office.

Photo by Chip Hires.

# Chapter 4

# Fairness to Minorities

Mr. Shelton Lewis, formerly of Mutual Radio's "Black Network News" and who was once the News Director for Harlem's Black-programmed WLIB, likes to tell the following story about a demonstration that was going on near the Columbia University campus one time.

## IT'S EASY TO ASSUME

The campus borders on Harlem itself, and many of those in the demonstration were Blacks. Within moments of the start, up rolled the familiar mobile units of New York City's various radio and TV stations. Microphones and cameras started to sprout among the corps of newsmen and engineers so that they could record for the rest of the world what was happening and why.

Up to the scene stepped a Negro dressed in black clerical clothes and wearing a typical clergyman's collar. He had a Bible under his arm, and offered to make a statement.

"Aha," thought the newsmen, "a spokesman." Immediately this Reverend whatever-his-name-was began "explaining" the reasons for the demonstration. The newsmen and engineers, almost all of them white, diligently recorded every syllable. Then they packed up their gear and headed for their stations, because, after all, there was that "Six O'Clock Report" to make.

Two stations passed up the opportunity to interview the good man-of-the-cloth. Strangely enough, they were the two stations from right there in Harlem (WLIB and WWRL). Why did they not record the statement along with the others?

"Because," says Mr. Lewis, "he wasn't a spokesman, he wasn't a minister, he wasn't from Harlem, and he didn't know anything about the demonstration. He's just some guy that goes around like that trying to get on television. We all know him pretty well."

By "we," of course Mr. Lewis was referring mostly to reporters from the Black community. The almost all-white news corps went back to their various stations and got down to the business of editing the "Reverend" down to the right number of seconds for that all-important six o'clock newscast, and the good "Reverend" probably went home and thoroughly enjoyed watching himself on television. The demonstrators at the Columbia campus probably were a little frustrated at the distorted news coverage they got, and probably concluded that "the media" (us) do not know what it is all about, anyway.

The problem of accurate and adequate coverage of minorities is certainly not new. Investigations and surveys by government commissions, universities, and others over the past several decades have tended to confirm that when white reporters talk to Blacks or other minority group persons, they tend to pick:

1. *The wrong people:* Interviewing an NAACP leader or a Black Congressman tells you little or nothing about the attitudes *within* the Black community. Whites often *think* they know who the most influential Blacks are, and are even accused of "creating" leaders (as in the example above).

2. *The wrong subjects:* Rats, roaches, crime, poverty, and busing are all too frequently on the minds of reporters, and they fail to view Blacks and other minorities as "normal." Instead of being asked about their achievements and their opinions on everyday nonracial issues, Blacks are often confined by newsmen to questions about racial problems or issues.

3. *Stereotypes:* Militants, colorful ghetto characters, criminals, star athletes, show personalities, and Blacks who are found in welfare, food-stamp, or unemployment offices seem to attract far more media attention than do normal, law-abiding, non-show-biz, middle-class Blacks. Black teachers, engineers, businessmen, and others are frequently overlooked in routine news coverage.

4. *The wrong times:* Mikes and cameras always seem to be right there on the scene when a Black man riots, rapes, steals, or kills. Somehow the same mikes and cameras are rarely so attracted by the normal interests of individual Blacks and their families. Crisis- and problem-oriented news coverage should always reflect a minority group's own expressed needs, not those of a program strategist trying to build ratings, and should rarely, if ever, overshadow advancement- and culture-oriented news about such persons.

5. *The wrong news reporters*: Blacks often complain that the news is always seen through white men's eyes, and that even Blacks in newsrooms are often assigned *only* to Black news or are somehow never quite "ready" to assume all the duties of their white counterparts. As an individual journalist or even as News Director, you may not have control of all the hiring at your station, but you should realize that the FCC and other groups have taken steps in recent years to ensure that minorities are being given their fair share in determining a station's editorial content. Management at every broadcast station will be under pressure to comply with these new demands, and you should do everything you can to assist with "Equal Opportunity" and "Affirmative Action" programs.

Assuming that either you are white yourself or that you are working for a station where most or all of the employees are white, how do you avoid making a fool of yourself as did those white newsmen talking with that "Reverend" in Harlem, and how do you *anticipate* the problems that are likely to rise?

To suddenly fill up your studio with Blacks and roll the tape will not do it; neither will suddenly taking Black clergymen, businessmen and politicians out to lunch. This approach is too much like trying to take the whole bottle of pills at one sitting when the doctor has prescribed one or two a day. By starting massive and spectacular coverage you will not only invite problems but chances are you will give up after a few weeks. To set yourself some limited goals and to get into the habit of achieving them regularly, day in and day out, you are more likely to find yourself in touch with the Black or any other minority community the way you should be.

## SOME NEW GROUND RULES

There will be some investigative projects and other ideas to help you develop an understanding of the minority community, and these will be given a little later on, but first here are some "ground rules" that go with *all* minority situations:

△ Act as though there are minority persons present. In the newsroom, in the studios, at the scene of a story—you are on the job. As a newsman, to walk around telling the familiar "Polish" jokes or "Italian" jokes, or to put on an "Amos 'n Andy" or "Frito Bandito" accent is very much like a surgeon walking into the operating room with dirty hands. Regardless of your private thoughts on any aspect of the nation's current racial problems, your behavior while at work should be impeccable. Jokes, accents, nicknames, and other behavior offensive to any minority group should be ruled out. When others indulge in this kind of behavior you may not be in a position to tell them to stop, but you certainly are in a position to discreetly let it pass and to not encourage it. Whenever it *is* possible, you should call for cooperation and understanding in this effort.

△ Keep at least a mental checklist (if not a written one) of the words, phrases, and approaches to news stories that minorities consider offensive or stigmatized. Do not use them in your own stories, and watch out for them in wire service stories that you tear off the machine. For example:

▶ *Stigmatized neighborhoods,* like a town's "mostly Negro north end" or "predominantly Negro south side."

▶ *Racial tags* on things like schools, stores, churches, and other institutions and locations unless there's some special *need* and *relevance* to the use of such a tag.

To report that violence has occurred in a "mostly Negro high school" without knowing the causes, the extent, or the parties involved is to imply that Negros were responsible for the violence. You wouldn't do the same with a *white* high school —or would you? In other words, seek to neutralize all racial overtones unless it becomes quite clear from an authoritative source that the problem itself is racial.

△ Do not assume racial causes for fires, crimes, disturbances or other such incidents just because a large number of minority persons live in the neighborhood. Just because a lady has a fire in her kitchen is no reason to add that it is a "predominantly Negro neighborhood." As was said in the previous chapter on civil disorders, ". . . never assume that a shooting, a fire, or a large gathering is racially caused, . . ."— and one might add here: "Be sure any spokesman who identifies such an incident as racially caused is qualified and authorized to do so." One patrolman or one firefighter under pressure who may hastily blame a situation on a particular minority group may be branding a whole neighborhood as harboring hostility toward authorities when actually it is only a few children throwing rocks.

△ In all cases involving minorities versus police, try to get the minority side of the story at least for your own reference if not for broadcast. This does not mean that you should seek to discredit the police or to broadcast information that might interfere with a fair trial, but it does mean that you should follow the time-honored newsmen's tradition of getting both sides of the story. If an accused person or his friends have denied the charges against him, and you ignore this in your story, are you being totally fair? (More on this is given in the next chapter, "The Police Beat and the Courtroom.")

△ If a minority person is the alleged victim of police brutality, you have a sensitive problem on your hands. First, be sure that that is exactly what was charged, not just something that "sounded like it." Recall from the first chapter, "The Basics," that in many a city those charges are cause for possible departmental discipline against the policeman involved.

You cannot ignore these charges if you plan to run the story, but you can take several steps to protect yourself:

▶ Get the name and address of the person making the charges. Get his title if he is an official of some group, a lawyer, or some kind of spokesman, and his relationship to the alleged victim.

▶ Get the specific charges, including the nature of the injuries. This is not necessarily for broadcast, but if anyone asks whether or not you bothered to check, your conscience is clear.

▶ Get a statement from the ranking police official involved as to whether or not they feel the charges are unfounded, whether they plan to investigate the incident, or just what their response is—even if it is no statement at all. Remember that the police are the accused party this time, and that you are still getting both sides of the story.

△ What minority groups consider a "peaceful" demonstration often comes out in wire service stories or other reports as a "disturbance." Some reporters will even take a look at a crowd marching down the street and file a story that "violence has erupted." Do not just blindly accept these terms. If the wire service gives no details to back up their claims of disruption or violence, call them up and get them to justify their story with specific details of the damage, injury, or other clear indications that the incident is not peaceful. Try to contact the minority people involved and see what *they* call it. If the versions do not match, use the least inflammatory version until there is clear justification for the stronger terms.

△ Draw up a "Minority Coverage List" with names and phone numbers, and give it just as much prominence in your newsroom as that all-too-familiar list of police phone numbers. Include the numbers of civil rights, housing, antipoverty, and other human relations agencies. Call them regularly.

It may be difficult getting stories from these sources at first. Over at police headquarters, your friend the desk sergeant has everything written out for him on the blotter in ready-made terms, but minority people often have no such device to help them organize their thoughts. You will have to ask more questions, and some of the people you will be calling may not seem as articulate as others because of educational differences. This means that occasionally you may have to help them put the story together.

By the way, if *they* call *you,* it must mean that it is important to them. Do everything you can to get the story on the air. A story about a minority person doing something *other* than getting arrested may not seem exciting to the white community, but it is vitally important to the minority people involved.

△ Get hold of as many human rights groups as you can at the state level and ask them to help you find their local branches. Also, get yourself on their mailing lists for releases at the state level. Look for agencies like:

▶ The State Commission on Human Rights (or Civil Rights)

▶ The State Welfare Department

▶ CORE, NAACP, Urban Coalition, Urban League

▶ Model Cities, Housing, Antipoverty groups

▶ Civic and Fraternal Societies whose names or locations indicate that they might be serving minority groups.

△ Screen out provocative implications from all stories. As was pointed out previously, all demonstrations are not necessarily violent, but now let us add a few similar situations where you must be on your guard:

▶ Two or three broken windows in one section of town should not give rise to a story that "violence has broken out" there, or worse, that "Negro youths" went around smashing windows. White youths are just as capable of smashing windows, but somehow you never see it written up that way.

▶ Pranksters with a slingshot gave rise to stories in one town that "snipers were firing at passing cars." Not only was it false when checked out, but the word "sniper" has pretty much been banned altogether by networks and wire services at this point. It leads to too many problems. (There are many words whose use is banned at larger stations for various reasons. See Chapter 9 on style.)

▶ A match thrown into a rubbish barrel brought fire engines into a tense neighborhood one night, and by the time the story had passed through many hands and many re-writes, one national TV network had that city listed on a big map of "racial hot spots" in the U.S., along with other towns where the National Guard had been called out.

△ Do not trust someone else's quotes, especially if they tend to be provocative or inflammatory. If a wire service, a newspaper, or some other source quotes a minority spokes-man, either try to contact the spokesman himself and confirm the quote, or write the name of the newspaper or wire service right into your story and make it clear that *they* quoted him this way, and you did not. Minority spokesmen say they are fre-quently misquoted or that only the inflammatory or controversial parts of their statements are quoted and the positive aspects omitted.

△ Be suspicious about numbers. Use the least inflammatory or least offensive figures available. Police in one town told re-porters that almost 500 people had been arrested for alleged curfew violations in the wake of a week of disturbances. Minority spokesmen pointed out that fewer than 90 were ar-rested in the troubled area, and that the other 400-plus had been picked up in other parts of town where they said they knew nothing of the curfew and little or nothing of the violence.

△ When a minority person is arrested, try to get his lawyer, his friends and relatives, court officials and police, or *someone* to be on the lookout for the outcome. Be sure an acquittal gets as much attention as the original arrest, if that is what the accused person would prefer. (Some may just want the whole matter dropped.) Local minority organizations may want to help you by setting up a courtroom "watchdog" system for this.

## SOME POSITIVE APPROACHES

As mentioned in the chapter on civil disorders, do not expect to call up the NAACP in the wake of some kind of disturbance and get them to "explain" it. The same goes for

CORE, the Urban League, and others. They did not *start* any trouble, they probably know a lot less about it than you would know sitting there in your newsroom, and for them to start issuing statements on the heels of such incidents would only tend to associate them with that kind of event (which is the last thing they want.)

What *do* you talk about, then? It may be helpful if you made an appointment and dropped by their office, seeking their help. Find out what their favorite topics are. In some communities, the topics will be "problem oriented," and they'll want help in such areas as housing, better police protection, education, employment, etc. In other towns, you will find a preference for "advancement oriented" stories such as the opening of a new medical or child-care facility, programs and cultural exhibits by performers or artists from a particular minority group, legislative or fund-raising projects, etc.

Pick up a copy of *Ebony, Essence, Jet,* or some other well-known Black publication. If you are dealing with a minority other than Blacks, then try to pick up a similar publication which applies to this particular minority group. It may be in another language, but what you are after are general topics as opposed to small details. Have someone help you find out what these topics are. In any case, find out what these people talk about when they talk with each other.

How can you accommodate these minority viewpoints into your general news coverage? For one thing, if your town is big enough to have its own branch of the NAACP or similar organization, then your newsroom should have a subscription to the appropriate minority publication to go with such a group. For another approach, try some of the investigative projects listed at the end of this chapter.

Thousands of members and volunteers have worked for minority-group organizations for years, advancing in such areas as housing, education, employment, community clean-up and self-help projects that are too often ignored by the news media. Phone calls from the news media to these organizations asking them to suddenly "explain" the reasons behind a confrontation or even an incident of violence are not only inappropriate but downright insulting. Try to see if you, as an individual, can improve this record of the news media.

One of the quickest ways to tell the members of a minority community that you really do not care about them is to mispronounce their names on the air, or to mispronounce one of their major holidays or religious events. They are not likely to call you up and correct you, but in their minds you and your station will definitely be regarded as outsiders. This is certainly no way to *warm up* contacts with the community involved. As soon as you are aware that pronunciation problems may occur, start a pronunciation chart to cover the situation. You may need several such charts. There are communities where groups holding public events include such widely ranging minorities as Portuguese, Lebanese, Ukranian, Jewish, German, Spanish, and several others. Sometimes the members of such a community are small in number and are usually only heard from in connection with a semiannual event at their church or social hall, while others constitute a major segment of your general public locally and you will be dealing with them in various situations the year round. Keep in touch with these groups.

In one city, for example, the writer's station had an arrangement with the local newspaper in which one of their reporters would read stories over our station in exchange for some advertising. The station was glad to get the stories most of the time, because the newspaper had dozens of reporters while the station had only three full-time newsmen and a few part-time "stringers." What made us wince in the newsroom, though, was listening to this newspaper reporter "anglicize" foreign names. There was a large Spanish-speaking community, and this fellow would consistently take a name like Miguel Rodriguez and pronounce it "MIG-well and rahd-RIG-ezz." (It should be more like "mee-GELL rohd-REE-gace"). He would also refer to someone like Jesus Gonzalez as "JEE-zuzz gahn-ZAH-lizz" instead of the more correct "hay-SOOS gohn-SAH-lace." It took a little persuading to convince the station manager that this was damaging, and the newspaper people wound up letting the station personnel read the stories on the air while still giving them credit.

Most romance languages (Spanish, French, Italian, Portuguese, etc.) have alphabets quite similar to ours when it comes to writing them. You should take the trouble to learn how these letters *sound* in another language, especially if it is a language used by a minority group in your area. In Spanish, for example, all but a few of the consonants are exactly the same as those in English. Learning the few exceptions and memorizing the five different vowel sounds will help you through many difficulties with pronounciation, even if you never get around to taking a course in the language itself.

At the end of this chapter are some investigative projects connected with minority-oriented news. You may find that many of them do not strike you as actual "news" stories (or as many newsmen call them, "hard" news). The reaction from your boss may be a yawn when you propose putting some of them on the air. In a special note to those who use the investigative projects, you will learn that these stories can be written in advance and used to replace the more worn-out ones. Eventually, depending on the size of your minority population and the results of your station's ascertainment studies, you should arrive at a policy for scheduling such stories *regularly* throughout the week, not just in the so-called ghetto-broadcast hours.

If your station does not already have a definite policy for placement and scheduling of investigative and minority-oriented stories, be sure to discuss the matter with your superiors before simply putting such stories on the air. It would be better to get a modest start at something like this than to put an ambitious piece of work on the air and have the manager call up to tell you not to do it again because it was "boring."

## EXTREMISTS

A cross burns on someone's lawn. It is unusual for your town, especially since you are not in an area that normally experiences racial tensions (or at least has not for some time.) The morning paper carries a front-page picture and story of the incident. The wire service has picked it up and done a few rewrites.

Photo by United Press International.

Maybe you run the story—maybe you do not—but later in the day the phone rings in the newsroom and there is a "Robert Kirk" or some such named person on the other end. (Usually the name is fairly bland but has an Anglo-Saxon ring to it.) He says he is the spokesman for the Ku Klux Klan and that he wants to fill you in on the cross burning.

You roll your tape, and he starts talking. He warns the community that the Klan is "on the move" and that the cross burning is only one of about a dozen they have already carried out or have planned. He says that there are at least six "Klaverns" or chapters throughout the area, and that the local one in your town has many members, including some prominent citizens and local policemen. "If they push us too far," he says, "we may take a more violent turn within the next few weeks." By "they," he does not necessarily mean a specific racial minority group. "They" usually refers to the opposition in a local issue that ranges anywhere from zoning, welfare, employment, or voter registration to school integration or busing. Your spokesman on the phone opposes any kind of outcome in these issues that would advance the cause of any minority.

All this is very intriguing. There you have it, right on tape. The mysterious voice of the Klan leader. Should you play it on the air? Excitedly you pick up your phone again and call police headquarters. They play a role in this, too. Of course they have heard about it. They are not at liberty to say what they have uncovered so far, but they would love to hear your tape. You play it for them. They thank you, and ask you to keep in touch and to call them if you get anything else.

Oh boy! It's very exciting now, and you put the whole thing on the air, complete with the name of the police officer who said very officially that they are working on the case. Congratulations! You, my friend, have just been taken in. Your "Klansman" must be dancing with delight by his radio, gleeful over the fact that you have broadcast—*without questioning them for one moment*—his assertions that they have all these chapters and members and plans for violence and the whole bit. Not only did you do that, but you even embellished his story a little bit by throwing in the police officer's statement to lend credibility to the whole thing.

In several major cities these so-called Klansmen have been checked out and unmasked for what they really are. In one town, it was just *one guy*—the proprietor of a local poolroom where business was a little slow and where he took up the slack by making crosses in the back room. In another town, the level of activity and the phone calls following each cross-burning were about the same, and chances are it could not have been more than two or three people at the most.

By day, many of these people lead a rather dull existence. Many of them work at menial jobs, which by the way, could probably be taken over by members of the minority group they fear. Many of them live in neighborhoods where a number of minority persons have been moving in. By night, these people get together and put on uniforms, hold ceremonies, meet in rooms decorated with their insignias and propaganda, and create for themselves the illusion that they are somehow important. It does not have to be the Ku Klux Klan; it can be anything from a motorcycle club to the American Nazi Party or some modification of one of these groups. Their devices for attention-seeking usually consist of some act like burning a cross or riding en masse on their motorcycles through a particular neighborhood, but sometimes they make mysterious calls to the news media or issue unsigned copies of a so-called news release or official statement. It is mysterious and fascinating, but it is also an appeal to sensationalism. Learn to recognize it.

Sometimes extremism is more subtle, and prejudices can easily slip through from unexpected sources if you are not on your guard. In one city, the wife of a leading political figure held some extreme views and skillfully used her husband's position to get some of her positions aired. She would call the newsroom frequently, at first giving "routine" bits of information from the town political committee on which her husband served, then giving "tips" about inside political developments which led to some fairly good stories. Finally, though, she started mentioning that "there was a lot of opposition" in area towns to certain pieces of legislation proposed at the state capital—legislation involving busing, special expenditures for ghetto schools, and some controversial measures like extra state aid for suburban schools who would take some students from a nearby city. A legislator from the same political party as this woman's husband finally called the newsroom to say that the stories broadcast were not quite as accurate as he would hope them to be, and questioned the source. The newsroom did not have to name the lady who had been giving the stories, because *he* named her in the next breath and said to watch out for her rather extreme viewpoints. Then it dawned on everyone in the newsroom: she had been giving much of the information on a "confidential" basis lately, and if little or no opposition existed to the legislation before she called the newsroom, the broadcast story would serve to arouse the kind of opposition she wanted.

You have to draw the line somewhere. To run a story on the air to the effect that there is some opposition to certain civil rights legislation is perfectly legitimate, but let the opponents of such legislation stand up and be counted by name! In this case, the station was guilty not only of *not* having a source it could name, but had allowed personal friendship with this lady on the phone to undermine its objectivity. She had managed to reach the point where the station wasn't questioning her stories as closely as it should have been, and she was able to express "opposition" to whatever measures she chose without naming anyone.

Prejudice can sometimes work its way into a newsroom more easily than flagrant extremism. Some reading in this area will help you increase your awareness of some of the techniques employed. One good book is *The Radical Right,* by Benjamin Epstein and Arnold Forster, published by Random House, and another excellent diagnosis of the symptoms of prejudice is found in *"Some of My Best Friends Are . . . . ."* also by Benjamin Epstein and Arnold Forster and published by Farrar, Straus and Cudahy.

## INVESTIGATIVE PROJECTS

Before you plunge into the personal lives of minority groups and individuals with any kind of investigative project, it is best to consider whether or not they want to be "investigated." American tourists wearing big straw hats, flashy clothing and expensive cameras often make themselves unwelcome in the remote villages of foreign countries by simply walking up to the natives and snapping pictures of them, smiling in a condescending manner, and approaching the local people as though they were "quaint." This same approach by newsmen toward minorities in our own country can do more harm than good for both the media and the minorities.

Rather than approaching your subject as though you were some kind of anthropologist studying a backwards culture, you must first determine the *needs* of the people with whom you are dealing. This is why we have divided the projects for this chapter into three main areas:

Advancement-oriented,

Culture-oriented,

Problem-oriented.

It may be that the people with whom you are talking want to be portrayed as in the mainstream of American life and not as minorities. In such a case, you would not use the old "Jackie Robinson" approach and ask the person why he is the first member of his particular race to be in whatever field it is. You would use an "advancement-oriented" topic and let the individual speak about his field of endeavor *as a person.* If, for some reason which you can support strongly, the racial aspect is the *most important* part of the story, then you may want to get the permission of your subject to mention it ever so subtly. (For example: the first Cuban immigrant to become a high school principal in a Florida town, a Black clergyman who takes on an all-white congregation as his next assignment, the first Black judge in a town where minority representation on the bench has been lacking, etc.)

Sometimes minority neighborhoods wishing to preserve a colorful part of their heritage would not mind sharing it with the public at large. Religious and other holiday celebrations are the most common among these "culture-oriented" topics. Music, processions, and descriptions of the history and customs connected with a certain event are a good part of the story on tape, and the "picture" possibilities are even greater in the case of TV coverage.

Finally, there *are* times when a minority group will feel that it is not getting its fair share, and that they would like the media to help. Topics can range from lack of heat or police protection in a public housing project to alleged discrimination in hiring or educational practices. If this is what your particular minority group seems to need, here are a few projects outlined which may be of some help.

These investigative projects have been divided into advancement-, culture-, and problem-oriented areas.

## Advancement-Oriented Investigative Projects

### 1. Professional Advancement

    a. *Minority-Owned Businesses*—What are some of the major success stories in your area among minority businessmen? Is there a firm that started out as a "ma and pa" operation some years ago that appears to be prospering now? Check with the owners and get them to tell you how they overcame difficulties and whether they would do it again.

b. *Management Positions in Local Industry*—Who are some of the leading minority people in charge of departments and other areas of local manufacturing plants, offices, and so forth? What is their view of advancement through the ranks? Is it tougher as a minority individual to acquire the "front office" or "white collar" jobs?

c. *Government Officials*—Since the major court decisions enforcing equality at the ballot box some years ago, minority groups have been more able to elect their own members to responsible government positions. How do these officials view their roles? Do they feel—as some of the nation's Black Congressmen do—that they serve a "double constituency"? What are some of the things they hope to accomplish in these positions? (Include elected and appointed officials at local, state and federal levels and executive, legislative and judicial branches in each case.)

d. *Doctors, Lawyers, Educators*—How are the minority people in your community advancing through the professional ranks? Are their numbers in the professions commensurate with their numbers as a group among the public at large? What are the obstacles toward achieving these positions? What is the future outlook for these people?

## 2. Group Recognition

a. *The Minority "Market"*—Just what effect does a minority group have on the local economy? Does their "buying power" give rise to specialized stores or products (like Soul Food, tortillas, African-style clothing, etc.)? Which products do these people buy that are rarely bought by the general public? Which ones are popular with the general public? Which special minority products now on the market were not around five or ten years ago?

b. *Industry Location*—Are industries fleeing large cities, or are they investing in disadvantaged areas where a large unskilled or semiskilled labor force may be helped by their presence? Have Chambers of Commerce and antipoverty groups put you in touch with the industries that are doing the most for minority groups. Then the "PR" men from these industries will be glad to help you put together a survey on this.

c. *Libraries*—How does the local public library serve the needs of the minority community? Do they have shelves or sections on the history, culture, and language of the minorities with whom they deal? How do the requests from borrowers who visit a travelling bookmobile differ from those who patronize the main library? Are there bilingual and/or minority librarians? Are there any state or federal funds helping the library to do a better job at serving minorities?

d. *Banks*—What specialized services are used more often in a minority neighborhood, and why? Are the people big users of deposit boxes, checking accounts, or just what? What efforts is the bank making to boost the economic well-being of this particular community? (PR men for the banks would love to help you with this one, but be sure you get several banks to answer this question, and get some answers from minority people who may have a different view.)

e. *The Disappearing Ghetto*—Urban renewal, upward mobility, and new generations have erased what used to be "minority" neighborhoods. Groups who used to be regarded as minorities (Italian, Irish, etc.) have moved into the mainstream of American life. Other groups are following. Is this happening in your area? Ask residents of one of these formerly minority-dominated neighborhoods where everybody went, how they got there, and why they went.

# Culture-Oriented Investigative Projects

## 1. Performing Arts

a. *Theatre, Dance, Music*—Is there a center for the performing arts of the particular minority represented in your area? Do they present "street plays" in the summer, form musical groups identified with their particular culture, and so on? Do children and older people take lessons in these areas to preserve the culture? Interview participants, perhaps at a rehearsal or staged event.

b. *Fiestas and Celebrations*—Your newsroom should have a calendar of cultural events which reoccur yearly so that you may anticipate them and give them continuous coverage from the moment committees are formed and chairmen named right up to the actual staging of the events themselves. Are block parties and dances held by these groups of some special significance which the public at large may not be aware? (See following item, "Religious Life.")

Check also to see if your local minorities "modify" their celebration of well-known holidays. (For example, look for Black or Spanish-speaking Santa Clauses around Christmas time.)

c. *Religious Life*—Certain holidays and other celebrations have more significance to the minority people involved than would appear to others. For example, a Purim carnival at a local Jewish synagogue is not necessarily just another "bazaar."

Check also on the "non-event" aspects of religious life in your area. What are the growth patterns of the various religions in your community? What percentage of the local population do the various religious groups make up, and what are their goals locally?

Interview clergymen from parishes where foreign languages are used all or part of the time. (Ukranian, Slovak, Spanish, Portuguese, Italian, German, and Hebrew, among others.) Is the need for the language growing or diminishing as the years pass, and why?

d. *Weddings*—Sometimes a minority group which has all but submerged itself in day-to-day life with the community at large will revive colorful parts of its heritage at a wedding. Are the flower arrangements unusually colorful and do they have a special significance? (Check with florists.) Will a special kind of musical group play or sing for the ceremony or for the reception? Is it more expensive or difficult to make arrangements for a wedding in these cases? (Problem-oriented: Is it more difficult to get engagement photos in the paper, and is news coverage of the wedding fair?)

e. *Beauty Pageants*—Although you see minorities represented in the Miss America and Miss Universe contests on television, you also find contests for Miss Black America and Miss Puerto Rican Day Festival, etc. Be sure to keep these events on your newsroom calendar and to give as much attention to them as you would to ordinary events of this type locally. The girls who compete in these contests take themselves quite seriously, and their goals and hopes make interesting interview topics.

## 2. Other Customs

a. *Athletics*—At an Italian gathering, you will often find the men engaged in a game of miniature lawn-bowling known as "Bocci." Little boys in Mexican neighborhoods may play with a toy known as a "balero." Latin-American minorities show a great deal of interest in soccer. Have the participants show how the game or toy works. Include the sounds of the activity on tape, perhaps with a little bit of play-by-play narration.

b. *Clothing and Hair Styles*—African dashikis and Mexican serape style clothes are no longer worn by just the individuals identified with the particular culture involved. They are sold in discount houses and department stores everywhere and worn by almost anyone. Afro hair styles are also widely imitated. Check with clothing stores and barber and beauty shops about which items are the most popular and why.

> *Special Note on Placement and Scheduling of Investigative Stories*
>
> The stories listed here obviously cannot compete with "hard" news stories. A plane crash, hotel fire, bank holdup, or parade in town would easily push these investigative stories off the air.
>
> One good time to schedule stories like these is in the "off" hours, such as a Saturday or Sunday afternoon and during other shifts when, at many stations, no newsman is on duty. Instead of having the people who are on the air at these times rotate old stories written by newsmen on previous shifts, why not give them a few of these investigative stories *on cartridge* with one-liner introductions?
>
> Just be sure to check with management on what the policy should be for this kind of story, and be sure to write and edit such stories so that they are attractive rather than long-winded and boring. See the chapter on "The Style of the Newscast."

## Problem-Oriented Investigative Projects

*Warning*—To simply walk up to a Black person at random and ask him about a "ghetto" problem implies to this person that you are operating under a basically false assumption: "All Blacks live in ghettos."

Is this what you *really* mean to imply? All too often, well-meaning but condescending newsmen will take this approach and be disappointed with the results. As you were cautioned earlier, you must first determine the *needs* of the people with whom you are dealing. If this is what *they* want to talk about, fine, then they could use your help. Find out whether this is true *before* you turn your microphone on, so that your questions do not create a problem where none existed.

### 1. Civil Liberties

Check with the local A.C.L.U. and see if there are any cases pending in which the rights of minorities are being defended. If current cases cannot be discussed because of possible conflict with "fair trial" proceedings, get a background briefing of past and future issues that might yield good stories. (See the chapter on "The Police Beat and the Courtroom" regarding coverage of legal cases.)

## 2. Municipal Services

How are the garbage collection, street and sidewalk repair, and other services in areas where minorities predominate? Do the residents feel that they are getting their fair share, compared to other parts of town? (Angry residents of several New York City neighborhoods burned their garbage in the streets once, after months of neglect from the Sanitation Department.)

For another view of the same question—survey the city departments involved and see if their progress reports match the complaints of the residents in the affected areas. If not, see if they are aware of the dissatisfaction and find out what they plan to do about it. (If "nothing," that is a story itself!)

## 3. Community Health

Check Health Departments, exterminating companies, pesticide stores, and others for the kinds of insects that "bug" ghetto areas the most. What preventive programs are underway? Are termites, cockroaches, etc., more active during certain seasons like summer? Are some pesticides just as harmful as the bites? What are the best precautions, especially around babies and young children?

Other problems: How are buildings in your area for such things as rats, lead poisoning in paint, broken plumbing, crumbling walls, fire hazards, and so forth? Follow the building inspector around for the day. What happens to his reports? How is he received by tenants, landlords, and the like?

## 4. Housing Problems

Since money has generally been tight in recent years on construction of *new* homes, is there a boom for remodeling in blighted areas or less affluent neighborhoods? Local contractors, plumbers, lumber firms, etc., can pinpoint the types of work. Who is paying for it? Is the kind of person who lives in such a neighborhood these days more prosperous or is he getting help from state or federal government sources?

Check the Federal Department of Housing and Urban Development. Are they involved in any local projects? (Get their booklet No. HUD-52-F, *Fixing Up Your Home and How to Finance It,* as a reference source.) What steps have been taken to shut off profiteering in mortgages (buying a dilapidated house, painting it, and getting an FHA mortgage to sell it to an unsuspecting disadvantaged person for ten times its actual value), a practice which flourished some years ago?

## 5. Utilities

Residents of economically disadvantaged neighborhoods frequently complain that telephone and electric service in their area is not on a par with that of more affluent parts of town. They claim that they must make higher deposits before a phone can be installed and that they are automatically assigned a lower credit rating for billing purposes just because of the neighborhood. They say that damaged public phone booths are left unrepaired longer in disadvantaged neighborhoods. Some of them also claim that power blackouts or dim-outs hit their neighborhoods first when electric companies are struggling with temporary power shortages.

How much of this is true in your area? Get both sides of the story in situations like this. Check with both the residents of allegedly short-changed neighborhoods and with the officials of the companies involved. Of course, the companies will have a more sophisticated answer. They have public relations people, and their officials are trained to handle such accusations. This is where you as a broadcast journalist will be challenged to examine the two versions and to determine the *real* story.

## 6. Cultural Needs

An issue in some cities where there is a cultural or "fine arts" center is that the plays, dances, musical performances, etc., are all geared to the tastes of the affluent WASP (White Anglo-Saxon Protestant) community and that the needs of the local minorities are being ignored. There are demands for Black theatre or dance groups, and in some towns there is a backlash when white taxpayers find their money being used to support street plays that portray whites and policemen as "pigs."

If no such problem exists in your community, *do not stir one up.* Approach this question from the *positive* angle, i.e., "What is being done to promote the cultural needs of the minority community? Can more be done, and, if so, specifically what?"

Also, does the demand for music lessons, ballet, and other after-school lessons follow the level of prosperity in a community, or are there some favorites in poverty areas? What are they, and who pays for them? (State, federal, local?) Which are girls' and which are boys' favorites? Do antipoverty groups outweigh the standard Cub Scout and Brownie programs found in the more affluent suburbs?

## 7. Employment vs. Unemployment

Take a specific area, perhaps a known disadvantaged neighborhood, and find out how heavily this area depends on government jobs and welfare. How much state and federal aid is being poured into this neighborhood compared with the state or national average? Do merchants in this area find that business is best on the day the welfare checks come out? How much of their monthly business does this account for? What other major sources of income are there in the neighborhood?

Check several surrounding towns with similar disadvantaged neighborhoods and compare the jobless rates. Which towns have the highest percentages, and why? Check State Employment Offices for the number of people drawing unemployment compensation checks. Do the same with the Welfare office. Has this number risen or fallen over the past few months? Why?

## 8. Food Stamps

Is the program really working the way it is supposed to? How do the banks and other stamp-issuing agencies feel about it? How do the merchants feel? What areas get the most food stamps in your town and why? Does the system discourage the earning of higher incomes? Can the average disadvantaged person hope to have a balanced diet, or are some important foods out of reach? Do merchants, public officials, and other shoppers feel that food stamps promote wise buying habits, or are they angered or disappointed at seeing food-stamp customers fill up their shopping carts with snacks, luxury items, novelties, and the more expensive frozen food products? What improvements are proposed in the program?

## 9. Schools

Do the schools in a certain part of town have a higher rate of teacher turnover than elsewhere? Why? Is this attributable to an economically disadvantaged or "blackboard jungle" situation? What is being done to alleviate the problem?

How is the minority student doing in local high schools lately? Has he had to vent his anger in demonstrations or are his needs being adequately cared for? Check students, faculty, parents, and administrators at several schools. See if the curriculum fits the needs of the minority students. (For example, if a foreign-language minority predominates, is proper attention being given to this factor?)

What about the extracurricular activities? What are the students themselves doing to improve the interpersonal relations? What is the outlook for each school in the months ahead, and why? (Here is a chance to throw the spotlight on schools where positive programs are *working,* and to give the reasons, rather than to wait for schools where minority relations are poor to have some kind of incident and report only the negative aspects.)

The old-fashioned "truant officer" has a new role now in many large cities. You can find him in bus terminals, amusement parks, and other areas where kids are liable to run away. Ask a local truancy official about disadvantaged youngsters. Are many of them hung up on dope? Do welfare and unemployment problems have an effect on truancy? What about the home situation? What is being done to get these kids the proper help? What other general solutions are being undertaken?

### 10. The News Media

You see the photographs of debutantes and well-to-do brides in the society pages of most newspapers, but how many pictures and articles are there about minority persons? Are the major newspapers in the area providing fair coverage? Are there any minority-oriented newspapers or magazines in your area providing alternate coverage, and, if so, is this coverage entirely acceptable, or do many minority persons still feel they are short-changed by the regular papers?

You may also ask about the *broadcast* media while you are at it. The results might not be very flattering. If they are not, it is a good hint for you to beef up your social coverage.

### 11. Child Protection

In one large city, a child climbs over a fence and dies of electrocution from a high-voltage railroad line. In still another city, a child climbs between the slats of a fence surrounding a construction site and drowns in the stream which is being rechannelled for an urban renewal and flood-control project. In both cases, the fences are at least 10 feet high and there are warning signs to "keep out," but in both cases angry demonstrations result, with demonstrators blaming the railroad and the construction company for not having adequate fencing. Company officials reply that parents should bear some of the responsibility and keep their kids out of places where potential danger exists. Who is right, and why? What are some of the solutions being proposed? Check your own community to see if such hazards exist and what is being done to avert such tragedies.

## 12. Community Safety

Find out from police statistics where the ten most dangerous areas for pedestrian accidents are in town. Many of them will be in areas where there is no direct police supervision, but are many of them also in disadvantaged neighborhoods? Perhaps with some traffic sounds in the background, interview pedestrians about the problem near these locations. What solutions are proposed by police and by area residents?

## 13. Civil Unrest—Predictable?

After residents burned garbage in the streets one summer to show displeasure with collection service, New York's Mayor John Lindsay called for weekly reports on the "pulse" of the community from various sources. Police precincts, neighborhood "city halls," and other municipal agencies were asked to file the reports in attempt to head off any future "predictable" symptoms of potential violence.

How do the symptoms of frustration become known to city authorities in your area? Do residents of potentially troubled neighborhoods approach any city agencies? Which agencies, and what are the steps for follow-up? (Is there an ombudsman in town, or *should* there be?) Conduct a survey to see if City Hall is responsive or not. Is bureaucracy apparent (for example, do the Mayor and various department heads give you this "My door is always open" line and then dismiss matters like these, or do they actively seek to resolve troublesome situations without waiting for organized protests or civil disturbances to make the problem visible?

## 14. Black Law Enforcers

The minority policeman is often called "the man in the middle." He must represent both the predominantly white establishment and its laws as well as the minority group of which he is a member. Interview the minority members of area police forces, sheriff's offices, and state police ranks. (Be sure to get permission from their superiors before you do, and determine whether or not you can use the men's names, voices on tape, or just the percentages from a "survey" story.) How do they view their present role as compared to the same role several years ago? Any improvement or deterioration? Why? What are some of their major problems and goals?

## 15. Ambulance and Fire Truck Drivers

What are some of the problems involved in covering a call in a disadvantaged neighborhood? Kids running around at night? Abandoned cars? Trash piled in the streets? Uncooperative or hostile neighbors? The most important question: *What can be done to improve the situation?* What is their department doing to improve the relations with these neighborhoods?

## 16. Arrests

What is it like to make an arrest in a disadvantaged part of your town lately? To what extent do officers get insults or arguments from those being arrested? From bystanders? How do the neighbors feel about the officers? What are some of the latest tactics used to "defuse" a situation so it does not lead to charges of brutality or to a civil disturbance? See if you can get to talk with both minority and white policemen, then compare their answers.

## 17. Courtroom Behavior

Disruptive elements have caused extremely tight security measures at certain trials over the past few years (for example, the "Chicago 7," "Black Panther," and "Angela Davis" trials). Are similar measures in effect for trials in your area? If so, do minority groups feel these measures are discriminatory? Why? What alternatives would they propose to ensure a fair trial? How do bailiffs and deputies feel about the kinds of defendants they have been bringing in lately? What solutions do they propose? (See the next chapter, "The Police Beat and The Courtroom," for some ground rules before you begin this project.)

18. **Criminal Rehabilitation and Drug Rehabilitation**

(See projects at the end of the next chapter if either of these topics is an important issue in your area.)

19. **University Research**

Many colleges have been the targets of "peace" demonstrators who claim that the colleges are only "Pentagon Think Tanks." Actually some colleges are actively engaged in programs to help the domestic quality of life in the community around them, especially in regard to minority and disadvantaged groups. What solutions to urban problems are being developed in your area? How many of these programs are financed by some level of government, and how many are doing it with private funds?

20. **Bartenders and Clergymen**

Both handle people's problems. How do these problems differ in disadvantaged areas? How do they differ among specific minority groups whether the area is "disadvantaged" or not? Have people been calling on them more lately for advice? What kind of advice? Have they felt they have been able to solve these problems? Is there any noticeable trend in the types of problems?

# IN-CLASS AND HOMEWORK ASSIGNMENTS

1. Prepare a list of racial, religious, and foreign-national minorities in communities within a ten-mile radius of your school. How many persons are in each of the groups you have named? Evaluate newspaper and broadcast coverage of each of these groups within the past few months. For

which groups has the coverage been advancement-oriented, for which groups has it been culture-oriented, and for which groups has news coverage been problem-oriented?

2. Do a profile report on a minority group assigned by your teacher. Trace the history of this group in your area, the present number of individuals in this group, and its status compared to that of the general public. Include such factors as neighborhood and housing conditions, occupations, school population, economic and social standing, employment and professional representation, etc. Evaluate local news coverage of this group, and give reasons for your evaluation.

3. Choose a topic from the investigative projects for this chapter and write an imaginary transcript which includes:

   a) 10- to 15-second introduction by newsman or disc jockey.

   b) Taped narration by investigative reporter, before and after.

   c) Excerpt of interview with minority person or other subject called for in project.

   Total reading time for items a, b, and c above should not exceed 60 seconds.

4. The following is an "agenda" for an imaginary 5-minute newscast on a small-town station late Sunday afternoon. Tell where you would insert your story written for assignment Question 3 (above) and which items you would omit in order to accommodate your story:

   a) Wire-service story: More than 100 killed in train-wreck in France. (35 seconds)

   b) Wire-service story: President working with advisors this weekend on budget cuts before presentation to Congress. (20 seconds)

   c) Wire-service story: FBI captures hijacker without firing a shot at San Diego Airport. (25 seconds)

   d) Local story: Large downtown hotel announced yesterday that it will close its doors after 44 years of operation in town.

e) Local story: Break-in on Friday night at grocery store. Seventeen dollars in cash missing from register, cigarette machine broken open. (25 seconds)

f) Wire-service story: Six traffic deaths in state so far this weekend; some details. (30 seconds)

g) Wire-service story: Governor opposed to proposed increase in state sales tax. (20 seconds)

h) Local story: Elderly couple from out-of-state injured in local auto accident last night. (25 seconds)

i) Commercial. (60 seconds)

j) Sports scores. (15 seconds)

k) Weather. (15 seconds)

Photo by Chip Hires.

# Chapter 5

# The Police Beat and the Courtroom

Go into the newsroom of a small-market, low-power, day-time radio station, and what will you find tacked up on the wall? Right!—the phone numbers for all the area police stations. To some of these outfits, this is all there is to news. Just rip a few stories from the AP or the UPI wire, mix them with the latest fender-benders and break-ins (all worded exactly the way the desk sergeant read them to you from the police blotter) and, by golly, you have got yourself a newscast ready to go!

Now consider a medium-sized market, say for instance in a city of 150,000 to 250,000 people. Now here are the *big* fellas; they have a police radio and a big "trade-out" vehicle with their call letters painted all over it, which they fondly refer to as their "mobile unit." Just let the police dispatcher call a signal number and location and they are first on the scene with lights flashing and press card in hand. Yes sir, hardly a sparrow falls in our town that they do not scoop-it-up on tape and make an "actuality" out of it somehow. They feel that they should win some kind of award for all this news gathering.

Award? For *what*? Just try to find an award in the broadcast industry for the kind of reporting described above.

## ARE YOU A BROADCAST JOURNALIST OR A TALKING POLICE BLOTTER?

Radio stations are known by their music formulas, such as rock, country, middle-of-the-road, etc., but terms like "all news" or even "rip-and-read" are being heard more often now. One formula which seems to be popular is "Cop-on-a-Cartridge." Just turn on your radio almost anywhere in the country, and before long you will pick up a station featuring the voices of police spokesmen describing run-of-the-mill holdups, traffic accidents, and the like.

At stations using the "Cop-on-a-Cartridge" formula, it doesn't really matter what each story is about, just so long as the policeman's voice is captured on tape, made into a cartridge, and played repeatedly during the day. There is a "Boy-Who-Cried-Wolf" effect from doing this, because a really *big* police story someday may sound just like all the fender-benders and break-ins which have been running all along.

Even some TV stations are not exempt from this category, covering little more than the old-fashioned police beat and other "event-oriented" stories which lend themselves to film or videotape coverage, such as fires, floods, deaths, and disasters. Many radio and TV stations operate at a level just barely above that of "Cop-on-a-Cartridge," covering routine meetings of city councils or other government bodies, press conferences, speeches, etc. Such stations are not really dealing with the "... problems, needs and interests" of the community as called for in the FCC's *Primer on Ascertainment,* and some group may challenge the station's application at license renewal time for not having kept the community well-informed. There are about twenty types of community groups listed in the "ascertainment" surveys filed by most stations with their renewal applications lately. Check with your station manager to see that they are all covered.

Although this chapter will discuss how to cover the police beat properly, you should broaden your horizons and take all other areas into account which deserve coverage. Be sure to check all the investigative projects in this book for a list of good topics to report on if you feel you are "hung up" on police stories.

# HOW NOT TO "BUG" THE DESK SERGEANT

"Why is that desk sergeant holding out on us? He probably gave the story to our competitors already. Boy, is he rude. He's not only leaving things out and slanting it his way, but he's trying to give us the impression that he doesn't have time to talk to us. Come on, come on! I heard it on the police radio already. Does he think it's some big secret or something? These cops have a gross ignorance of what the problems are in putting a newscast together. They have no sense of what news is at all. Now he's trying to make like he's our friend and that he's doing us the favor. I thought so; he wants it on the air *his* way or there won't be any more favors."

Does some of the above sound familiar to you? It certainly sounds familiar to policemen—familiar as a broken record! It is a checklist of favorite gripes lodged by newsmen against police. If that is the attitude you portray toward them when you call, you are just one more newsman they can do without. Look at it through the eyes of the desk sergeant for a moment. A survey of policemen's favorite gripes about newsmen revealed that police think newsmen:

- ▶ demand too much (like details that are not checked out, are not authorized for release, that violate constitutional rights of the accused, and the like).
- ▶ do not understand police problems.
- ▶ are not considerate.
- ▶ are looking primarily for scandal.
- ▶ take minor things and build them up into major problems.
- ▶ do not dig deep enough and wind up airing surface facts which are often incomplete and misleading.
- ▶ play politics.
- ▶ emphasize disagreements between factions rather than build up the many good relationships which exist.

The police also blame newsmen for:

- ▶ running as the top story an item about occasional police misconduct while overlooking the many good, clean, honest policemen who deserve mention once in a while.
- ▶ being in too much of a hurry and wanting everything

"now" instead of allowing an investigation to unfold in an orderly manner.

▶ giving prominence to their favorite agency or officer when several police agencies may have worked on the same case.

Newsmen, according to police, often think they are better investigators than policemen are. Sometimes it seems like each newsman is trying to win the Pulitzer Prize by attempting to prove that police arrested the wrong man, or did not arrest the right one. In fact, say the police, newsmen build up some stories so much that it is hard to make the charge stick in court. They prejudice jurors with all that publicity, and while they are out fighting for their "right to know" under the First Amendment, they seem to forget all about the right to a fair trial under the Sixth Amendment.

Finally, say the policemen in the survey, when they tell newsmen they can not give them a story, or certain details of one, the newsmen go around the corner and get it from somebody else and it comes out warped on the air. Since it is hard to tell which newsmen are the reliable ones and which newsmen are not, . . .

> *"We just have to treat all newsmen as*
> *though they were unreliable."*

There you have it, straight from the mouths of policemen themselves in a survey taken some years ago in the Columbus, Ohio, area. The final conclusion—about *all* newsmen being presumed unreliable—is probably the most damaging of all.

What doesn't help, of course, is the fact that as one newsman you cannot account for the conduct of all your colleagues throughout the industry, including those from the newspapers. The local stations in your area may enjoy a pretty good rapport with the policemen in your town under normal conditions, but just let a murder take place or a bomb go off and hundreds of reporters from out-of-town will either call or show up in person at the local precinct, shoving their microphones in the face of that tired detective who has been trying to work on the case all night. You may have unknowingly done this yourself at one time or another if you have worked in this business before. Have you ever called a police station in a distant town to get a statement on tape about a major crime or catastrophe? It might just be that you are the 99th station or newspaper to call, and that the desk sergeant is getting pretty tired of giving out that statement.

As more than one Police Chief has hinted, it would be nice to have newsmen do some *other* stories about police work. There are some things police would rather talk about, like a report on how the men on the force are earning college credits in Police Science, how some of them are working in their free time with minority or disadvantaged or youth groups, etc. Maybe they could use some help with an educational series on the drug problem or pedestrian safety in town. If you as a newsman are just following the calls on the police radio or calling the desk sergeant every hour or two to see what is on the blotter, you are missing a great deal that goes on behind the scenes. You are also *building resentment,* because the only time they talk to you is when they are under pressure. If this is the case at your station, it is time you had a "chat with the Chief" to find out what his department would *like* to talk about. Be sure to see some of the investigative projects at the end of this chapter before you drop by his office.

## SOME PITFALLS TO AVOID

Policemen are not medical spokesmen. One station that had an all-night "stringer" who drove around with a police radio in his car ran into some problems with this. Newsmen reading this fellow's stories the next morning would often get calls from area hospitals saying that the stories had given the victims' conditions incorrectly. Sometimes a morning newsman calling to see if an individual described in a story as "near death" would be told by hospital officials that the person had simply been "treated and released" after the accident. It finally dawned on the people in the newsroom that their all-night man was getting his "medical" reports from well-meaning but unqualified policemen at the scene. It may be the policeman's *opinion* at the scene that someone does not appear to be too badly hurt or, to the contrary, that a certain victim will be "lucky if he manages to live," but this is just a *tip*. The official word—the information you use on the air—comes only from qualified and authorized spokesmen at the hospital.

"Police brutality" is a dangerous term for newsmen to use. As already has been mentioned several times in this book, a policeman charged in court with some sort of injury, assault, etc., upon someone else is not necessarily charged with brutality. Brutality may not be a word officially recognized for the purpose of court prosecution at all in your state, but it *may* at the same time be a word recognized by the police department as a formal charge requiring a disciplinary hearing. It may come before, during, or after any court action, depending on the laws in your state, but in any case it is an extremely sensitive term and not advisable for broadcast use unless you can actually quote the person who used it and be sure that those were his *exact words,* not some term that "sounded like it."

The police radio is to be used for *"tips"* only, never as a bona fide news source. It is against FCC regulations to take a police message from the police radio and broadcast it, so you *must* get it confirmed by the authorities themselves before you can air it. Furthermore, all such messages are understood to mean that something may *possibly* have happened, not that it *has* happened, and that policemen being dispatched to the scene are investigating a *possibility,* not a confirmed fact.

One newsman the writer knew once heard a "Signal 37" on the police radio, called the desk sergeant and asked, "Sarge, was that a Signal 37 you just announced?"

"Yes, it was," said the sergeant.

Thinking he had properly confirmed that a bank holdup was indeed in progress, the newsman went on the air, interrupting the program to name the bank and to say what presumably was taking place. Bank officials protested vehemently, and the newsman claimed that he had confirmed it with police headquarters.

"I never told you there was a holdup going on," said the sergeant later on. "I told you that we had a Signal 37, which means we've received an *alarm* for a holdup." It turned out that the alarm was set off accidentally, and one newsman who thought he was first with the big story of the day found himself writing a retraction! When *you* call headquarters, do not just confirm the coded signal; confirm whether or not the incident implied by such a signal is actually taking place.

## POLICE JARGON—HOW TO TRANSLATE IT

Terms taken from a police blotter are usually too awkward for normal conversation. They are intended for use in the courtroom, not on the air. So that you do not sound as though you were reading from such a blotter, you have to "translate" for broadcast purposes:

| IF POLICE SAY: | WRITE IT: |
| --- | --- |
| Lacerations, abrasions, and contusions. | Cuts and bruises. |
| Charged with larceny over $15 and under $250. | Accused of stealing a small amount of . . . (cash, goods, or whatever it was). |
| Failure to grant right-of-way at an intersecton. | Just say that police "charged" or "blamed" whomever they gave tickets to. |
| Held in lieu of $25 bond for a September 13th court arraignment before Judge Milton Brown. | Do not specify bonds under $1000. No court date or judge's name unless it is a big case attracting state or national attention. |
| At 2:38 a.m. | Early this morning, *or* just after 2:30. |
| Investigated by officers Enrico Kryzakowski and Joseph Gablanowitz. | Sorry, but *leave it out* unless an officer did something heroic, controversial, or was injured. (See reasons in Chapter 9, "The Style of the Newscast.") |
| Fire gutted a house at 128 Main Street occupied by 31-year-old Mrs. Tom Smith and owned by a Harry B. Todd of 56 Maple Avenue. | Leave out absentee owners' names unless they were somehow involved. Leave out ages unless they are babies, elderly people, or the age is highly significant for some reason vital to the story. |
| Mrs. Edmonds was treated at the scene for a bruised knee by ambulance attendant Oscar V. Carey. | Forget it! (Unless everybody else was killed or something, then just say Mrs. E. was not seriously hurt.) |

| | |
|---|---|
| Apprehended by Trooper Wood of the Fishkill Barracks "B.C.I." | Other than fellow policemen, only one listener in a hundred will know what the initials mean. It is a corny way to imply that you are "in" with the police crowd. |
| The Chief warned . . .<br>The Mayor said . . .<br>The City Council Voted . . . | *Which* Chief? (Police? Fire?) Which city? Your station does not stop at the city line, and even if you are the Springfield station, call him: "Springfield Police Chief . . ." |
| Jones struck Smith on the head. | *Police say* Jones struck Smith *(the radio station did not). According to Police,* . . . or . . . Jones *allegedly* or *reportedly* did whatever it was, just so long as it is clear that police, not the station, are making the accusation. |

## USE OF PRESS CARDS AND CREDENTIALS

Every year, the managers and editors of the nation's news outlets—including radio and TV news departments—receive application forms from police and other government agencies for renewal of their Press Cards. At the larger stations and network operations, there is no doubt about who is a "newsman" and who is not. At smaller stations, though, the list of reporters named by the management is quite amusing. The boss's wife, the janitor, salesmen, copy writers, and practically everybody on the payroll plus a few friends are likely to be listed as qualified broadcast journalists for the purpose of getting these credentials.

At one small station, it took a lot of courage for the News Director to drop many of these names one year. When the Press Cards finally arrived for the remaining few names on the list, they were passed on to the recipients with a letter telling them that they were taking on a responsibility for the use of the cards.

This letter should be quoted in full as a guide for those newsmen carrying Press Cards:

Dear _____,

Attached is a Police Press credential for your use as a WXXX "news" staff member.

Along with it, may we please bring to your attention the fact that every so often police officials have had some questions as to the validity of the names we present to them as "newsmen" in order to get these credentials? While we are fairly certain that WXXX personnel would never deliberately abuse a press card, may we offer some suggestions as to how you might help us uphold the station's integrity:

1) For the record: under no circumstances is this credential a pass to park illegally or to "chisel" your way into paid performances with no intention of giving news coverage when it is expected. Police and fire officials may allow some leeway at the scene of a bona fide emergency to reporters who appear to be doing their job, but they are likely to question the indiscriminate use of such passes for nonemergency situations and routine business of a nonnews nature.

2) Since we tell the people to whom we apply for this pass that you are employed as a "news" staff member for this station, we would expect that in return you would act the part in as professional a manner as you can. Just one individual who abuses "press" privileges, whether from this station or any other, casts doubt on the validity of every reporter who must depend on the same Press Card.

In particular, if access to the scene of a news story, or information about such a story, is withheld by those in charge, extreme care must be used to exercise courtesy. A show of frustration or anger at the scene of a story upon not getting all you want is likely to alienate these people for future occasions. Express any unhappiness you may experience about covering a news event to us here at the station, not to those at the scene.

3) Not all on-the-scene stories demand the use of a Press Card. In fact, very few do. Any veteran reporter will tell you he has never been asked to show his credentials more than once or twice in a year's time, and he will probably add that you can tell the "Cub Reporter" or the rank beginner because the latter always flashes a Press Card at the drop of a hat. In some cases, the ostentatious shoving of a Press Card under someone's nose, as though demanding to get in, will result in the "bum's rush."

4) Finally, it almost goes without saying that we would appreciate your call whenever you *do* happen to come across a story, whether you get to use your Press Card or not. At least a portion of our station's listenership and income is based on the quality of its news operation, and you can do your part to help improve that aspect.

News stories will not always happen at the most convenient time, or in the most convenient place, or under the most comfortable circumstances. It could be the middle of the night, raining, and the people in charge could be a bit irritable because they are working under pressure. Whatever the case, we hope and trust you will do the very best you know how, and that this credential will be of some help to you whenever it is needed.

With your understanding and cooperation, we shall have no qualms about assuring police and other officials that you are qualified to hold this pass, and that the credentials they have issued are in good hands.

Yours truly,

.............................

News Director

—and what was the reaction to the letter? Well, some of the disc jockeys who thought they were "stars" did not like someone else telling them what broadcasting was all about, but somehow management eventually decided that perhaps the News Director was trying to raise the standards a bit and increase the level of responsibility called for on the part of the station's Press Card holders, so they backed the News Director and the opposition subsided. The following year, everybody who received a Press Card got the same letter and there was no opposition.

Unfortunately, it will be a long time before the broadcast industry follows this pattern. Many stations still hand out *their own* so-called Press Cards with the words "Press" or "News" printed in big red letters across the middle of them. Even the National Association of Broadcasters will send the managers of its member stations any number of official-looking wallet cards or visor cards they may ask for. All of them are very impressive-looking documents with the words "Radio News" displayed prominently across them, but somehow no Press Card can really make you a bona fide reporter. When certain agencies require their own official authorization before admitting newsmen to the scene of a story, these mass-produced and indiscriminately awarded credentials are then not worth very much anyway.

# A LOOK AT COURTS AND LAWYERS

If you have ever tried to carry a portable tape recorder into a courtroom, you may have found your welcome less than cordial. Court officials may look at you suspiciously, and one or two of them may be seen whispering into the judge's ear, giving every indication that they are talking about *you.* Eventually, a bailiff or deputy may step over to where you are seated and ask if your machine is turned on, or whether you plan to use it. In fact, they may ask you to leave the room or even the building with it. "Why," you may ask yourself, "is everybody so uptight about a tape recorder?"

Over the years, it seems, we have inherited a set of ground rules for coverage of court cases which are based on repeated abuses by the news media—more recently the *broadcast* news media—that have made things very difficult. It will take years, perhaps decades, to turn the situation around.

Let's go to Flemington, New Jersey. The year is 1934. The case on trial will go down in history as a courtroom landmark. It is the famous Lindbergh Kidnapping Case, and before it is over our friends from the print media will have learned quite a few lessons about the rights of the accused to a fair trial versus the public's "right to know."

Famed journalist Walter Lippman is quoted from a speech he gave to a 1936 gathering of the American Society of Newspaper Editors, just a year or so after the trial concluded, and the account, in Rivers and Schramm's *Responsibility in Mass Communications,* is nothing that newsmen can be proud of. Lippman says, among other things, that:

▶ Papers ran police claims of having an "iron-clad" case against the accused, carpenter Bruno Hauptmann.

▶ Reporters asked people on the street at random what they thought, and from 12 of these people concluded that "Bruno Guilty, But Had Aides."

▶ When the courtroom was already crowded (capacity 260) constables let in 275 more spectators without passes.

▶ Attorneys for both sides issued as many as a hundred subpoenas in one day to their friends to get them in as spectators.

▶ Pictures were taken despite orders forbidding it, and no action was taken.

▶ Reporters filed stories with their papers that Hauptmann "made senseless denials" on the stand and that he looked like "a thing lacking human characteristics."

▶ Both lawyers held news conferences and issued statements to the press, almost from the day of Hauptmann's arrest:

▶▶ The defense attorney told reporters before one session that he would name the kidnappers, and that they were from the Lindbergh household.

▶▶ The prosecuting attorney said that Mrs. Lindbergh's testimony later that day would be "loaded with importance" and on another occasion that he would "wrap the kidnap ladder around Hauptmann's neck."

Of course the lawyers were violating Canon 20 of the American Bar Association Code of Ethics with their statements and news conferences. The police who talked about their "iron-clad" case and the officials who not only allowed the courtroom to become so overcrowded but who also looked the other way when all those pictures were being taken and all those other abuses were occurring did not help things either, but in the long run *the newsmen* were blamed for the travesty! Two years later, the American Bar Association passed Canon 35, barring the photographers and the so-called electronic media from the courtroom. At first, "electronic media" just covered radio and telegraph, but later the term was expanded to include television.

One would think that after 20 years or more the news media might have learned something from the Lindbergh experience, but apparently not. In 1954, say Rivers and Schramm, "Many of the patterns of the Hauptmann case were repeated." It was the famous murder trial of Dr. Sam Sheppard, accused of killing his wife:

Hordes of reporters and photographers descended on Cleveland. Information was leaked. Notes were passed to reporters by the accused. Lawyers talked. Self-styled crime experts analyzed the evidence, even added evidence, in public print. Biographies of the accused were published and broadcast. The photographic coverage was extensive. The sex element was played big, and the crime was described in gruesome detail."

At the time, all this failed to prevent the conviction and sentencing of Dr. Sam Sheppard to life in prison, but ten years later the Supreme Court ruled that because of the "carnival atmosphere" at the trial, Dr. Sheppard was entitled to another. Rivers and Schramm quote Justice Thomas Clark's opinion, which includes a scathing denunciation of the judge. Justice Clark says the judge should have asserted his authority and control of the courtroom by:

► restricting the number of newsmen and their use of court facilities, and regulating their conduct in the courtroom.

► insulating witnesses.

► controlling the release of leads, gossip, or any other information to newsmen by police officers, witnesses, and lawyers for both sides.

In connection with the last item, Justice Clark is quoted as saying: "The prosecution repeatedly made evidence available to the news media which was never offered in the trial. Much of the evidence disseminated in this fashion was clearly inadmissible. The newspapers described in detail clues that had been found by the police, but not put into the record."

In 1966—12 years later—Dr. Sam Sheppard was given another trial under tight controls and was acquitted. Unfortunately, the news media will never quite be "acquitted" as conclusively. Most newsmen will face severe restrictions in the years ahead whenever they go near a courtroom because of the abuses in these and countless other trials. Over the years, the necessity to order defendants strapped to their chairs and gagged (as in the case of National Black Panther Chairman Bobby Seale in the "Chicago 7" trial) to avoid their screaming of obscenities and their wrestling with deputies and others for the benefit of the news media—coupled with the appearance of flamboyant lawyers whose purpose often seems aimed more at winning an award for acting rather than at winning a court case—points out even more clearly that participants are sharply aware of the presence of the news media and feel somehow compelled to make headlines whether or not they make a tight case in legal terms.

There are several factors working against newsmen that prevent any quick solution to the problem. For one thing, professions like law and medicine require their members to acquire certain degrees, to pass certain examinations, and to swear to uphold the Hippocratic Oath or the Canons of Ethics. No such restrictions govern the coming and going of newsmen, and those with the least training and lowest standards can sit next to the Pulitzer Prize-winners in almost any news conference. For another thing, though, the "show biz" image somehow taints every newsman who comes from a radio or TV station. He must compete with his colleagues from other stations. This competition, combined with the temptation of opposing attorneys, witnesses, defendants, and of police and other public figures to seek favorable treatment by the news media, is enough to keep the lid on courtroom news coverage for quite some time to come.

## FREE PRESS VERSUS FAIR TRIAL: A BRIEF HISTORY

The problem of a *Free Press* versus a *Fair Trial* is certainly not a new one. It has been with us ever since the United States has existed, and it has grown more and more complex with the years. Literally hundreds and hundreds of volumes have been written about the issue over the decades by newsmen, lawyers, judges, journalism and law school professors, and so on. This book cannot pretend to cover the topic in depth in the space of one thin chapter, but it can give you some of the major highlights and point you toward some helpful references should you wish to pursue the matter at greater length.

The first Chief Justice of the United States Supreme Court, John Marshall, was aware that newspaper articles were having an effect on the outcome of the Aaron Burr trial. Marshall said he did not mind what he termed "light impressions" in newspapers which could easily be corrected by testimony and fair presentation of evidence in the courtroom, but he was quite concerned about articles in the Alexandria *Expositor* in nearby Virginia which he said created "strong and deep impressions" which would be hard to erase from the minds of jurors in spite of any testimony or evidence which may be presented against them. This has been the issue ever since.

Back in Chief Justice Marshall's day, the news traveled only as fast as horse and buggy could carry it, so there were a number of handy procedural devices that could be used to ensure a fair trial. These included:

- ▶ change of venue (moving the trial to another location where jurors presumably might be more impartial)
- ▶ sequestration (isolating the jury)
- ▶ continuance (postponement of court sessions until the furor and publicity die down a bit)
- ▶ instructions from the judge (telling the jury to disregard certain kinds of evidence)
- ▶ *voir dire* examination (careful screening of prospective jurors to determine whether they are "objective" or not)
- ▶ motions for new trials, mistrial declarations, appeals, habeas corpus, etc.

Many of these procedures are still used, of course, and in routine, day-to-day robbery, burglary, and narcotics cases they still work. It is still quite possible to pick a jury which has heard little or nothing about the case. It is in the sensational cases (like the *Sheppard* and *Lindbergh* cases just used as examples) that all the procedural devices available to the court are not enough to keep pace with all the rampant publicity and "strong impressions" which are likely to enter the minds of prospective jurors.

Justice Marshall never heard of the Chicago Seven, Billie Sol Estes, Richard Speck, Lee Harvey Oswald, and Jack Ruby, or even Bruno Hauptmann and Sam Sheppard, nor could he have begun to imagine the problems that these cases would create in the 20th century. Today, living almost anywhere in the world, you can easily form an opinion about Angela Davis in San Jose, Richard Nixon in San Clemente, the Black Panthers or the Simbionese Liberation Army, or of any person or group whose name comes up in the news. As you hear the stories break on the radio, or see them in print or on television, you are gaining impressions which cannot be eradicated. In today's supersonic age of jet travel and instantaneous news delivery, the old methods of avoiding the saturation of jurors' minds with details of a sensational crime just do not work.

It comes down to this, then: does the public's "right to know," guaranteed in the First Amendment to the Constitution as a protection against secret tribunals and secret government operations, take precedence over an individual's right to a fair trial, guaranteed in the Sixth Amendment as a protection against "lynch mobs?" Both of these guarantees are written into our Bill of Rights, yet they have apparently conflicted with one another over the decades. The following is a brief history of some of the cases, codes, rulings, and other milestones bearing upon this important issue:

**Spanish Inquisition**
**British Star Chamber**
**French Lettres du Cachet**

The secret tribunals of the European governments prior to the 1700's were so entirely distasteful to people in the colonies that were soon to become a democracy that there was no chance that such procedures would survive. It was written into our Constitution in the sixth of ten amendments that were to become known as the "Bill of Rights" that every citizen is guaranteed a *public* trial before a jury of his peers. Secret tribunals were strictly prohibited.

**John Peter Zenger Trial (1734)**—This is the famous case that established "freedom of the press" in the colonies even before the nation gained its independence. Censorship and licensing had disappeared in England by 1695, when Parliament refused to renew such laws, and although these practices continued in the New World under the authority of the colonial governors until about 1730, Zenger managed to draw the fire of Governor William Cosby by establishing his New York *Weekly Journal* in 1733 and openly criticising British authority. He was charged with seditious libel and sent to jail simply on orders of the governor after a grand jury failed to indict him. The governor even disbarred Zenger's lawyer, who then had to turn to someone else to plead the case. They came up with Andrew Hamilton of Philadelphia, who had the reputation of being just about the best lawyer in the colonies. Zenger waited for eight months in jail to be tried, but finally Hamilton managed to convince the jury in a ringing plea that was quoted for years afterward that they would earn the "love and esteem" of their fellow

citizens and of everyone who preferred freedom to slavery, to uphold the right to expose and oppose arbitrary power by speaking
and writing the truth. The jury's acquittal of Zenger will remain in
the history books as the official precedent establishing "freedom
of the press," a verdict which influences court decisions and legislation to this day.

**United States vs. Aaron Burr (1807)**—Col. Burr, who had recently
finished a term as Vice President of the United States (1801-1805)
had been arrested in February of 1807 and charged with treason.
Specifically, he was accused of planning to seize New Orleans and
make it the capital of a new country under his own rule, and of preparing to carry out a military expedition against Mexico. As mentioned earlier in this chapter, Chief Justice Marshall was concerned
about the impressions the jurors might get from published accounts
of the trial and the developments which had led to Burr's arrest. After
a trial of almost seven months, Burr was acquitted. Much of the
"evidence" published in the papers or disclosed in testimony by
third-party individuals who were not involved directly in the case
was not admitted in court because it was hearsay or ruled inadmissible for other reasons.

**Mooney and Billings (1916)**—Thomas Mooney and Warren Billings
were two well-known labor leaders in the San Francisco area just
after the turn of the century. The nation was in a period of turbu-
lence which began with the assassination of President William
McKinley in 1901, grew with the coming of World War I in 1914,
and was aggravated by labor violence and the growth of the bomb-
throwing "anarchist" movement. When bombs went off during the
July 22nd "Preparedness Day" parade, a nationwide hunt was
touched off for these two men, among others. Mooney, who consistently maintained that he and his wife had watched the parade
from their own rooftop more than a mile from the scene of the
bombing, first became aware that he was wanted when he picked
up a newspaper almost a week later. He and his wife had rented
a tent and a rowboat and had been enjoying a popular vacation
area for several days when they finally saw his picture on the front
page of a newspaper, along with a detailed story of his radical career written just about the way the prosecutor would like to have
seen it. Bankers, industrial leaders, and the "establishment press,"
which they controlled, saw the likes of Mooney and Billings as symbols of radicalism and a threat to patriotism, law, and order. Not
only did management of the press tend to inflame public opinion
about such defendants, but it was common practice in those days
for reporters to depend upon the District Attorney's office or the
police as their only source of information about a case. Billings
got life, Mooney was sentenced to hang. This was commuted to life
imprisonment when it began to appear that Mooney would become

an international martyr and a symbol of capitalist oppression of the working class. After more than twenty years behind bars, Mooney and Billings were freed by the governor of California in 1939, but the role played by the press at the time of the trial can never be looked upon with pride by professional journalists.

**The Lindbergh Kidnapping: New Jersey vs. Hauptmann (1934)—** Carpenter Bruno Hauptmann was charged with kidnapping the infant son of famed aviator Charles Lindbergh and of demanding ransom, shortly after Lindbergh made his record-breaking flight across the Atlantic Ocean. It is a classic case in the history of journalism, involving abuses by just about everybody concerned: police, prosecution, defense, court officials, the press, and not least of all the judge who failed to control the situation. After Hauptmann had been executed, the affair was termed by an 18-member committee of lawyers and newspaper executives as "the most spectacular and depressing example of improper publicity and professional misconduct ever presented to the people of the United States in a criminal trial."

**Baltimore Radio Case (Maryland vs. Baltimore Radio Show) (1948-1950)—** When an 11-year-old girl was dragged from her bicycle and stabbed to death in Baltimore, four radio stations began to play upon the public alarm by increasing the excitement in their newscasts. When a black suspect by the name of Eugene James was finally booked after an all-out police search, one station screamed, "Stand by for a sensation!" as it began the news of the arrest. Other newscasts told all about James' confession, his "long" criminal record, and about his having dug up the murder weapon and reenacted the crime for police. The municipal courts fined the stations for contempt, charging them with broadcasting items which were not admissable in court as evidence and which were likely to influence potential jurors. The stations paid the nominal fines but appealed, saying that no one had proved that the broadcasts had any effect on the jury's impartiality. The Maryland Court of Appeals reluctantly accepted this argument, overturning the contempt citations, and the U.S. Supreme Court refused to hear the case.

It was to be one of the last times they would do so, as Justice Felix Frankfurter wrote in an outraged dissent, "It hardly seems necessary for the court to say to men who are experienced in the trial of jury cases that every time defense counsel asked a prospective juror whether he had heard a radio broadcast to the effect that his client has confessed to the crime or that he has been guilty of similar crimes, he would by that (very question) be driving just one more nail into James' coffin."

"The broadcast(s)," concluded the dissenting justice, "must have had an indelible effect upon the public mind and . . . that effect was bound to follow the members of the panel into the jury room." Within a few years, a majority of the court would agree with this position on future cases. (See "Irvin vs. Dowd," later in this discussion.)

**The Brinks Robbery Case (Commonwealth vs. Geagan) (1950-1959)**—Shortly after 7 p.m. on January 17, 1950, seven armed men wearing rubber Halloween masks forced two Brinks' employees to give up more than $1.2 million in cash and securities at the Brinks' headquarters building in Boston. Within the hour there was a 14-state alarm out and roadblocks throughout the area. A $100,000 reward was offered by the firm for clues and information leading to convictions, but despite 10,000 letters within the first week, no one was captured. It began to look like the "perfect crime," and police and the press suspected an inside job. Although state laws allowed six years, the federal statute-of-limitations law said that no one could be held accountable for the crime in a federal court after three years. In November of 1952, a grand jury was convened to set everything up for indictments, except for the names, just in case anyone was arrested before January 17, 1953. As the six-year deadline approached in 1956, strange things suddenly began to happen. Boston underworld figure "Specs" O'Keefe was ambushed not once, but twice. There were rumors that he threatened to talk to authorities about not receiving what was apparently his share in the gigantic robbery, and that the mob was trying to kill him. The FBI got to "Specs" before the mob did, and on January 12, 1956, just five days before it would have been too late, they cracked the case by naming eleven men, all with well-known criminal records. Because of all the widespread national publicity over the years, defense claimed that there was no way a fair trial could take place. Moving the trial location, delaying the trial, locking up the jury—all possible judicial remedies—were considered useless. Some 1200 motions to this effect were all denied, and some 1700 candidates were questioned for weeks before they came up with an all-male jury to hear the case.

Continuance after continuance was granted, with defense attorneys hoping that the publicity would die down, but the intense news coverage would resume every time a new trial date was set. Finally, in October of 1966, all eleven defendants were found guilty. Joseph F. McGinness, considered the "brains" of the operation, was given eight concurrent life sentences, while the seven men who were inside the Brinks headquarters on the night of the robbery all received at least life terms with other terms "tacked on" to account for other charges. All attempts to appeal the case on the grounds of unfair publicity failed.

**U.S. vs. Accardo (1962)**—Tony Accardo had just become the new head of Chicago's original "Al Capone" mob in 1957 when the federal government challenged his income tax returns. It seems they questioned his $178,000 annual salary as a "beer salesman" for the syndicate-operated Fox Head Brewing Company. Accardo, long suspected of being one of the gunmen in the 1929 "Valentine's Day Massacre," drew a six-year sentence on income tax evasion charges in 1962, but was granted a second trial because of unfavorable newspaper publicity and was acquitted. The Supreme Court said that the judge's warnings to the jury as they started and his instructions to them later in the trial to ignore the publicity were not enough. The justices concluded that, ". . . there is no certainty that all jurors would volunteer information about violating the admonitions or admit that they were influenced by publicity."

**Billie Sol Estes Case (1962-1965)**—The Estes case, like the Hauptmann (Lindbergh Kidnapping) trial, is a notorious example of abuses by the news media while the trial is in progress. Texas had not adopted the American Bar Association's Canon 35 which forbids camera and TV in the courtroom, but had its own "Texas Canon 28," which leaves such matters up to the judge. Billie Sol Estes was a flamboyant financier with White House connections. In 1962, he was charged wits swindlend farmers by selling them nonexistent fertilizer tanks. Even at a preliminary hearing before the actual trial began, the tiny second-floor courtroom was described as a "forest" of equipment. Two TV cameras were up front, inside the bar, and four more cameras were outside the gates. Cables and wires were snaked across the courtroom, and there were microphones all over the judge's bench, the jury box, and the counsel tables. Newspaper photographers wandered at will throughout the courtroom and a total of twelve cameramen were busy televising and taking "still" shots and movies. The proceedings were broadcast "live" on radio and TV, and when Estes' attorney presented eleven volumes of news clippings to indicate the national notoriety the case had gained, the judge denied a motion to shut off the broadcasting and picture-taking.

The actual trial began about a month later, with some changes. The TV cameras were in a booth at the back of the courtroom which had been painted to match the rest of the room. Live broadcasting was cut back to exclude testimony by witnesses and the questioning of would-be jurors. Even so, everyone in the courtroom was well aware of those "telltale red lights," as Supreme Court Justice Tom Clark later described them. The high bench reversed the original conviction and ordered a new trial, contending that it was not just the physical presence of the camera but the "awareness" of the telecasting that made everyone self-conscious and impaired not only the quality of the testimony of the witnesses but the judgment of the jurors. Estes was finally convicted in a later trial, without the "circus" atmosphere that had prevailed at the first trial and preliminary hearing.

**Rideau vs. Louisiana (1961-1963)**—On February 16, 1961, a lone gunman held up a bank at Lake Charles, Louisiana, kidnapping three bank employees and killing one of them. Within a few hours, police had captured Wilbert Rideau and held him overnight in the Calcasieu Parish jail in Lake Charles. Over the next three days, station KLPC in Lake Charles broadcast a 20-minute TV filmed "interview," in which the Sheriff of Calcasieu Parish asked Wilbert Rideau all about the holdup and got him to admit that he had committed the robbery, the kidnappings, and the murder. Even though close to 100,000 out of the 150,000 who lived in the Parish (county) saw the "interview," a defense motion to move the trial elsewhere was denied. Three members of the jury were seated even though they admitted seeing the show, and two of their fellow jurors were deputy sheriffs of Calcasieu Parish. Rideau was found guilty and sentenced to death. The Louisiana Supreme Court upheld the conviction, but the U.S. Supreme Court overturned it. Amazingly enough, they were not as concerned about the role of the television station as they were about the fact that Rideau's confession was made in a "kangaroo court" manner without a defense lawyer. They acknowledged the impact of the pretrial publicity rather obliquely, saying only that failure of the court to grant him a change of trial location (change of "venue,") in view of such publicity was violating his right to a fair trial.

**"Mad Dog" Irvin (Irvin vs. Dowd) (1955-1961)**—In November of 1954 and March of 1955, the citizens of Vanderburgh and Gibson counties in the vicinity of Evansville, Indiana, were alarmed by a series of six murders. The news media covered the crimes extensively. On April 8, 1955, Evansville authorities picked up Leslie Irvin, a parolee, on a charge of writing bad checks and suspicion of burglary. A few days later, the Evansville police and the Vanderburgh County Prosecutor's office came out with news releases claiming that "Mad Dog Irvin" had confessed to all six of the murders. Within two weeks a grand jury had handed down an indictment. Irvin's court-appointed defense attorney asked for a change of venue because of the "impassioned atmosphere" in Vanderburgh County, and got one—to adjoining Gibson County. The defense attorney asked that the trial be moved a little farther away, but was told that Indiana law permits only one change of venue. Out of 430 candidates screened for the jury, 370 said they already believed that Irvin was guilty. At least four people with this admitted belief wound up on the jury anyway, because the defense attorney had used up all his challenges. Motions to dismiss the case because of obvious jury bias, or even to delay the trial because of the publicity, were all denied. The news media were having a field day, constantly using the "Mad Dog" nickname and referring to Irvin as the "confessed slayer of six." They talked about his juvenile record and his previous convictions for arson, burglary, parole violation, and going AWOL in the Army.

Irvin was quickly convicted and sentenced to death. Within a month, his defense attorney appealed, citing what he considered at least 415 violations of Irvin's constitutional rights. Unfortunately, Irvin didn't help matters any by escaping from the Gibson County jail the night before the motion was filed, and the Indiana courts ruled that they could not grant a new trial while he was a fugitive or consider any appeals after 30 days even if he was recaptured. Having exhausted all state and even lower-eschelon federal court remedies, Irvin's lawyer turned to the Supreme Court on constitutional grounds and got a landmark decision. It was the first time the Supreme Court had ever reversed a criminal conviction from any state solely on the grounds of pretrial publicity. The decision was unanimous, and Justice Felix Frankfurter, who had been warning the press about prejudicial publicity ever since the **Baltimore Radio Case** (discussed earlier in this section), said that cases like Irvin's would be reversed ". . . . because prejudicial publicity had poisoned the outcome," and that the Court ". . . has not yet decided that," . . . ". . . the poisoner," (meaning the news media) ". . . is constitutionally protected in plying his trade."

Sizing up the issue in the concise terms we use today (first-versus-sixth amendments) Justice Frankfurter wrote, "This Court has not yet decided that the fair administration of criminal justice must be subordinated to another safeguard of our constitutional system —freedom of the press . . ." Irvin was given a new trial in a less emotional atmosphere, convicted, and sentenced to life imprisonment.

**People vs. Van Duyne (N.J., 1963)**—After making the rounds of the taverns in Patterson, New Jersey, one night in April of 1963, construction worker Louis Van Duyne went to the apartment of his estranged wife, chased her into the nearby alleyway, and beat her to death. As the trial got underway, the defense attorney pointed out to the judge that copies of local newspapers were in the jury room and were being circulated among the jurors. The papers carried stories quoting Van Duyne as telling police, "You've got me for murder," and threatening to "kill a cop," and ran stories of Van Duyne's background and previous arrests. Although the New Jersey Supreme Court upheld the conviction when the case was appealed, it issued a sweeping order to police, prosecutors, and defense attorneys not to talk to newsmen about any confessions or damaging admissions made by a defendant. It also barred these officials from making any mention of a suspect's prior criminal record, but it could not prohibit the press from doing so because that would mean putting a "gag" on the news media *prior* to publication—clearly violating the first amendment to the Constitution. New Jersey newspapers comp'ained that the ruling amounted to a "blackout" of news coverage between arrest and trial, and felt that law enforcement agencies would use it as a pretext to cover up *everything*, even the items of legitimate public concern. Columnists and editorial writers hinted that they would have to depend more on the court-house "grapevine," and that rumors and other misstatements were likely to come out in print.

Issued before the days of "Press-Bar Guidelines" (to be discussed later in this chapter) the New Jersey ruling had a chilling effect on the release of pretrial information. At least one paper, the New York *Times,* thought it placed the responsibility squarely where it be-longed—on lawyers and police who talk to newsmen. Said the *Times,* "Once the police and members of the bar recognize that prejudicial statements about a defendant are unethical and unprofessional be-havior, then sources for this kind of news will dry up for all of the press, and the problem will largely disappear."

**Lee Harvey Oswald ("JFK Assassination" 1963)**—The suspect ac-cused of killing President Kennedy never came to trial, but most judicial sources agree that he probably could never have received a fair and unbiased trial if he had lived to see the courtroom. The scene at the Dallas Police Station before Oswald was shot by Jack Ruby was again a "forest" of TV cameras, microphones, cables, floodlights, technicians, and reporters, lending a "show business" aura to the whole affair just as it did in the *Billie Sol Estes* case which was just discussed. In addition, the American Bar Association later proclaimed that "widespread publicizing of Oswald's alleged guilt, involving statements by officials and public disclosure of the details of 'evidence' would have made it extremely difficult to em-panel an unprejudiced jury and afford the accused a fair trial."

The Warren Commission, later investigating the assassination, severely criticized the coverage, saying that "part of the respon-sibility for the unfortunate circumstances following the President's death must be borne by the news media . . ." The Commission said that newsmen lacked self-discipline and needed some kind of pro-fessional code of ethics to show they supported the Sixth Amend-ment for a fair trial as well as the First Amendment for free speech. It was the Commission's recommendations that led to many years of self-examination by both the news media and the legal profession, some of which is still going on. The American Bar Association's famous "Reardon Report," and other guidelines issued by the Justice Department, New York's "Medina Committee," and various state Press and Bar Associations, all came from the Warren Commission's call for a code of professional conduct.

**The Jack Ruby Trial (1963)**—No one could possibly doubt who shot Lee Harvey Oswald. As the accused presidential assassin was being brought from his cell at the Dallas Police Station on November 24, 1963, Jack Ruby stepped in front of the watching eyes of a nationwide television audience and shot him. Aside from the "circus" atmosphere which already prevailed as a result of the presidential assassination which had occurred less than 48 hours prior to Ruby's act, the "trial by mass media" which followed brought into high gear a controversy which raged throughout the 1960's between the press and the bar on the rights of the accused to a fair trial versus the public's "right to know." The assassinations and attempted assassinations of Robert F. Kennedy, Dr. Martin Luther King, Jr., and Governor George Wallace of Alabama which were to follow all brought the issues into clearer focus, but the abuses by the news media in the "Ruby" trial were what forced the print and broadcast journalism industries to come up with guidelines and pooling policies to avoid becoming the main characters in the news stories they were trying to cover.

Specifically, you will recall in the discussion of the **Estes** trial that "Texas Canon 28" allowed judges to decide just what broadcast and photographic coverage could take place in their courtrooms. Judge Joe Brown in the Jack Ruby trial gave in to pressure from the national and local bar associations to prevent TV coverage during the actual trial, but he allowed photos and broadcast interviews out in the hallway and said they could come into the courtroom for the jury's verdict if they used only one "pool" TV camera and shut it off the moment he left the bench. Instead, they used several TV cameras and left them on to capture an outburst by defense lawyer Melvin Belli discrediting the court and the jury after the verdict was announced. The stampede of newsmen to give Belli a nationwide audience for his criticism caused the New York *Times* to comment that "The case of Jack Ruby was virtually retried on live coast-to-coast television yesterday after the Dallas jury had returned its verdict and the court had been recessed . . ."

**"Escobedo" and "Miranda" Decisions (1964 and 1966)**—In the wake of cases like **Rideau, Irvin, Van Duyne, Estes** and **Ruby,** police throughout the country were under pressure from the courts not to talk to newsmen. Things like prior convictions, confessions, evidence, etc., were all "taboo." Law enforcement officials found themselves criticized by the press for concealing too much and by the judiciary for revealing too much. To add to their frustration, a pair of related Supreme Court decisions in the mid-60's forced them to drastically change their ways of questioning suspects. It would be harder to get confessions, and hence harder to publish or broadcast them as a result.

Danny Escobedo was arrested shortly after his brother-in-law had been found murdered on January 19, 1960, but was released on a writ of habeas corpus by his lawyer. When a suspect who was later indicted along with Danny implicated him on January 30th, Danny was rearrested and made a confession. The Supreme

Court ruled that he had not been warned of his rights to remain silent under the Fifth Amendment involving self-incrimination, and that therefore any statement he had made was not admissable in court.

The Supreme Court went a step further in 1966 by adding the Sixth Amendment right to have a lawyer present. An Arizona youth, Ernesto Miranda, had been charged with the kidnapping and rape of an 18-year-old girl, but the decision which bears his name was aimed at a total of four similar cases from both state and federal courts. The coupling of the Fifth Amendment immunity against self-incrimination and the Sixth Amendment right to assistance of counsel struck at the very heart of traditional police interrogation procedures and forced minimum standards on police throughout the country. It gave desk sergeants another strong pretext to shrug their shoulders at inquiring newsmen.

## REPORTS AND GUIDELINES

**The Warren Commission**
**The Katzenbach Guidelines**
**The Mitchell Revisions**
**The Reardon Report**
**State Press—Bar Guidelines**

With the assassination of President John F. Kennedy in 1963, a commission headed by Supreme Court Chief Justice Earl Warren investigated not only the killing itself but the tragic events which followed it. The commission issued a report that sharply criticized police and prosecutors for their handling of Lee Harvey Oswald and Jack Ruby, but the commission also concluded that "part of the responsibility for the unfortunate circumstances following the President's death must be borne by the news media . . ." Rude behavior and extremely unprofessional conduct were cited by the commission, which called on journalists to adopt some kind of code for future coverage of this sort.

As a result, there were many press-and-bar meetings throughout the 1960's to come up with "codes" of conduct for law enforcement agencies, lawyers, and the news media. The Attorney General could easily control the actions of Justice Department personnel, which is what Nicholas deB. Katzenbach did in 1965. His guidelines were later "tightened" by Attorney General John Mitchell in 1971 to include civil as well as criminal cases and to require lawmen to withhold comment as soon as a person became "the subject of an investigation"—not waiting until he was identified as a suspect or even a defendant.

The legal profession was able to control its members through the Canons of Ethics, revisions of which were proposed in the

"Reardon Report." Adoption of the Reardon proposals by any state bar association, legislature, or court system would make the proposals binding on judges and lawyers.

It remained for someone to "control" the news media. The Constitution would not allow judges or legislatures to do it, because that would violate freedom of the press. Instead, a special committee on radio and television for the Association of the Bar of the City of New York under Judge Harold R. Medina did a survey entitled, **Radio, Television, and the Administration of Justice.** This documented report on newscasts and other activities by radio and TV stations up until about mid-1965, pointing to and commenting upon some of the most serious abuses by the broadcast media and their influences upon grand juries, police, prosecutors and defense attorneys, and jurors and judges, was used as a basis for guidelines later produced by various state press-and-bar committees. Included in the Medina committee's report was a survey of police departments in 37 large cities across the U.S. and their policies toward newsmen, and some of the court rulings, state laws, canons of ethics, and voluntary guidelines in use at that time.

By 1974, more than half of the states had adopted some form of voluntary guidelines for their lawyers and newsmen, most of them based on a combination of **Katzenbach, Medina** and **Reardon.** Under "The Police Beat and the Courtroom: Some Guidelines," of this chapter, there are reprinted some of these guidelines for your use as "models" in the event that you may not have copies of up-to-date codes used in your state or even your municipal area. While these will give you a general idea of the professional ethics expected of newsmen as they cover police and courtroom situations, the writer would advise you to get a copy of the latest rules for your area from your state broadcasters' or state bar associations.

**Candy Mossler and Melvin Powers (1966)**—Mrs. Candice Mossler, described as a "wealthy and vivacious blonde" in her 40's, and her 24-year-old nephew, Melvin Lane Powers, were charged with the midnight murder of Mrs. Mossler's 69-year-old millionaire husband, Jacques, in the luxurious Mossler apartment at Key Biscayne, Florida. Hundreds of spectators crowded the Miami courthouse for one of Florida's longest trials, which attracted nationwide publicity because of the money and sex angles which were being played up by the news media. The elderly victim was head of the Mossler Acceptance Company, a complex of banks and loan companies, and he reportedly was worth anywhere from seven to thirty-three million dollars. Testimony in the trial started with the love affair between Powers and his aunt. It was an item which the prosecution could prove beyond a reasonable doubt, and it was precisely what drew the large crowds and the extensive news coverage. Unfortunately for the prosecution, the news coverage is what eventually led to an acquittal for the couple, who got married in December of 1967, suing the *Saturday Evening Post* along the way for eighty-three million dollars in connection with articles Mrs. Mossler considered libelous.

**Carl Coppolino (1966-1967)**—Dr. Coppolino was an anesthesiologist who was charged with killing not only the husband of his alleged lover, Marjorie Farber, but of killing his own first wife, bypassing Mrs. Farber, and marrying a wealthy and attractive divorcee named Mary Gibson. There was intense nationwide interest in the "dual" murder cases developing in New Jersey and Florida, and the news media carried all the sensational details. Besides mystery, murder, society, sex, and suspense, there was the added angle that Dr. Coppolino used hypnosis as part of his practice and was known to have used a drug named succinylcholine chloride, which could kill without leaving a trace. Papers across the country hinted that the states of Florida and New Jersey were in a race to see who got to prosecute Coppolino first: Florida, for the death of his wife, Carmela, or New Jersey, for the death of retired army Colonel William Farber. By December of 1966, there was an acquittal in the "Farber" case in New Jersey, and defense attorney F. Lee Bailey held a party for the press and some friends at a nearby motel. Complications developed in the Florida trial, however, when Bailey was unable to get a change of venue to Miami where there would be a better chance of getting an unbiased jury. Instead, the trial was moved from Sarasota to the town of Naples, Florida. Both towns were on the west coast of Florida, where Bailey's surveys had indicated that most people already believed Coppolino was guilty and that he had been acquitted in New Jersey through some kind of legal trickery. Besides, in smaller towns like Naples there was more chance that jurors knew each other and that gossip would be more powerful than the evidence itself. The local newspapers, reasoned Bailey, would blow the story up to much greater proportions because this would be the biggest thing to happen in Naples for quite some time and because the smaller the newspaper, the less experienced and more opinionated the writers are likely to be. All of this would permeate the minds of jurors before the trial even got underway.

The trial was a battle of medical and scientific testimony from expert witnesses for both sides. The witnesses gave their "opinions" and "hypotheses" but admitted that the state of the scientific and medical professions still did not permit publication of their statements as proved facts. No one on the jury was a chemist or a doctor, so presumably they were being asked to make a judgment which science itself was not ready to make about the nature of the mysterious drug which had been modeled somewhat along the lines of the legendary South American Indian poison for arrows, "curare." The jury brought in a verdict of guilty, and appeals since then have been fruitless.

Although the acceptability of the medical testimony would no doubt be a key factor in overturning the conviction, Bailey made no secret of his displeasure with coverage by the news media, telling a Press and Bar Association gathering at the University of Kansas in May, 1967, that, ". . . I find written pontifically and with the usual expertise, an article in *Time* magazine summing up a case that never was, including the case of Carl Coppolino written by a man who appeared on the scene the day of final arguments and did most of his research, because I was there, in the privacy of the bar . . . (at the) . . . Buckaneer Motel."

**Dr. Sam Sheppard (1954 and 1964-66)**—In one of the most notorious murder cases ever to be reported in the history of American criminal trals, the Sheppard case certainly ranks with the Lindbergh kidnapping trial as a prime example of prejudicial publicity before and during a trial. As was already discussed at some length in this chapter, Cleveland osteopathic surgeon Dr. Samuel Sheppard was convicted of the killing of his wife in 1954, but the Supreme Court ordered a new trial ten years later and the conviction was reversed. Supreme Court Justice Tom Clark wrote that "bedlam reigned at the courthouse during the trial and newsmen took over practically the entire courtroom, hounding most of the participants in the trial, especially Sheppard." (See the earlier discussion for more on the Supreme Court ruling.) Whenever the issue of "Free Press versus Fair Trial" is mentioned, the **Sheppard** and **Lindbergh** cases are most likely to come up in any discussion.

**Richard Speck Murders (1966-1972)**—On the night of July 13, 1966, 25-year-old Richard Speck gained entrance to an apartment house in Chicago occupied by some nurses who worked at a nearby hospital. Apparently drunk and/or "high" on drugs, Speck took eight young nurses, one by one, to a room where he brutally killed and mutilated them. Speck failed to notice that there had been nine girls in the group which he had originally herded into one room at knifepoint, and a small Filipino girl named Corazon Amurao managed to hide under a bed and live to tell police and the court what had happened. The "Speck" case comes up whenever someone defends the public's "right to know" in connection with freedom of the press. Obviously, it would be unreasonable to expect the news media to sit around biting their nails, wanting to break a story that eight nurses had been slaughtered and that the killer was still at large, but unable to release the story for fear of giving out pretrial publicity that would deny a suspect his right to a fair trial. The press was credited with helping to capture Speck, because police who brought him to the "gin" ward of a local hospital did not know who he was; they thought he was just another drunk who had tried to kill himself with a broken bottle, but the doctor recognized the tattoo on Speck's arm with the slogan "Born to Raise Hell," which had been reproduced in the Chicago newspapers. The big controversy which arose following Speck's apprehension was not over Police Chief O. W. Wilson's statement that a suspect had been apprehended, but that he went on to say things to the effect that "this is the killer," and "we've found his fingerprints at the scene," and other statements that could immediately be challenged as release of prejudicial pre-trial publicity. Despite Chief Wilson's apparently well-meant intention of assuring the terror-stricken Chicago area after a manhunt of several days that law enforcement agencies had done their job and that they had someone in custody, he was subjected to a barrage of criticism from those who felt that his discussion of potential "evidence" would overturn the case and free the killer. As a result, there were further attempts to regulate police statements about arrests. (See "Katzenbach Guidelines," "The Reardon Report," and "Sample State Guidelines for Reporting Criminal Proceedings," in this chapter.) Speck was sentenced to death, but he and 38 other death-row inmates throughout the country were affected by the 1972 Supreme Court order barring the death penalty and he was later resentenced to eight prison terms of 50 to 150 years apiece.

**The Gault Case (1967)**—In what was to become a judicial landmark for juvenile cases, the Supreme Court overturned an Arizona decision which had remanded a 15-year-old youngster to the reformatory for a term ranging from six months to six years. Gerald Gault's parents pointed out that the maximum "adult" penalty for conviction was just two months, and successfully claimed the youth had been denied his rights. The State had claimed that young Gerald was just being "detained" as a juvenile offender for making obscene phone calls, but that he had not officially been convicted of a "crime" in the true sense of the word. "You can call it a crime or a not-crime," said Supreme Court Justice Abe Fortas, "or you can call it a horse. He's still deprived of his liberty." The Supreme Court decision touched off a sweeping revision of outdated juvenile statutes throughout the country, guaranteeing them full Sixth Amendment rights instead of making them "wards of the court," under the old, well-meaning, but often misguided custom. Along with state-by-state changes in the basic laws regarding juveniles were many changes regarding coverage of juvenile proceedings by the news media. (See "Sample State Guidelines" in this chapter.)

**The Giles Case (1961-1968)**—It took a seven-year legal battle by a citizens' committee in the Washington, D.C., suburb of Rockville, Maryland, to free three young black men who originally had been sentenced to death for raping a white woman. John and James Giles, along with Joseph Johnson, were accused of attacking the woman who had been sitting alone in a car in a "lover's lane" somewhere in Maryland's Montgomery County. Extensive investigation by area citizens and the news media, including at least one local radio station, revealed that the woman apparently had a "habit" of getting "raped" like that quite often, and that the prosecution had apparently withheld a number of things about her personality and moral character that would have tended to exonerate the three young men from blame. Although the Giles brothers were freed after several court reversals in 1966, it took until February of 1968 to overturn the life sentence which Joseph Johnson had been serving since the summer of 1961. Advocates of the First Amendment rights such as free speech, free press, public's right-to-know, etc., claim this as a significant case in which investigative reporting helped to secure justice where traditional court methods had failed.

**Jim Garrison and Clay Shaw (1967-1969)**—A politically ambitious district attorney in New Orleans used "the leak," a tactic that was to become better known to the American public in later years, to promote the notion that he had somehow "solved" the assassination of President John F. Kennedy in 1963. When a local paper, the New Orleans *States-Item*, picked up the bait and ran the story, it gave Garrison a pretext to hold a news conference.

"Arrests were probably just a few weeks away," said District Attorney Jim Garrison, "until the disclosures of the investigation by the local newspapers. Now," he said, "they are almost certainly months away." This broad hint that perhaps President Kennedy had been killed as the result of a conspiracy after all was certain to gain instant nationwide attention. It played upon the lingering doubts in the minds of many, and Garrison's news conferences, TV appearances, and dramatic statements over the months that followed were to fan the flames of this suspicion.

The leaks and statements continued, all geared toward giving the impression that it *had* been a conspiracy: "There were other people besides Lee Harvey Oswald," and, "Arrests will be made, charges will be filed, and convictions will be obtained." It was also implied that Garrison's investigation had uncovered a great deal of evidence and new information: "We know what cities are involved, how it was done in the essential respects and the individuals involved." What the news media had begun to notice by now was that Garrison was clearly beating his own drum and seeking attention. All of this was at the very height of the "free press—fair trial" debate that was going on across the country. Indeed, the American Bar Association was about to adopt a revision of its old "Canon 20" of professional ethics. (See the "Reardon Report," in this chapter.) The new section clearly stated: "It is the duty of the lawyer not to release or authorize the release of information or opinion for dissemination by any means of public communication . . ." in connection with any upcoming trial in which the information might prejudice the case. Newsmen wondered when a court order or bar-association disciplinary action might shut Garrison off, but none did.

A former army officer who headed the New Orleans Trade Mart was charged with playing a role in the alleged "conspiracy," and the case finally appeared headed for the courtroom where it belonged, instead of through the news media. Clay Shaw had been formally charged.

The networks, the wire services, the national news magazines, and the nation's major newspapers sent their best men to cover the proceedings. It soon began to dawn on all of these top-flight journalists that actual, hard evidence to back Garrison's theories was lacking. There were contradictions in testimony, and potential witnesses began to admit that they had either been coerced or bribed into making inaccurate and misleading statements. Finally, *Newsweek* commented that the only "conspiracy" in New Orleans was "a plot of Garrison's own making," and both NBC and CBS did documentaries on what was becoming known as nothing more than a very convincing fabrication. As NBC's Walter Sheridan (a former Justice Department and FBI investigator) concluded, "Justice is in real danger down here."

Clay Shaw was acquitted on March 1, 1969, due at least in part to the highly professional "watchdog" and "critic" role played by the news media.

**James Earl Ray (Dr. Martin Luther King Assassination, 1968)—** Dr. Martin Luther King, Jr., had come to Memphis, Tennessee, to lead a march supporting garbage workers for better wages and working conditions. He had dressed for dinner on the evening of April 4, 1968, and had stepped out onto the balcony of his motel room with several aides when a shot rang out. In the world-wide hunt that followed the killing, James Earl Ray was picked up at Heathrow Airport in London and flown back to Memphis for trial.

Although the press corps and technicians at Dallas in 1963 had created the chaos that led to the shooting of Lee Harvey Oswald and the turmoil which accompanied coverage of the **Jack Ruby** trial, almost five years had passed, and press and bar alike had been discussing and drawing up ground rules for orderly coverage of such events. The **Reardon Report** was ready for adoption by the American Bar Association, and newsmen gave every indication of their willingness to adopt such arrangements as "pooling" and take other measures to show professionalism and ethical conduct.

None of this impressed Memphis police or Judge W. Preston Battle, who was to preside at the trial. Deputies with sawed-off shotguns ringed the courthouse where Ray was to be brought back from London, forcing newsmen across the street. There were armed policemen in nearby windows and on the rooftops. Five men carrying submachine guns jumped out of the unmarked car which had been escorting Ray's procession from the airport. As CBS Television turned on some floodlights to film the arrival, a policeman stuck his shotgun into the face of the TV newsman holding the lights and ordered them off. When the CBS crew claimed that the judge's rules allowed them to film this event, the policeman snarled back that, "We make our own rules" here. The lights remained off.

When the trial began, Judge Battle went to extremely severe measures to control the news media and the lawyers, issuing wholesale contempt orders over almost anything that was reported about the case. The fact that King had been shot in broad daylight and that the suspect had apparently been able to escape as far as England led to nation-wide speculation that a conspiracy was involved, yet prosecution was trying to prove that this was all the work of one man. Judge Battle's contempt actions whenever the news media tried to discuss this apparent controversy were seen by many as little more than censorship *prior* to broadcast or publication, a clear violation of First Amendment rights.

James Earl Ray was sentenced to 99 years in prison, and has since tried a number of ways to get out of this predicament, including appeals, requests for new trials, a 1971 escape, and a 1974 hunger strike. No further attempt was made to investigate the possibility of any conspiracy, and Judge Battle refused to sentence any newsmen for all the contempt citations which had piled up, denying them the chance to appeal what they felt were unfair and arbitrary rulings. John Siegenthaler, in his book *A Search for Justice,* claims in connection with the **Ray** trial and others that "already there are some defendants who are appealing criminal convictions contending in principle that the courts, in imposing press restrictions, violated their rights to a public trial."

**Sirhan Sirhan (Robert Kennedy Assassination, 1968-69)**—The late President's younger brother had just delivered a victory speech to a tumultuous crowd upon winning the California presidential primaries, and was leaving by way of the kitchen when a swarthy-skinned, bushy-haired young man stepped out from a corner and fired a gun several times at point-blank range. Wrestled to the ground and immediately disarmed by those accompanying Kennedy, the suspect was placed under extremely tight security by Los Angeles police, who clearly wished to avoid a repetition of the **Lee Harvey Oswald** incident in Dallas. Newsmen were frisked for weapons upon entering a press conference a while later, and Police Chief Thomas Reddin revealed that his men were not asking the suspect any questions for fear of damaging the case.

This time it was not the news media nor the policemen or lawyers who jeopardized the case against Sirhan Sirhan, but the mayor of Los Angeles. Mayor Sam Yorty began holding press conferences at which he read from the suspect's diary and commented on what he felt was the suspect's "definite Communist leanings." The state Attorney General phoned Yorty to warn him that the statements were prejudicial, and the Chief Counsel for the California Chapter of the American Civil Liberties Union objected to such statements by a public official but said that newspapers, television, and radio were not to be criticized for carrying Yorty's words. By now, the nation's news media and law enforcement officials had learned restraint in such situations, and the trial of Sirhan Sirhan bore no resemblance to the **Ruby, Oswald, Estes,** and other affairs before the days of the **Reardon Report** and the **Katzenbach Guidelines.**

Although all reporters were thoroughly searched, and items such as pocketbooks, cameras, and tape recorders were confiscated by Sheriff's deputies before the carefully screened journalists could enter the courtroom (see photo below), no one needed any explanation for the extreme security measures. They were far more reasonable than the heavy-handed tactics used by Memphis police and Judge W. Preston Battle in the **James Earl Ray** trial.

Sirhan Sirhan was sentenced to die in the gas chamber on April 23, 1969, but this was changed to life imprisonment on August 7, 1972, because of a U.S. Supreme Court ruling which barred practically all executions anywhere in the country.

Photo by United Press International.

**Arthur Bremer Case (George Wallace Shooting, 1972)**—At about 4 p.m. on the afternoon of May 15, 1972, Alabama Governor George Wallace made a campaign speech to a shopping center crowd in

Laurel, Maryland, a suburb of Washington, D.C. Wallace, seeking delegates toward the Democratic presidential nomination in primaries that were to be held in Maryland and Michigan the following day, had just stepped out from behind a bulletproof podium to mingle with the crowd briefly when a man pulled out a gun and began to fire repeatedly at him. Three others were wounded in the melee as the crowd subdued Arthur Bremer. By August of 1972, Bremer had been tried and sentenced to a total of 63 years on the various charges.

Once again, massive pretrial information would have been unavoidable. A nation which had seen both Kennedy assassinations and the killing of Dr. Martin Luther King, Jr., within the decade was stunned by yet another assassination attempt upon a major political figure. There were reports that Bremer had also stalked candidates Richard Nixon and Hubert Humphrey before the attempt on Wallace. Biographies on Bremer pointed to the similarities in his life with aspects of the lives of Lee Harvey Oswald, James Earl Ray, and Sirhan Sirhan, including such items as "poverty, difficult childhood, derelict fathers, domineering mothers, sexual inadequacy, repeated failure, and isolation."

President Nixon issued a statement deploring the violence, all major presidential candidates stopped campaigning, and the news media were busy running interviews with Bremer's former teachers, employers and neighbors, and publishing detailed maps of Bremer's travels as he apparently followed Wallace and other candidates over a period of several months.

The Maryland and Wisconsin offices of the American Civil Liberties Union (ACLU) sharply criticized news coverage of Bremer as irresponsible and sensational, and Bremer's attorney tried unsuccessfully after the conviction to get a new trial on grounds that at least one juror had seen the TV newsfilms of the shooting prior to their presentation in the trial itself. Although Bremer remains in prison, the ACLU criticism and the defense challenge on grounds involving news coverage indicate that the issue of "Fair Trial versus Free Press" is still with us and deserves continued study and discussion for many years to come.

### RADICAL CONSPIRACY TRIALS (1969-1972)

**The "Chicago Eight"**
**Black Panthers (New York)**
**Black Panthers (New Haven)**
**Angela Davis**

The four-year period which closed the 1960's and ushered in the 1970's saw a new element injected into courtroom proceedings which seriously challenged the so-called objectivity of juries and news media alike. A degree of political polarization in the court-room was achieved by defendants trying desperately to bring home the point that they were not really being tried by a jury of their "peers," as the Constitution provided, but by a panel composed in most cases of middle-class whites (in some cases, all-white juries facing all-black defendants) who had no identification whatsoever with radical causes. These defendants also felt that news coverage of their trials was seen through an "angle of refraction" by report-ers who were also part of the American establishment as mostly middle-class whites and nonbelievers in radical thinking them-selves and who, therefore, were really unable to understand the is-sues. Space will not allow discussion of all the cases in detail, but we may just examine them as a group to see how some of the principles involved apply to the topic.

The stage had been set during the 1968 Democratic National Convention in Chicago, when hundreds of young radicals (identified by various names such as "hippies," "Yippies," "Weathermen," etc.) newsmen, policemen, delegates, and others tangled violently in the streets of Chicago. Polarization was achieved in living rooms throughout the country as television viewers sided with either the club-wielding Chicago police or with the young radicals—newsmen wound up somewhere in the middle as these two groups collided, but that is another story.

In the years that followed, the American public came to view these "Chicago" groups, the Black Panthers, and others much as Americans fifty years before them had viewed the anarchists: news media reports tended to stigmatize individual defendants by identi-fying them, perhaps not all that consciously, with a mythical nationwide "network" of radicals involved in shootings, bombings, murders, and other assorted violence.

News reports on the "Black Panther" trial at New Haven, for ex-ample, linked the defendants to the Black Panthers in New York, ". . . where members . . . were arrested several weeks ago for plot-ting to blow up several large department stores . . ." The reports also identified the New Haven group with national Black Panther Chairman Bobby Seale months before he was himself named as a codefendant in the alleged New Haven "conspiracy." This, in turn, effectively linked all of the New Haven defendants with every bit of Black Panther associated violence which had occurred in the five years since the Black Panther Party had been born in the streets of a ghetto in Oakland, California.

In New Haven, it took four months and the screening of more than a thousand candidates to seat a jury. Costing over a million dollars, it was Connecticut's longest and most expensive trial in his-tory. The New York City "Panther" trial, where 13 Black Panthers had been accused of a conspiracy to bomb police stations and de-partment stores, also became New York's longest trial and cost more than two million dollars, ending in acquittal for all of the defendants. By this time, the nation's viewers and readers had become accustomed to bail figures in the millions and months of pretrial investigations and legal maneuvering.

It was in vogue during these years for defense attorneys to subpoena all newscasts and articles from every newspaper and broadcast station in the area of the trial, hoping to find among them some flaw that would overturn any of these cases on the basis of alleged prejudicial publicity either before or during the trial. This was a warning to every newsman in the country that from now on—at any moment—he could expect to become part of the story rather than just a neutral observer, and that every phrase he banged out on his typewriter could possibly be brought into court in an attempt to reverse a conviction.

Panther Chairman Bobby Seale played a major role not only in the trial at New Haven, but in Chicago, where few Americans watching TV newscasts or reading newspaper or magazine coverage at the time can forget the descriptions of Seale shouting obscenities, throwing furniture, being wrestled to the floor by deputies, and being gagged and tied to his chair in the Chicago courtroom of Judge Julius Hoffman. The elderly judge's "no-nonsense" approach, climaxed by his sentencing of Seale to a four-year term for contempt of court, served as a symbol of the ethnic and social polarization which the Panthers were generally protesting in claiming that their trials were unfair.

Specifically, the New Haven group was charged with holding a "kangaroo court" at Panther headquarters which resulted in the shooting, burning, and mutilation death of one Alex Rackley, a Panther said to have turned informer to police. Two of the defendants were convicted of the actual murder plot, but an alleged "conspiracy" among the rest was too difficult a charge to prove. In fact, the New York *Times* had editorialized a few days earlier upon the acquittal of the New York group that ". . . conspiracy . . . tends to be viewed by the general public as a 'dragnet' kind of device—which it often is—used by authorities more eager for political conviction than criminal justice."

The Chicago, New York, and New Haven cases were already underway when troubles began for Angela Davis in California. She had been fired from the UCLA faculty in 1969 as an avowed Communist, had been reinstated, and then had been ousted again after being charged with going around the country making "inflammatory" speeches which allegedly incited crowds to violence. As she was about to be tried for these activities in 1970, the younger brother of one of her best friends broke into the courtroom heavily armed, freed three black convicts, and kidnapped the judge and several hostages. In the shootout that followed, the judge and two of the convicts were killed along with the young man who had perpetrated the whole scheme. Miss Davis wound up charged with supplying the guns for the tragic incident, and waited for almost two years in jail to come to trial as other judges who were friends of the slain jurist all disqualified themselves. Finally, in 1972, Angela Davis spoke as co-counsel in her own defense to an all-white jury and almost miraculously managed to win acquittal on the kidnapping, murder, conspiracy, and other charges despite nation-wide sensationalism which had built up ever since her original firing from UCLA.

In all of these cases, it was feared that jurors, even if they had not seen or heard any specific news items which could be labeled "prejudicial," would inevitably link all of this violence with any defendant wearing a "radical" label, whether he was simply black or a member of the Panthers, Weathermen, Yippies, SDS or any number of groups which had become identified with causes which were tainted in any way by violence or the threat of it as portrayed by the news media. Such juries would have little sympathy for the political beliefs symbolized by the defendants, would probably show little or no reluctance to impose the heaviest possible penalties (including execution where it was still allowed), and would have great difficulty presuming that such defendants were innocent. It was also felt that newsmen, in their allegedly "myopic" view of radicals, had either consciously or unconsciously managed to *link* defendants in these cases in a sort of "guilt-by-association" image which implied that "if you've seen one, you've seen 'em all."

These trials and others like them provided a new wrinkle in the old "Free Press versus Fair Trial" debate—not a direct frontal attack by the bar and the judiciary attempting to uphold the Sixth Amendment in well-defined terms, but a serious challenge to what all journalists had come to take for granted as their "objectivity." It served to put all reporters on the defensive for future coverage where minorities, radicals, and other defendants whose values and/or life styles which differed from those of the average newsman were likely to become involved.

**Spiro Agnew Resignation (1973)**—Leaks from the news media became one of the major issues in the case that suddenly ended with the first "forced" resignation of a U.S. Vice President in disgrace. The nation's major news organizations were already in high gear as they pursued the "Watergate" scandal in the administration of President Richard M. Nixon, and picked up momentum in the spring of 1973 when disclosures that a federal investigation into kickbacks for roadbuilding contracts in Maryland had begun to turn up evidence implicating Vice President Spiro Agnew. It was said that Agnew had not only received thousands of dollars in payoffs while he was Baltimore County Executive and Governor of Maryland, but that he had continued to receive the money in his offices at the White House and the Old Executive Office Building.

By midsummer the embattled Vice President told a nationally broadcast news conference that "defamatory statements are being leaked to the news media by sources that the news reports refer to as 'close to the investigation.' " Leaked allegations and daily stories increased, with the alerted news media turning loose an army of reporters to investigate Agnew's past. In September, Agnew specifically blamed the Justice Department for the leaks, saying, "They call themselves informed sources close to the investigation . . . and they don't have any hesitancy about violating my civil rights." He tried to make it clear that he was not blaming the newsmen, but it was too late—he had traveled the length and breadth of the nation in recent years calling newsmen "an effete corps of impudent snobs" and "a tiny, enclosed fraternity of privileged men elected by no one . . ." The media would never reveal their sources, nor would they slacken for one moment their microscopic public scrutiny of everything they could learn about Spiro Agnew.

The Vice President's lawyers filed a motion on September 28, 1973, accusing the Justice Department of leaking damaging stories about him, and President Nixon ordered the Attorney General to conduct an investigation into the possible sources of the leaks. Members of Agnew's staff, along with his friends and supporters, began to suspect the White House as the source, speculating that President Nixon was trying to divert public attention away from himself and the Watergate scandal.

CBS and NBC were subpoenaed as the issue began to come to a head, along with *Time, Newsweek,* the New York *Times* and *Daily News,* and the Washington *Post* and *Star-News.* Judge Walter Hoffman, presiding over the Baltimore grand jury, had a reputation for hostility toward the news media, and threatened to turn the proceedings into a landmark case on freedom of the press. This shift in direction anguished Justice Department officials, who feared that if something were to happen to President Nixon, a felon would succeed to the Presidency. They believed they had a tight case against the Vice President for conspiracy, extortion, bribery, and tax evasion, and they didn't want to see the target of their investigation disappear behind the Constitutional protection of the impeachment process, something which Mr. Agnew had tried briefly but unsuccessfully to do even as Vice President.

The news organizations geared for battle; they were not to be taken lightly after their victory in the "Pentagon Papers" case and their momentum in "Watergate." They had grown much bolder in their use of the term "informed sources," and some of them reportedly had spent more than $30,000 in legal fees and other expenses as they approached Judge Hoffman's hearing on October 10, 1973, ready to protect these sources or see some of their top newsmen and executives go to jail. The judge warned everyone that they would not be permitted to leave at any time during the course of the proceeding, and had the courtroom locked.

Suddenly, Spiro Agnew's lawyers announced to the court that he had just resigned as Vice President, and private citizen Agnew pleaded "nolo contendere" (practically the equivalent of "guilty") to a charge of income tax evasion. Justice Department spokesmen were allowed to make a statement revealing that they had enough evidence to go much further, but had brought the case to a swift conclusion in the national interest.

What had *not* been brought to a conclusion was the matter of the leaks and their potential threat to a fair trial, nor the matter of the news media's insistence on protecting their sources. As Judge Hoffman had warned the grand jury a week earlier, "We are rapidly approaching the day when the perpetual conflict between the news media . . . and the judicial system . . . must be resolved." Judge Hoffman never got around to it in the **Agnew** case, and it will remain alive as an issue for some years to come.

**Watergate (1972-1974)**—From the break-in at National Democratic Headquarters in June of 1972 to President Nixon's resignation in August of 1974, newsmen covering the various aspects of the Watergate scandal saw themselves as sentries against corruption and fearless bearers of the truth. Not every reader and listener in the land agreed with this point of view, and public opinion polls taken just before the final month of the Nixon administration showed that many people were "tired" of all the bad news coming out of Washington or considered the coverage biased, unfair, or inaccurate in some way.

When prosecution of the case appeared to be limited to just the break-in itself, or as White House News Secretary Ron Ziegler put it, "nothing more than a third-rate burglary" which he did not care to comment upon, newsmen were suspicious, and it was this suspicion which undoubtedly led to greater disclosure of the growing scandal than that which would have come from official sources. The beleaguered Nixon administration was particularly outraged at the growing use of unattributed stories quoting "informed sources" and at the means by which the news media were getting their information. Amazingly few inaccuracies did result, despite charges by Mr. Ziegler, an arrogant press secretary disliked by the media. We shall discuss his role and this "press relations" aspect further in the chapter on government and politics.

As for the "Free Press versus Fair Trial" issue, lawyers and civil liberties supporters across the country were shocked by the intrusion of the press into the privacy of grand jury proceedings. Attempts by Washington *Post* reporters Carl Bernstein and Bob Woodward to get grand jury members to violate their "secrecy" oath and publication of grand jury testimony by Columnist Jack Anderson caused some alarm among reporters and news executives who felt that a judicial backlash might occur at any moment in the form of harsh contempt sentences or other penalties, jeopardizing future court news coverage in general. Many newsmen attempted to justify such actions in these cases by arguing that, without the pressure of publicity, the outcome of the proceedings would have been different and many facts would not have been disclosed.

Newsmen also came under sharp criticism from the White House and Mr. Nixon's supporters for violating the principle that an accused person should be treated as innocent until proved guilty. True, argued the news media, *in the courtroom,* but they insisted that outside the courtroom someone has to bring certain accusations and other information to the public attention before any individual can become a defendant. If newsmen were not allowed to *interpret* facts and occasionally imply that something might be wrong, the media would become quite sterile, reporting just dog-bite cases, car accidents, and other after-the-fact situations. If that were the case, unchecked rumors would soon fill a gap not covered by today's increasingly sharp investigative reporters, because society is no longer that naïve.

Supporters of the troubled president, when turned back on such issues as secrecy, informed sources, and presumption of innocence (see above) turned to the motives of the press and accused newsmen of sensationalizing and overplaying "Watergate," attempting to chase a president out of office in much the way that hounds chase a fox. It is true, admitted *Time* magazine in a cover story on press treatment of Watergate, that ". . . Washington is the world's most densely populated press room, and it sometimes operates on a pack mentality." Although the magazine conceded that the press occasionally reaches too far, it was effectively pointed out by many news organizations that impeachment proceedings were not the same thing as a criminal trial. Despite many arguments to the contrary, the "high crimes and misdemeanors" required by the Constitution for impeachment proceedings were not necessarily violations of specific laws and statutes, and a president facing impeachment was not entitled to the same guarantees as the Sixth Amendment rights of a defendant in an ordinary criminal trial. This became quite clear when the "grand jury" phase of the case to be presented against Mr. Nixon was televised, "live" in the form of debate by the House Judiciary Committee. The highly ethical demeanor portrayed by the Congressmen as they debated the issue and the professionalism of the broadcast and print news media as they covered both the House Judiciary hearings of 1974 and the Senate Watergate hearings of 1973 was a strong hint that in future years the news media might be seen as mature enough to handle themselves in such proceedings without distorting the outcome as in most of the trials we have discussed.

The situation will be analyzed for years to come, but it is the writer's opinion here that if the news media seemed to "overplay"

Watergate, it was to fill a void created by the failure of others to play an effective role in dealing with the problem. Many Congressmen and Senators were notably silent, making no indignant speeches despite such things as gaps in presidential tapes, discrepancies in transcripts, implicit approval of "hush money" for the original defendants, perjury by the President's staff and other close associates, and a determined cover-up effort that lasted for more than two years. The questions raised by the whole complex of alleged and proved misdeeds as they relate to "Free Press versus Fair Trial" will probably not be definitely resolved for some time, because the tension that brought the nation's news media into a collision course with the government slackened considerably after Mr. Nixon's resignation as president.

## SHIELD LAWS AND CONFIDENTIAL SOURCES: THE NEWER ISSUES

Just as most of the finer points in the "Free Press versus Fair Trial" issue had been settled in the 1960's, along came a new issue involving a reversal of traditional roles in the relationship between newsmen and the courts—that of reporters wanting to *conceal* and *protect* their sources of news rather than to advocate their release by broadcast or publication. Until about 1969, there had been very few cases involving a newsman's refusal to testify about his sources, but then from 1969 to mid-1971 it was estimated by one network official that CBS and NBC alone had received more than 120 subpoenas, not only for broadcasts themselves but for notes and films and tapes which had *not* been broadcast!

The print media had been facing contempt charges for some time. Reporter Annette Buchanan for the University of Oregon campus newspaper was convicted on contempt of court charges for refusing to reveal the names of seven students who had given her information for an article on marijuana use. Earl Caldwell of the New York *Times,* based in San Francisco, refused to appear or testify before a grand jury about Black Panther activities. When cases like these began to reach the U.S. Supreme Court, the high bench said it was not convinced that the newsmen's sources would "dry up" if they were forced to reveal them in testimony. The Court said simply that evidence "failed to demonstrate" the newsmen's claim, but hinted at a possible solution: While the U.S. Constitution did not specifically "shield" newsmen's sources, there was nothing to stop Congress and the state legislatures from passing "Shield Laws" that would do so.

Newsmen lost no time in "getting the hint," pressing Congress and their various state legislatures for shield laws. More than fifty bills were filed in Congress, and by the end of 1973 at least twenty states had some sort of statute on the books to afford at least partial protection to journalists similar to that provided to clergymen, doctors, and lawyers in dealing with their parishioners, patients, and clients. Although most bills introduced wanted an "absolute" guarantee of immunity for newsmen, legislators added many "if's" to the proposals allowing the government to require disclosure if:

- ▶ all other sources had been tried and the information was vital to the public interest,
- ▶ a superior court ordered disclosure,
- ▶ the reporter was defending himself against libel charges,
- ▶ disclosure was ruled "necessary" to prevent a potentially unfair ruling or other injustice,
- ▶ the material had already been broadcast or published and its truth was challenged in court,

. . . and other loopholes, reducing the likelihood that many states, or even Congress, would pass an "unqualified" bill giving complete protection to any newsman for whatever reason. Another problem came up as states began to legislate on the question; they had to define "reporter," and many of them began to limit such privileges to those who worked for licensed broadcast stations or other well-defined mass media, excluding smaller "newsletter" operators who use mimeograph or ditto machines and people like researchers, scholars, lecturers, etc., thereby opening themselves to the possibility of a challenge to the effect that these smaller operators were being denied their First Amendment rights. The issue is far from settled, and it is necessary, if you wish to put your mind at ease on the matter, to run a careful check on the status of such legislation and court rulings in your own state if you do not wish to run afoul of the law.

Where does this all leave us today? You can go to any number of luncheons and seminars on such issues as "Shield

Laws" and "Free Press versus Fair Trial," but somewhere you eventually will get the feeling that there is a weakness in this relationship between the Press and the Bar. Typically, participants at such gatherings enjoy cocktails in luxurious surroundings, then adjourn to an air-conditioned meeting room with wall-to-wall carpeting and hold a dialogue among well-tailored members of the legal community and what they believe to be their counterparts from the news media. Within a couple of months, many of the matters they thought they had resolved surface again as sources of irritation. All the agreements seem to have fallen through. What has happened?

First of all, broadcasters are not as fully represented at such conferences as it would first appear. While newspapers have a hierarchy of editors and other supervisory personnel, the radio and TV people, except in large cities and at network operations, rarely do. All too often, the so-called News Director of a local radio station wears several hats and cannot make it to the luncheon. He can be found doubling as a disc jockey or a transmitter engineer back at the station. Maybe he is doing commercials in the production room, or it could be that his on-the-air shift usually conflicts with the time of these gatherings. One way or another, he is tied to the station. It is also possible that after he gets through working his full time at the station, it is just too much for him to drive to that distant city (often the state capital) because management would never think of giving him the time off to do so, or to pay his extra time and expenses. He was hired because he had a Third Class FCC ticket and a nice, deep voice with fairly decent reading ability on those commercials, not because he was a journalist. If anybody is at that Press-Bar gathering from his station, it is likely to be the General Manager or the Sales Manager who intercepted the luncheon invitation for "PR" reasons. These nonnewsmen will pay "lip service" to the lawyers during the panel discussions, but not much will reach the newsroom later on.

Secondly, mobility in the broadcast industry appears to be far greater than that in the print media. Those newsmen sitting in on today's discussion are likely to be working for a bigger station somewhere else within the next year or two. By the time a murder trial comes to town, it will be covered by that new kid in the newsroom who has just been thrust into the situation "cold" after being hired with hopes of becoming a disc jockey. He will probably make all those mistakes that should not be made, the lawyers will all feel betrayed, and the "Press" will be in trouble all over again.

Finally, the topic of "Free Press versus Fair Trial" is getting a little bit old by now. It was kicked around all during the 1960's by press and bar associations all over the country. It is not the "in" thing anymore. There are new issues coming up all the time, like the ones just mentioned under "Shield Laws and Confidential Sources." Lyndon Johnson's "Credibility Gap" and Richard Nixon's "Watergate" have opened up whole new areas outside the courtroom which we shall discuss in the "Government and Politics" chapter. These new issues include not only the question of your access to government information, but ways in which you must determine as a journalist whether the government is telling the *truth* or not! The broadcasting and journalism schools will still cover the "Free Press versus Fair Trial" topic adequately, of course, but their graduates are not seeking jobs at that little thousand-watt daytime station in Podunk; they are going where the money is, and you can guess who that leaves to be "News Director" in small stations throughout the country.

Where does this leave you, as you read this book? If you are about to work for a small station, or *are* working for one, find out just where the management stands on these issues. Will they allow you to travel to conferences if the opportunity comes up? Have they had any experience with court coverage before, and if so, what was the outcome? Do they have any up-to-date guidelines or other reference materials handy? If not, can they help you get some? These and other questions will come up again in Chapter 11, "A Word From Your Sponsor, the Outfit That Signs Your Paycheck" so that you may ask the boss all about these things in a convenient "checklist" style before you have to find them out the hard way.

If you are new in broadcast news, or you are a student, or for some other reason you were not around for any of those conferences between the news media and the bar associations that have just been discussed, you have some catching-up to do. Be sure you are familiar with the major cases just listed in the section on "Free Press versus Fair Trial," but do not stop there. Get hold of some of the readings listed in the bibliography on this topic, so that you may gain a full appreciation of how the whole concept has developed over the years. The trials themselves were very exciting to the readers, listeners, and viewers of news at the time they occurred, and they make fascinating reading material even now. Get in touch with the nearest bar association office and see if they can provide you with the latest developments on this important topic.

In the meanwhile, one of the worst mistakes you can make is to assume that everyone will be as "responsible" and "professional" as you try to be whenever you cover the police beat and the courtroom. It would be easy, in writing this book, to tell you all about the virtues of a free press, impartial trials, honest lawyers, unbiased jurors, and highly competent policemen— but if all this reading is to do you any good when you are on the job, you will have to assume that you will be covering stories in an imperfect world in which your colleagues and competitors will not always broadcast their stories without some kind of "slant," in which lawyers will seek some way of gaining publicity for selfish purposes, in which policemen will show their prejudices, in which unbiased jurors will be very hard to find, and in which any or all of these potential forces can improperly influence a trial or put pressure on you to reveal a confidential source at any time.

A glimpse of this "imperfect world" in which you may expect to operate when you get out there and start covering stories is very effectively captured in the book *The Trial of Jack Ruby,* by Kaplan and Waltz (see Bibliography). The authors talk about the next-to-last witness in the trial, Jack Ruby's girl friend, Alice Nichols, who had managed to keep her composure through all the testimony and who had just left the witness stand:

Alice Nichols' ordeal was not over, however. Just as she left the courtroom, the flashbulbs began exploding in her face, and this additional stress was enough to destroy her brittle composure. She broke into tears and struggled to get away from the pursuing photographers. She ran out of the courthouse and down the steps, followed by a mob of some twenty photographers snapping pictures all the way. They had been told to get a picture of Ruby's girl friend and this they intended to do. Finally, about a half block from the courthouse, the strange procession ended when Miss Nichols, out of breath, permitted herself to be surrounded by her pursuers, who snapped picture after picture as she sobbed and shouted incoherently.

## THE CHANGING ROLE OF POLICE: COOPERATION VS. EVASION

As mentioned in the introductory example under "A Look at Courts and Lawyers" in this chapter, concerning the Lindbergh Kidnapping Trial, police felt for many years that they were duty-bound to prove the guilt of those they had arrested. Statements to the press, such as those given in the Lindbergh case, were considered part of the game in winning a conviction.

Along came a few cases in which convictions were overturned because police had allegedly been "promoting" evidence which would not have been admitted in court and the term "trial by newspaper" was coined. Still, somehow, police felt more or less duty-bound to answer all questions put to them by newsmen, apparently feeling that the press would bear the responsibility for what came out in print. This did not seem to please anyone, either. The press accused them of concealing too much and the courts and lawyers accused them of revealing too much.

Gradually, the "fair trial" forces began to gain the upper hand over the "free press" forces. The theory was that if you could not control the news media for fear of violating their constitutional "freedom of the press" rights, then you could shut off their information at the source, which was the police. Any form of collaboration between the police and the news media as to information affecting the fairness of a criminal trial not only became subject to court orders and even laws, but also to censure and other disciplinary measures within police departments themselves. It is no wonder, then, that police began to conclude that it would be safer in many cases to simply decline comment. Whenever newsmen complained, policemen would simply blame it on the courts.

It was not long, though, before police began to refuse information that even the courts themselves would approve for release. The news media, through their broadcasters' and publishers' associations, along with their combined "freedom-of-information" committees, began to cry "police state" and to complain about secret law enforcement and "Star Chamber" proceedings. Constitutional challenges were launched in many parts of the country against the closing of public records of any kind, especially police blotters and criminal records.

In spite of a few decisions upholding freedom of the press (see the section "Free Press vs. Free Trial" of this chapter), it is still far more comfortable for police to say "no comment" on many occasions to newsmen or to use some tactic of evasion or delay in order to avoid the possibility of releasing anything that might get them in trouble with the courts. If you feel that they are using such tactics when you call, and that other stations or newspapers are getting the stories while you are getting "the run-around," it may be a symptom that your relations with some of these police forces are not what they should be, or that your knowledge of their procedures is insufficient.

Some of these seemingly "evasive" tactics will be considered in just a moment, but you should not assume that all of these tactics are deliberately done just to spite you and to make your job rougher. Also, we must warn you not to blame the poor fellow who answers the phone at headquarters, because frequently the approach he is using toward you is dictated by someone else for reasons of which you may never become aware. Both the policeman who answers the phone and his superiors are "marching to a different drummer." They have their orders, and it may never occur to them as they follow these orders that they are putting some roadblocks in your way as you try to gather the day's news. To "lose your cool" and accuse them of holding out on you will only breed hostility. It may be that you or your News Director needs to have a chat with the Chief. This will be covered after an outline of some of the tactics.

*"I'm Not Authorized"*—A common plea from lower-ranking policemen who say that only some higher-ranking officer can give out any information. Usually that means a Lieutenant, Captain, or Chief, and unless you have learned when to call it often seems that he is never there.

*"Not Our Jurisdiction"*—If you have ever had a bank holdup or a plane crash in your area, you may have already discovered that local police are not allowed to discuss it with you. This is because a federal agency has jurisdiction in cases like these, and local authorities are simply to seal the area off and say nothing until the FBI, the FAA, or other agency having jurisdiction arrives. The local people may perform any emergency actions such as saving lives, putting out fires, capturing suspects, etc., *but they may not talk about it!* (More on this is given in Chapter 7, "Searches, Rescues, and Disasters.")

The same phenomenon may occur within your state or county governments, and it may be quite frustrating to you as a newsman if you are not aware of these limitations in advance. Many small towns throughout the country have law enforcement people who *on the surface* appear to be regular policemen but whose authority is actually limited and who must call in the County Sheriff or the State Police to handle certain major crimes.

Some of these smaller forces, following orders to "keep quiet," may not even acknowledge that a major crime has occurred even if it has happened right under their noses. One small New England town where the First Selectman also wore the hat of "Police Chief" and where the few policemen in town were just "constables" insisted to a newsman who called them every hour that it had been "a quiet night—nothing much going on." When a friend called the radio station later to "tip" them about a murder in town, the newsman drove over to the police station and found six State Police cars parked outside and a full-scale investigation underway. When accused of trying to cover up the story, the First Selectman and constables only shrugged and claimed it was not under their jurisdiction. Technically, it was not, but apparently from fear of saying the wrong thing they chose to claim it had been a "quiet night," which was pretty far from the truth.

*"Can't Give It to You Right Now"*—Delaying the release of information can be very frustrating to a newsman, especially a newsman who has an important newscast coming and for whom the story will be "stale" later on, but there are a great many reasons for such delay. A common one occurs when a crime has been committed by several suspects and only *one* of them has been taken into custody. Police fear that a story on the air about the one arrest will cause the others to realize that the deed has been discovered and that it will cause them to flee, thus jeopardizing the chances of their arrest. Another reason might concern the possible safety of hostages or prospective "victims" in the case, such as in the kidnapping of a child. To report that one suspect has been booked, or even that a manhunt is on, may cause the remaining suspect(s) to harm the child on the theory that it is useless to wait around for the ransom. In any case, police feel that somehow the release of certain information, which normally would be all right by itself, would under these circumstances affect the final outcome. If such a delay is an isolated case, you may just have to take it "on faith" that police have good reasons for it. If delays seem to be a habit with certain police stations, then you may want to recheck your relations with them and see if a chat with the Chief about the problem is warranted.

*"Nothing that I know of."*
*"I just came on duty."*
*"Not on my shift."*
*"Nothing since midnight."*
*"Nothing for you today."*

These are all familiar phrases mumbled by desk sergeants across the country. On occasion, even *half the number of times* you call them, they may be valid excuses not to give you any news. It may just be true that there is nothing going on. On the other hand, it may be that the individual answering the phone has programmed himself to say that to *all* newsmen to keep them off his back. It may be his way of saying, "I *do know* something, but I'm not about to tell you about it." He is leading off with an *excuse,* so that he can always claim that the big story he did not give you happened on someone else's shift, before he came on duty, or that *officially* he did not know about it. There are ways of dealing with these "buckpassers," but the least advisable way is to collide with them head-on in some kind of complaint or accusation tangle. The writer would recommend:

▶ *Go around him*—Find out when he is on duty and arrange to call just before or just after his shift. Talk with someone else and ask them what happened during the time period for which he was on duty. Find out who the best spokesmen are at headquarters and build up your relationships with them, so that you are calling when they are available to talk with you.

▶ *Drop in personally*—This kind of individual may be glad to let you look over the blotter or the box of news releases, or whatever, just so long as *you* are doing all the work, not him. He is just too lazy to give any of this information over the phone. While you are there, you may meet someone who is more likeable, and then you may be able to gradually make friends with that other person and ask for him by name when you call up.

▶ *Have a chat with the Chief*—You may never have to name the buckpassing individual about whom you have come to deal with, and you may never have to complain or accuse, but sometimes the fact that you have taken the trouble to visit the higher-ups and express an interest in "closer communications" with the department, asking when are the best times to call, etc., may get through in the form of a hint to the Chief, followed by an order to your buckpassing friend to cooperate a little more with the news media. (At the end of this list of "evasive" tactics is a brief discussion of what items you may wish to include in your personal visits to Police Chiefs and your overall public relations program with various police departments. Be sure to see it before you drop in.)

▶ *Last resort: Tighten up your questions and keep score*—Do not just ask this evasive individual if "there's any news today." Ask him exactly how many people were booked on the blotter during his shift and the previous shift. Ask him who was the officer in charge during the previous shift and who will follow him, and the times involved. Ask him exactly how many "emergency" calls were made which involved hospitals, fire departments, or other agencies, whether they involved arrests or not, and find out exactly which agencies they were so that you may contact them for details. Make a note of the time you called him and what he said. Then, as soon as the newspaper or some other station in town has a story that you did not get and that seems to have occurred during the shift on which this particular "evasive individual" works, tell him about it and ask him if you are doing anything wrong. (Do not accuse *him* of the problem just yet.) Try to get him on your side by asking what he would suggest so that you will not miss these stories in the future. Thank him for his suggestions and follow them as much as you can, but continue to keep score and to state your questions so that he cannot just use one of those little evasive catch-phrases to answer them. *If all else fails,* then confront him or his superiors with the track record, but be sure you have a well-documented case over a period of several months, complete with times and specific questions asked—and specific stories missed directly attributable to this individual. This is only to be done as a *last resort,* after you have tried every public relations trick in the book and can prove that you have done so. Unless you have an "airtight case," you may just be trying to gather honey by kicking over the beehive, and the whole thing will backfire. As a matter of fact, *get the backing of your station management* before you go to any police station with accusations. They may have a few solutions you have not tried, and it would be better to settle such controversies peacefully than to strain the relations with an important news source.

*"Let's see what's in the box."*—This is an excuse in itself for not giving you any news that may be *outside* that little box of authorized news releases that is on the desk in many police stations. It may be a *valid* excuse as far as the officer answering the phone is concerned, because he may be under orders not to release anything else. It is also a sign that there may be

some stories that occasionally exist outside the normal channels, and that you will have to find other ways of getting them.

For example:

▶ The Detective Bureau may keep its own blotter of arrests, and none of these arrests will appear on the regular blotter out front where the desk sergeant answers the phone. The writer has seen cases where Detectives must file news releases on their arrests and put them in "the box" for anyone who calls, but in some stations they arrange to put them in the box at 11:55 p.m., knowing that the box of releases is emptied at midnight! The only newsmen who benefit from this little "sleight-of-hand" trick may be the newspaper reporters who know about this practice and who sit there at 11:55 p.m. waiting for the detectives to drop their releases on the desk. The radio stations who call the next morning are simply out of luck, and when challenged on this suspected practice the policemen involved will usually say something like: "Gee, it's a shame you didn't call. The story was right there in the box."

▶ The existence of "the box" also controls just what kind of information can be given out. There may be some important facts right there on the blotter to which you are entitled and which no court would ever challenge, but since the officer answering the phone is ordered to give you *only* what has been authorized for release in the box, the person who wrote those releases is, in effect, managing the news. This is very comfortable for him, because he is never around when you are talking to that poor unauthorized individual on the phone. By the time you reach him to get any additional information cleared, the story is stale. If you suspect that stories are slipping through your fingers in this manner, it is time to set your public relations program in motion, have a chat with the Chief, and get some of these loopholes closed up.

*Deluge of minor details*—Some police stations manage to create the impression that they are really cooperating with you by flooding the conversation with minor details that you really do not need for broadcast purposes. They may give you such gems of information as:

▶ make, type, year, etc., of vehicles involved in an accident.

▶ names, addresses, ages, etc., of all occupants, bystanders, and cast of "extras" who are not essential to the story. (See Chapter 9 on style.)

▶ where the vehicles were towed to.

▶ complete list of merchandise stolen, property damages, etc.

▶ exact charges, court dates, amount of bail, names of all arresting officers and those who were helping out, etc.

This practice is not deliberately done as a "smokescreen" in all cases. In fact, it may be the result of contacts over the years with poorly trained newsmen who for some reason use all of these details whether they are needed or not. It may be, too, that they do not make a distinction between newspaper reporters and radio people, and that some small-town newspaper actually prints all this. Do not "put them down" for it; just thank them and go your way. *You* are the newsman, they are not.

*"Can you come down and see what's here?"*—Whenever the writer has run into this approach, it is usually a valid plea for help. It tells you that the policeman who answers the phone really does not want to hide anything from you, and that you are welcome to look over the blotter, the releases, and any other information that can possibly be released. It is just that he is snowed under with the duties of running a police force, or part of one, and that he may be tied up with such details as dispatching patrol cars, inspecting reports brought in by other officers, etc. He is admitting frankly that he just does not have time to drop everything and hold a little press conference right there on the phone. Rarely will police deliberately withhold at least the mention of a major crime, but if you are calling from one of those small stations that is interested in all the little fender-benders, stolen cars, drunk arrests, etc., they may be trying to discourage you from getting it all over the phone. In this respect, the writer is on their side—that kind of material just does not belong on the air.

And then, of course, there is just the distinct possibility that they do not like you, they do not like your station, or that they do not like newsmen in general. This is life, it happens. Somewhere in their history of dealing with newsmen, someone may have done something to strain the relations and they have never forgotten it. It may have been an unfavorable story about their department or a member of their force, it may have been an accusation by a newsman or by someone reacting to a news story, or it could just be that some newsman, somewhere, "bugs" them with his behavior. Who knows? You will just have to go back through your own approaches and see if you are doing anything wrong. Check with your own station management. Check with other newsmen from newspapers or other stations.

Maybe you are not calling at the right times or asking the right questions. Some stations just ask if there is any news and always get "no" for an answer. Some daytime stations just call early in the morning and late in the afternoon, missing all the news that is authorized for release during the four-to-midnight shift, never suspecting when they call in the morning that the desk sergeant is only going back as far as midnight when he tells them that nothing happened "overnight." If you ever expect to get more than just the barest minimum out of any police station, they should become more than just a phone number to you which you dial once or twice a day while you are on duty in the newsroom. You should have a vigorous and positive program of "public relations" underway at all times to see just what makes these people "tick" and for them to see what makes *you* tick.

## A CHAT WITH THE CHIEF:
## A POSITIVE PROGRAM OF POLICE RELATIONS

As mentioned earlier in this chapter, newsmen come in all shapes and sizes from the Pulitzer Prize-winners and the Walter Cronkites right down to the grubbiest, least-qualified individuals who can hardly spell their own names. There is no really standard definition of the term "newsman," especially the kind that comes from radio and TV stations. So people like policemen and other "news-source" individuals must always assume the lowest common denominator when they are dealing with people from the news trade. It will take an active program of "police relations," if you will, to *earn* the respect of the various local law enforcement agencies with whom you deal. It will not come overnight, and it will start over again with every new newsman who joins your station's staff.

Your approach should never be how *they* can help you, but how *you* can help *them.* If you walk into the Chief's office to complain about that desk sergeant who is sitting on "your" stories, you can expect a polite but very cool reception and no real change after you leave. Instead, you should try to get the Chief (or your host) talking about the things that interest *him* first, like:

- ▶ "I'll bet you've seen quite a few changes in the force over the past few years, right?"

- ▶ "Has it actually been tougher to do the job with all those recent Supreme Court rulings, or do you think the men are getting used to them?"

- ▶ "Is there some college credit required for promotion in the force now? Where do most of the men go for courses?"

Do not have your pencil and pad on your lap or your tape recorder running for this conversation. This is *not* an interview for an on-the-air story. You will freeze up the whole situation right away if you give the impression that everything you are talking about is "on the record." Remember that your purpose in visiting is not to get a story but to "pass the time of day," as it were, in order to warm up relations and to find out what kind of people you are dealing with and how they run their operation.

Once your conversation gets going, you might gradually bring it around to relating the police department with the news media, but still focused on *their* needs, not yours. For instance:

- ▶ "Have you had any trouble with newsmen lately? Are there some who make life a little difficult? What are some of the things they do?—Because we'd certainly want to be sure of not making the same kind of mistakes.

▶ "When are your busiest times of day? When would you *least* prefer to deal with the news media? When would you say are the *best* times?

▶ "Have you had any problems with court cases becoming fouled-up because of news stories? Do you have any suggestions regarding this business of "Free Press versus Fair Trial?"

▶ Are there some ways in which we can be of help?"

Finally, you can begin to talk about some of the things *you* are most interested in, but still tied to *their* needs. Be sure to check the investigative topics at the end of this chapter for some interesting subjects which you may both have in common to talk about. In the long run, you will find that police—just like anyone else—like to talk about themselves, *but on their own terms.* This is only human. You must remove the fear that someone is going to criticize them or accuse them of violating some court order every time they open their mouths. Look back at the beginning of this chapter and read the criticisms noted in "Are You A Broadcast Journalist or A Talking Police Blotter?" Is this all you are doing with police right now? Is your news confined to the "run-of-the-mill crimes of violence, traffic accidents, and the like . . ." or are you *really interested* in some of the positive things that they are doing, *and showing it?*

Once you have broken the ice with the Chief and the top officials on the force, keep some follow-up activity going at all times. Schedule an investigative project at least three or four times a year. Let them talk with you in person. Ask each division Captain about his specialty. Make sure you are not just another phone call every few hours asking for the old-fashioned "fender-benders" and sordid crimes from the blotter. Not only will your relations with police improve, but so will the quality of your news coverage.

## THE POLICE BEAT AND THE COURTROOM: SOME GUIDELINES

As explained in earlier sections of this chapter, "Codes of Professional Ethics" and "Guidelines" were sorely lacking for newsmen during the 1960's when the nation went through a period of major assassinations and sex-and-murder trials. The various sets of guidelines you see here are the result of many years of work by law enforcement agencies, bar associations, and various newspaper and broadcasters' associations.

It cannot be repeated too often that these are just *models.* They may not agree in every respect with current rules in force in your area, so be sure to get a copy of the latest guidelines on this topic from local police, bar, and broadcasters' associations at your earliest opportunity if you plan to be doing any police or court coverage.

**Katzenbach Guidelines (1965)**—In the wake of cases like **Irvin, Rideau, Van Duyne, Estes,** and **Ruby,** the Attorney General under President Lyndon Johnson, Nicholas deB. Katzenbach, issued guidelines in April of 1965 aimed ostensibly at "Justice Department Personnel," but in practice applied to most law enforcement agencies in the country. Speaking in strict Constitutional terms, he could not direct them at the news media without violating their First Amendment rights. It is interesting to note that in Section 8 (below) he makes an exception in cases like that of Richard Speck, where the public's need to know in order to protect itself is greater than that of protecting the rights of a potentially dangerous fugitive.

## OFFICE OF THE ATTORNEY GENERAL
### WASHINGTON, D.C.

Statement of Policy Concerning the Release of Information by Personnel of the Department of Justice Relating to Criminal Proceedings.

The availability to news media of information in criminal cases is a matter which has become increasingly a subject of concern in the administration of criminal justice. The purpose of this statement is to formulate specific guidelines for the release of such information by personnel of the Department of Justice.

1. These guidelines shall apply to the release of information to news media from the time a person is arrested or is charged with a criminal offense until the proceeding has been terminated by trial or otherwise.

2. At no time shall personnel of the Department of Justice furnish any statement or information for the purpose of influencing the outcome of a defendant's trial.

3. Personnel of the Department of Justice, subject to specific limitations imposed by law or court rule or order, may make public the following information:

(A) The defendant's name, age, residence, employment, marital status, and similar background information.

(B) The substance or text of the charge, such as a complaint, indictment, or information.

(C) The identity of the investigating and arresting agency and the length of the investigation.

(D) The circumstances immediately surrounding an arrest, including the time and place of arrest, resistance, pursuit, possession and use of weapons, and a description of items seized at the time of arrest.

Disclosures should include only incontrovertible, factual matters, and should not include subjective observations. In addition, where background information relating to the circumstances of an arrest would be highly prejudicial and where the release thereof would serve no law enforcement function, such information should not be made public.

4. Personnel of the Department shall not volunteer for publication any information concerning a defendant's prior criminal record. However, this is not intended to alter the Department's present policy that, since federal criminal conviction records are matters of public record permanently maintained in the Department, this information may be made available upon specific inquiry.

5. Because of the particular danger of prejudice resulting from statements in the period approaching and during trial, they ought strenuously to be avoided during that period. Any such statement or release shall be made only on the infrequent occasion when circumstances absolutely demand a disclosure of information and shall include only information which is clearly not prejudicial.

6. The release of certain types of information generally tends to create dangers of prejudice without serving a significant law enforcement function. Therefore, personnel of the Department should refrain from making available the following:

(A) Observations about a defendant's character.

(B) Statements, admissions, confession, or alibis attributable to a defendant.

(C) References to investigative procedures, such as fingerprints, polygraph examinations, ballistic tests, or laboratory tests.

(D) Statements concerning the identity, credibility, or testimony of prospective witnesses.

(E) Statements concerning evidence or argument in the case, whether or not it is anticipated that such evidence or argument will be used at trial.

7. Personnel of the Department of Justice should take no action to encourage or assist news media in photographing or televising a defendant or accused person being held or transported in federal custody. Departmental representatives should not make available

photographs of a defendant unless a law enforcement function is served thereby.

8. This statement of policy is not intended to restrict the release of information concerning a defendant who is a fugitive from justice.

9. Since the purpose of this statement is to set forth generally applicable guidelines, there will of course, be situations in which it will limit release of information which could be prejudicial under the particular circumstances. If a representative of the Department believes that in the interest of the fair administration of justice and the law enforcement process information beyond these guidelines should be released in a particular case, he shall request the permission of the Attorney General or the Deputy Attorney General to do so.

**Mitchell Revisions (1971)**—John Mitchell, the Attorney General under President Richard Nixon, tightened the Katzenbach Guidelines so that they applied not just when a suspect was *arrested* or *indicted,* but ". . . from the time a person is the subject of a criminal investigation." Mitchell also widened the scope of the guidelines to prevent Justice Department officials from discussing civil as well as criminal cases.

The Mitchell revisions were very much in force even after Mitchell resigned as Attorney General. In their best-selling book, *All the President's Men,* authors Carl Bernstein and Bob Woodward tell what it was like to investigate the "Watergate" scandal:

During a routine check with a Justice Department official that morning, Bernstein had asked if the official had ever heard of Donald Segretti. It had been a throwaway question.

"I can't answer your question because that's part of the investigation," the Justice official replied.

Bernstein was startled. Woodward and he had thought they were alone in pursuing Segretti.

There could be no discussion of Segretti because he was part of the Watergate investigation, right?

That was correct, but the official would not listen to any more questions about Segretti. Bernstein went down his list of checks, crossing out each item, writing 'no' or 'nothing' in the margin.

Herbert W. Kalmbach?

"That's part of the investigation, too, so I can't talk about it," the official said.

**Sample State Guidelines (1969)**—As the 1960's drew to a close, much had been done to improve relationships between the bar and the press. The nation had seen both "Kennedy" assassinations, plus that of Dr. Martin Luther King, Jr. and the attempt on Alabama's Governor George Wallace. The sensational "sex-and-society" trials of Sheppard, Mossler, and Coppolino had made their mark, juvenile rights had been updated by the "Gault" decision, and the Reardon

Report had been adopted by the American Bar Association's House of Delegates in August, 1968.

Joint committees formed by the news media and the legal profession came out with guidelines for the coverage of criminal trials, such as these from the state of Wisconsin:

### Statement of Principles of the Wisconsin Bar and News Media

The bar and news media of Wisconsin recognize that freedom of the news media and the right to a fair and swift trial are fundamental to the basic liberties guaranteed by the First and Sixth Amendments of the United States Constitution. The news media and the bar further recognize that these basic rights must be rigidly preserved and responsibly practiced according to highest professional standards.

The bar and the news media, and indeed all citizens, are obliged to preserve the principle that any person suspected or accused of a crime is innocent until found guilty in a court under competent evidence fairly presented and accurately reported.

The bar and the news media recognize that access to legitimate information involving the administration of justice is as vital to the public's concern in the commission of crimes against society as is guaranteeing the suspect and the state a fair trial free of prejudicial information and conduct. The same principles apply in all civil proceedings.

To promote understanding toward reconciling the constitutional guarantees of freedom of the press and the right to a fair, impartial trial, the following principles, mutually drawn and submitted for voluntary compliance, are recommended to all members of these professions in Wisconsin.

1. The news media have the right and responsibility to disseminate the news. Free and responsible news media enhance the administration of justice. Members of the bar should co-operate, within their canons of legal ethics, with the news media in the reporting of the administration of justice.

2. All parties to litigation, including the state, have the right to have their causes tried fairly by an impartial tribunal. Defendants in criminal cases are guaranteed this right by the Constitutions of the United States and Wisconsin.

3. No trial should be influenced by the pressure of publicity from any news media or the public. Lawyers and journalists share responsibility to prevent the creation of such pressures.

4. All news media should strive for accuracy and objectivity. The public has a right to be informed, the accused the right to be judged in an atmosphere free from undue prejudice.

5. The news media and the bar recognize the responsibility of the judge to preserve order in the court and to seek the ends of justice by all appropriate legal means.

6. Decisions about handling news rests with editors. In the exercise of news judgment, the communicator should remember that:
   (a) An accused person is presumed innocent until proven guilty.
   (b) Readers, listeners and viewers are potential jurors.
   (c) No person's reputation should be injured needlessly.

7. The public is entitled to know how justice is being administered. No lawyer should use publicity to promote his side of a pending case. The public prosecutor should not take unfair advantage of his position as an important source of news. These cautions shall not be construed to limit a lawyer's obligation to make available information to which the public is entitled.

8. Journalistic and legal training should include instruction in the meaning of constitutional rights to a fair trial, freedom of press, and the role of both journalist and lawyer in guarding these rights.

9. A committee of representatives of the bar and the media, possibly aided by or including representatives of law enforcement agencies and other interested parties, should meet from time to time to promote understanding of these principles by the public and especially by all directly involved persons, agencies, or organizations. Its purpose may include giving advisory opinions concerning the interpretation and application of these principles as specific problems arise.

## Guidelines on the Reporting of Criminal Proceedings

1. There should be no restraint on making public the following information concerning the defendant:
   (a) The defendant's name, age, residence, employment, marital status, and other factual background information.
   (b) The substance or text of the charge, such as complaint, indictment, information or, where appropriate, the identity of the complaining party.
   (c) The identity of the investigating and arresting agency, and the nature of the investigation where appropriate.
   (d) The circumstances surrounding an arrest, including the time and place of arrest, resistance, pursuit, possession and use of weapons, and a description of items siezed at the time of arrest.

2. The release to news media of certain types of information, or publication, may create dangers of prejudice to the defense or prosecution without serving a significant law enforcement or public interest function. Therefore, all concerned should be aware of the dangers of prejudice in making pretrial public disclosures of the following:
   (a) Opinions about a defendant's character, his guilt or innocence.

(b) Admissions, confessions, or the contents of a statement or alibis attributable to the defendant.

(c) References to investigate procedures, such as fingerprints, polygraph examinations, ballistic tests, or laboratory tests.

(d) Statements concerning the credibility or anticipated testimony of prospective witnesses.

(e) Opinions concerning evidence or argument in the case, whether or not it is anticipated that such evidence or argument will be used at trial.

Exceptions to these points may be in order if information to the public is essential to the apprehension of a suspect, or where other public interests will be served.

3. Prior criminal charges and convictions are matters of public record, available through police agencies or court clerks. Law enforcement agencies should make such information available upon legitimate inquiry but the public disclosure of it may be highly prejudicial without benefit to the public's need to be informed. The news media and law enforcement agencies have a special duty to report the disposition or status of prior charges.

4. Law enforcement and court personnel should not prevent the photographing of defendants, or suspects, when they are in public places outside the courtroom. They should not promote pictures or televising nor should they pose a defendant or a suspect or a person in custody against his will. They may make available a suitable photograph of a defendant or a person in custody.

5. Photographs of a suspect not in custody may be released by law enforcement personnel provided a valid law enforcement function is served thereby. It is proper to disclose information necessary to enlist public assistance in apprehending fugitives. Disclosure may include photographs as well as records of prior arrests or convictions.

6. Freedom of news media to report proceedings in court is generally recognized. The bench may utilize measures, such as cautionary instructions, sequestration of the jury, and the holding of hearings on evidence in the absence of the jury, to insure that the jury's deliberations are based upon evidence presented to them in court. All concerned should cooperate toward that end.

7. Sensationalism should be avoided by all.

### Guidelines for Reporting Juvenile Offenses

The news media and the bar recognize the distinction between juvenile and adult offenders established by law. We also recognize the right of the media to have free access to all matters concerning juvenile offenders and juvenile proceedings and to report the same, except as prohibited by law.

The bar and the media further recognize that they share, with the courts and other officials, responsibility for developing sound public interest in and understanding of juvenile problems as they relate to the community.

We therefore recommend:

1. In the handling of juvenile matters, basic principles of fairness and cooperation, as defined in the Statement of Principles of the bench-media committee of Wisconsin, shall apply. When a juvenile is regarded as an adult under criminal law, the bar-media guideline for reporting crime and ordinance violations shall apply.

2. When news media attend sessions of the juvenile court, they may disclose names or identifying data of the participants, unless prohibited by law. News media should make every effort to fully observe and report such sessions, and the disposition thereof by the court, with regard for the juvenile's rights and the public interest.

**Massachusetts Bar-Press Guidelines for the Broadcast News Media**—Although similar in substance to the "Wisconsin" guidelines just quoted, the Massachusetts Bar-Press Committee broke its guidelines down into sections addressed specifically to print media, broadcast media, and lawyers. The **Reardon Report,** which quotes the Massachusetts guidelines in their entirety, notes that the following "broadcast" section was adopted by the Massachusetts Broadcasters' Association soon after its approval by the Bar-Press Committee:

The broadcast news media in news stories originated by them concerning a crime should keep in mind that the accused may be tried in a court of law.

To preserve the individual's rights to a fair trial, news stories of crime should contain only a factual statement of the arrest and attending circumstances.

The following should be avoided:

(1) Broadcasting interviews with subpoenaed witnesses after an indictment is returned.

(2) Broadcasting of the criminal record or discreditable acts of the accused after an indictment is returned or during the trial unless made part of the evidence in the court record. The defendant is being tried on the charge for which he is accused and not on his record. (Broadcasting of a criminal record could be grounds for a libel suit.)

(3) Broadcasting of confessions after an indictment is returned unless made a part of the evidence in the court record.

(4) Broadcasting of testimony stricken by the court unless reported as having been stricken.

(5) Editorial comment preceding or during the trial, tending to influence judge or jury.

(6) Broadcasting of names of juveniles involved in juvenile proceedings unless the names are released by the judge.

(7) The broadcasting of any "leaks," statements, or conclusions as to the innocence or guilt, implied or expressed, by the police or prosecuting authorities or defense counsel.

**The Reardon Report (1968)**—Adopted by the American Bar Association House of Delegates in August, 1968, this approved draft of **Standards Relating to Fair Trial and Free Press** was aimed ostensibly at lawyers, judges, and other court officials or employees, because these are the people who are legally under the jurisdiction of a court or a bar association. In cases where these standards were addressed to "law enforcement agencies," they were simply *recommended,* hoping that the agencies themselves would adopt the rules for the conduct of their own members. Even though newsmen were not directly named in the Reardon standards, the recommendations in Part IV that a judge be able to bring contempt action against: "a person who . . . disseminates by any means of public communication . . ." certain kinds of statements or information, touched off a furor from the news media who saw these contempt powers hanging over them as nothing less than naked censorship. As a result, the Reardon recommendations, while serving as a model, have not always been adopted "100%" as court orders, laws, or even voluntary guidelines across the country, but have been modified to reflect prevailing needs and opinions in each state or region where such codes have been approved.

**American Bar Association Project on**
**Minimum Standards for Criminal Justice**
**STANDARDS RELATING TO**
**FAIR TRIAL AND FREE PRESS**
*Recommended by the*
*Advisory Committee on Fair Trial and Free Press*
*Paul C. Reardon, Chairman*

PART I. RECOMMENDATIONS RELATING TO THE CONDUCT OF ATTORNEYS IN CRIMINAL CASES

1.1 Revision of the Canons of Professional Ethics.

It is recommended that the substance of the following standards, relating to public discussion of pending or imminent criminal litigation, be embodied in the Code of Professional Responsibility:

It is the duty of the lawyer not to release or authorize the release of information or opinion for discussion for any means of public communication, in connection with pending or imminent criminal litigation with which he is associated, if there is a reasonable likelihood that such dissemination will interfere with a fair trial or otherwise prejudice the due administration of justice.

With respect to a grand jury or other pending investigation of any criminal matter, a lawyer participating in the investigation shall refrain from making any extrajudicial statement, for dissemination by any means of public communication, that goes beyond the public record or that is not necessary to inform the public that the investigation is underway, to describe the general scope of the investigation, to obtain assistance in the apprehension of a suspect, to warn the public of any dangers, or otherwise to aid in the investigation.

From the time of arrest, issuance of an arrest warrant, or the filing of a complaint, information, or indictment in any criminal matter until the commencement of trial or disposition without trial, a lawyer associated with the prosecution or defense shall not release or authorize the release of any extrajudicial statement, for dissemination by any means of public communication, relating to that matter and concerning:

(1) The prior criminal record (including arrests, indictments, or other charges of crime), or the character or reputation of the accused, except that the lawyer may make a factual statement of the accused's name, age, residence, occupation, and family status, and if the accused has not been apprehended, a lawyer associated with the prosecution may release any information necessary to aid in his apprehension or to warn the public of any dangers he may present;

(2) The existence or content of any confession, admission, or statement given by the accused, or the refusal or failure of the accused to make any statement;

(3) The performance of any examinations or tests or the accused's refusal or failure to submit to an examination or test;

(4) The identity, testimony, or credibility of prospective witnesses, except that the lawyer may announce the identity of the victim if the announcement is not otherwise prohibited by law;

(5) The possibility of a plea of guilty to the offense charged or a lesser offense;

(6) Any opinion as to the accused's guilt or innocence or as to the merits of the case or the evidence in the case.

The foregoing shall not be construed to preclude the lawyer during this period, in the proper discharge of his official or professional obligations, from announcing the fact and circumstances of arrest (including time and place of arrest, resistance, pursuit, and use of weapons), the identity of the investigating and arresting officer or agency, and the length of investigation: from making an announcement, at the time of seizure of any physical evidence other than a confession, admission, or statement, which is limited to a description of the evidence seized; from disclosing the nature, substance, or text of the charge, including a brief description of the offense charged; from quoting or referring without comment to public records of the court in the case; from announcing the scheduling or result of any stage in the judicial process; from requesting assistance in obtaining evidence; or from announcing without further comment that the accused denies the charges made against him.

During the trial of any criminal matter, including the period of selection of the jury, no lawyer associated with the prosecution or defense shall give or authorize any extrajudicial statement or interview, relating to the trial or the parties or issues in the trial, for dissemination by any means of public communication, except that the lawyer may quote from or refer without comment to public records of the court in the case.

After the completion of a trial or disposition without trial of any criminal matter, and prior to the imposition of sentence, a lawyer associated with the prosecution or defense shall refrain from making or authorizing any extrajudicial statement for dissemination by any means of public communication if there is a reasonable likelihood that such dissemination will affect the imposition of sentence.

Nothing in this Canon is intended to preclude the formulation or application of more restrictive rules relating to the release of information about juveniles or other offenders, to preclude the holding of hearings or the lawful issuance of reports by legislative, administrative, or investigative bodies, or to preclude any lawyer from replying to charges of misconduct that are publicly made against him.

1.2 Rule of Court.

In any jurisdiction in which Canons of Professional Ethics have not been adopted by statute or court rule, it is recommended that the substance of the foregoing section be adopted as a rule of court governing the conduct of attorneys.

1.3 Enforcement.

It is recommended that violation of the standards set forth in Section 1.1 shall be grounds for judicial and bar association reprimand or for suspension from practice, and, in more serious cases, for disbarment. It is further recommended that any attorney or bar association be allowed to petition an appropriate court for the institution of disciplinary proceedings, and that the court have discretion to initiate such proceedings, either on the basis of such a petition or on its own motion.

## PART II. RECOMMENDATIONS RELATING TO THE CONDUCT OF LAW ENFORCEMENT OFFICERS, JUDGES, AND JUDICIAL EMPLOYEES IN CRIMINAL CASES

2.1 Departmental Rules.

It is recommended that law enforcement agencies in each jurisdiction adopt the following internal regulations:

(a) A regulation governing the release of information, relating to the commission of crimes and to their investigation, prior to the making of an arrest, issuance of an arrest warrant, or the filing of formal charges. This regulation should establish appropriate procedures for the release of information. It should further provide that, when a crime is believed to have been committed, pertinent facts relating to the crime itself and to investigative procedures may properly be made available but the identity of a suspect prior to arrest and the results of investigative procedures shall not be disclosed except to the extent necessary to aid the investigation, to assist in the apprehension of the suspect, or to warn the public of any dangers.

(b) A regulation prohibiting:

(i) the deliberate posing of a person in custody for photographing or televising by representatives of the news media and

(ii) the interviewing by representatives of the news media of a person in custody unless, in writing, he requests or consents to an interview after being adequately informed of his right to consult with counsel and of his right to refuse to grant an interview.

(c) A regulation providing:

From the time of arrest, issuance of an arrest warrant, or the filing of any complaint, information, or indictment in any criminal matter, until the completion of trial or disposition without trial, no law enforcement officer within this agency shall release or authorize the release of any extrajudicial statement, for dissemination by any means of public communication, relating to that matter and concerning:

(1) The prior criminal record (including arrests, indictments, or other charges of crime), or the character or reputation of the accused, except that the officer may make a factual statement of the accused's name, age, residence, occupation, and family status, and if the accused has not been apprehended, may release any information necessary to aid in his apprehension or to warn the public of any dangers he may present;

(2) The existence or contents of any confession, admission or statement given by the accused, or the refusal or failure of the accused to make any statement, except that the officer may announce without further comment that the accused denies the charges made against him;

(3) The performance of any examinations or tests or the accused's refusal or failure to submit to an examination or test;

(4) The identity, testimony, or credibility of any prospective witnesses, except that the officer may announce the identity of the victim if the announcement is not otherwise prohibited by law;

(5) The possibility of a plea of guilty to the offense charged or to a lesser offense;

(6) Any opinion as to the accused's guilt or innocence or as to the merits of the case or the evidence in the case.

It shall be appropriate during this period for a law enforcement officer:

(1) to announce the fact and circumstances of arrest, including the time and place of arrest, resistance, pursuit and use of weapons;

(2) to announce the identity of the investigating and arresting officer or agency and the length of the investigation;

(3) to make an announcement, at the time of seizure of any physical evidence other than a confession, admission, or statement, which is limited to a description of the evidence seized;

(4) to disclose the nature, substance, or text of the charge, including a brief description of the offense charged;

(5) to quote from or refer without comment to public records of the court in the case;

(6) to announce the scheduling or result of any stage in the judicial process;

(7) to request assistance in obtaining evidence.

Nothing in this rule precludes any law enforcement officers from replying to charges of misconduct that are publicly made against him, precludes any law enforcement officer from participating in any legislative, administrative, or investigative hearing, or supersedes any more restrictive rule governing the release of information concerning juveniles or other offenders.

(d) A regulation providing for the enforcement of the foregoing by the imposition of appropriate disciplinary sanctions.

2.2 Rule of court or legislation relating to law enforcement agencies.

It is recommended that if within a reasonable time a law enforcement agency in any jurisdiction fails to adopt and adhere to the substance of the recommendation recommended in Section 2.1(c), as it relates to both proper and improper disclosures, the regulation be made effective with respect to that agency by rule of court or by legislative action, with appropriate sanctions for violation.

2.3 Rule of court relating to disclosures by judicial employees.

It is recommended that a rule of court be adopted in each jurisdiction prohibiting any judicial employee from disclosing, to any unauthorized person, information relating to a pending criminal case that is not part of the public records of the court and that may tend to interfere with the rights of the people or of the defendant to a fair trial. Particular reference should be made in this rule to the nature and result of any argument or hearing held in chambers or otherwise outside the presence of the public and not yet available to the public under the standards in Section 3.1 and Section 3.5(d) of these recommendations. Appropriate discipline, including proceedings for contempt, should be provided for infractions of this rule.

## 2.4 Recommendation relating to judges.

It is recommended that with respect to pending criminal cases, judges should refrain from any conduct or the making of any statements that may tend to interfere with the right of the people or the defendant to a fair trial.

## PART III. RECOMMENDATIONS RELATING TO THE CONDUCT OF JUDICIAL PROCEEDINGS IN CRIMINAL CASES

## 3.1 Pretrial hearings.

It is recommended that the following rule be adopted in each jurisdiction by the appropriate court:

Motion to exclude public from all or part of pretrial hearing.

In any preliminary hearing, bail hearing, or other pretrial hearing in a criminal case, including a motion to suppress evidence, the defendant may move that all or part of the hearing be held in chambers or otherwise closed to the public, including representatives of the news media, on the ground that dissemination of evidence or argument adduced at the hearing may disclose matters that will be inadmissible in evidence at the trial and is therefore likely to interfere with his right to a fair trial by an impartial jury. The motion shall be granted unless the presiding officer determines that there is no substantial likelihood of such interference. With the consent of the defendant, the presiding officer may take such action on his own motion or at the suggestion of the prosecution. Whenever under this rule all or part of any pretrial hearing is held in chambers or otherwise closed to the public, a complete record of the proceedings shall be kept and shall be made available to the public following the completion of trial or disposition of the case without trial. Nothing in this rule is intended to interfere with the power of the presiding officer in any pretrial hearing to caution those present that dissemination of certain information by any means of public communication may jeopardize the right to a fair trial by an impartial jury.

## 3.2 Change of venue or continuance.

It is recommended that the following standards be adopted in each jurisdiction to govern the consideration and disposition of a motion in a criminal case for change of venue or continuance based on a claim of threatened interference with the right to a fair trial.

(a) Who may request.

Except as federal or state consitutional provisions otherwise require, a change of venue or continuance may be granted on motion of either the prosecution or the defense.

(b)  Methods of proof.

In addition to the testimony or affidavits of individuals in the community, which shall not be required as a condition of the granting of a motion for change of venue or continuance, qualified public opinion surveys shall be admissible as well as other materials having probative value.

(c)  Standards for granting motion.

A motion for change of venue or continuance shall be granted whenever it is determined that because of the dissemination of potentially prejudicial material, there is a reasonable likelihood that in the absence of such relief, a fair trial cannot be had. This determination may be based on such evidence as qualified public opinion surveys or opinion testimony offered by individuals, or on the court's own evaluation of the nature, frequency, and timing of the material involved. A showing of actual prejudice shall not be required.

(d)  Same; time of disposition.

If a motion for change of venue or continuance is made prior to the impaneling of the jury, the motion shall be disposed of before impaneling. If such a motion is permitted to be made, or if reconsideration or review of a prior denial is sought, after the jury has been selected the fact that a jury satisfying prevailing standards of acceptability has been selected shall not be controlling if the record shows that the criterion for the granting of relief set forth in subsection (c) has been met.

(e)  Limitations; waiver.

It shall not be a ground for denial of a change of venue that one such change has already been granted. The claim that the venue should have been changed or a continuance granted shall not be considered to have been waived by the waiver of the right to trial by jury or by the failure to exercise all available peremptory challenges.

## 3.3  Waiver of jury.

In those jurisdictions in which the defendant does not have an absolute right to waive a jury in a criminal case, it is recommended that the defendant be permitted to waive whenever it is determined that (1) the waiver has been knowingly and voluntarily made, and (2) there is reason to believe that as a result of the dissemination of potentially prejudicial material, the waiver is required to increase the likelihood of a fair trial.

## 3.4  Selecting the jury.

It is recommended that the following standards be adopted in each jurisdiction to govern the selection of a jury in those criminal cases in which questions of possible preudice are raised.

(a)  Method of examination.

Whenever there is believed to be a significant possibility that individual talesmen will be ineligible to serve because of exposure to potentially prejudicial material, the examination of each juror with respect to his exposure shall take place outside the presence of other chosen and prospective jurors. An accurate record of this examination shall be kept, by court reporter or tape recording whenever possible. The questioning shall be conducted for the purpose of determining what the prospective juror has read and heard about the case and how his exposure has affected his attitude towards the trial, not to convince him that he would be derelict in his duty if he could not cast aside any preconceptions he might have.

(b) Standard of acceptability.

Both the degree of exposure and the prospective juror's testimony as to his state of mind are relevant to the determination of acceptability. A prospective juror who states that he will be unable to overcome his preconceptions shall be subject to challenge for cause no matter how slight his exposure. If he has seen or heard and remembers information that will be developed in the course of trial, or that may be inadmissable but is not so prejudicial as to create a substantial risk that his judgment will be affected, his acceptability shall turn on whether his testimony as to impartiality is believed. If he admits to having formed an opinion, he shall be subject to challenge for cause unless the examination shows unequivocally that he can be impartial. A prospective juror who has been exposed to and remembers reports of highly significant information, such as the existence or contents of a confession, or other incriminating matters that may be inadmissable in evidence, or substantial amounts of inflammatory material, shall be subject to challenge for cause without regard to his testimony as to his state of mind.

(c) Source of the panel.

Whenever it is determined that potentially prejudicial news coverage of a given criminal matter has been intense and has been concentrated primarily in a given locality in a state (or federal district), the court shall have authority to draw jurors from other localities in that state (or district).

3.5 Conduct of the trial.

It is recommended that the following standards be adopted in each jurisdiction to govern the conduct of a criminal trial when problems relating to the dissemination of potentially prejudicial material are raised.

(a) Use of the courtroom.

Whenever appropriate in view of the notoriety of the case of the number or conduct of news media representatives present at any judicial proceeding, the court shall ensure the preservation of decorum by instructing those representatives and others as to the permissible use of the courtroom and other facilities of the court, the assignment of seats to news media representatives on an equitable basis, and other matters that may affect the conduct of the proceeding.

(b) Sequestration of jury.

Either party shall be permitted to move for sequestration of the jury at the beginning of trial or at any time during the course of the trial, and, in appropriate circumstances, the court shall order sequestration on its own motion. Sequestration shall be ordered if it is determined that the case is of such notoriety or the issues are of such a nature that, in the absence of sequestration, highly prejudicial matters are likely to come to the attention of the jurors. Whenever sequestration is ordered, the court in advising the jury of the decision shall not disclose which party requested sequestration.

(c) Cautioning parties, witnesses, jurors, and judicial employees; insulating witnesses.

Whenever appropriate in light of the issues in the case or the notoriety of the case, the court shall instruct parties, witnesses, jurors, and employees and officers of the court not to make extrajudicial statements, relating to the case or the issues in the case, for dissemination by any means of public communication during the course of the trial. The court may also order sequestration of witnesses, prior to their appearance, when it appears likely that in the absence of sequestration they will be exposed to extrajudicial reports that may influence their testimony.

(d) Exclusion of the public from hearings or arguments outside the presence of the jury.

If the jury is not sequestered, the defendant shall be permitted to move that the public, including representatives of the news media, be excluded from any portion of the trial that takes place outside the presence of the jury on the ground that dissemination of evidence or argument adduced at the hearing is likely to interfer with the defendant's right to a fair trial by an impartial jury. The motion shall be granted unless it is determined that there is no substantial likelihood of such interference. With the consent of the defendant, the court may take such action on its own motion or at the suggestion of the prosecution. Whenever such action is taken, a complete record of the proceedings from which the public has been excluded shall be kept and shall be made available to the public following the completion of the trial. Nothing in this recommendation is intended to interfere with the power of the court, in connection with any hearing held outside the presence of the jury, to caution those present that dissemination of specified information by any means of public communication, prior to the rendering of the verdict, may jeopardize the right to a fair trial by an impartial jury.

(e) Cautioning jurors.

In any case that appears likely to be of significant public interest, an admonition in substantially the following form shall be given before the end of the first day if the jury is not sequestered:

> During the time you serve on this jury, there may appear in the newspapers or on radio or television reports concerning this case, and you may be tempted to read, listen to, or watch them. Please do not do so. Due process of law requires that the evidence to be considered by you in reaching your verdict meet certain standards—for example, a witness may testify about events he himself has seen or heard but not about matters of which he was told by others. Also, witnesses must be sworn to tell the truth and must be subject to cross-examination. News reports about the case are not subject to these standards, and if you read, listen to, or watch these reports, you may be exposed to misleading or inaccurate information which unduly favors one side and to which the other side is unable to respond. In fairness to both sides, therefore, it is essential that you comply with this instruction.

If the process of selecting a jury is a lengthy one, such an admonition shall also be given to each juror as he is selected. At the end of each subsequent day of the trial, and at other recess periods if the court deems necessary, an admonition in substantially the following form shall be given:

> For the reasons stated earlier in the trial, I must remind you not to read, listen to, or watch any news reports concerning this case while you are serving on this jury.

(f) Questioning jurors about exposure to potentially prejudicial material in the course of trial; standard for excusing a juror.

If it is determined that material disseminated during the trial goes beyond the record on which the case is to be submitted to the jury and raises serious questions of possible prejudice, the court may on its own motion or shall on motion of either party question each juror, out of the presence of the others, about his exposure to that material. The examination shall take place in the presence of counsel, and an accurate record of the examination shall be kept. The standard for excusing a juror who is challenged on the basis of such exposure shall be the same as the standard of acceptability recommended in Section 3.4(b), above, except that a juror who has seen or heard reports of potentially prejudicial material shall be excused if reference to the material in question at the trial itself would have required a mistrial to be declared.

3.6  Setting aside the verdict.

It is recommended that, on motion of the defendant, a verdict of guilty in any criminal case be set aside and a new trial granted whenever, on the basis of competent evidence, the court finds a substantial likelihood that the vote of one or more jurors was influenced by exposure to an extrajudicial communication of any matter relating to the defendant or to the case itself that was not part of the trial record on which the case was submitted to the jury. Nothing in this recommendation is intended to affect the rule in any jurisdiction as to whether and in what circumstances a juror may impeach his own verdict or as to what other evidence is competent for that purpose.

**PART IV. RECOMMENDATIONS RELATING TO THE EXERCISE OF THE CONTEMPT POWER**

4.1  Limited use of the contempt power.

It is recommended that the contempt power should be used only with considerable caution but should be exercised under the following circumstances:

(a)  Against a person who, knowing that a criminal trial by jury is in progress or that a jury is being selected for such a trial:

(i) disseminates by any means of public communication an extrajudicial statement relating to the defendant or to the issues in the case that goes beyond the public record of the court in the case, that is wilfully designed by that person to affect the outcome of the trial, and that seriously threatens to have such an effect; or

(ii) makes such a statement intending that it be disseminated by any means of public communication.

(b)  Against a person who knowingly violates a valid judicial order not to disseminate, until completion of the trial or disposition without trial, specified information referred to in the course of a judicial hearing closed pursuant to Sections 3.1 or 3.5(d) of these recommendations.

As indicated, many of the rules spelled out in these guidelines have the force of law behind them in some states, while in other states there may be major differences. Even in the same state, there may be differences between state and federal courts. For example, in the 37 cities surveyed in the "Medina" report (see "Free Press versus Fair Trial" section), some police forces allowed cameramen inside their police stations to photograph suspects as they were being "booked," while others forbade the practice. First of all, you will have to know which rules do apply and do not apply by inquiring *in advance* of any coverage in any jurisdiction you plan to cover. Occasionally, seasoned reporters may "bend the rules" a bit in order to correct an alleged injustice. Some of the common reasons for this practice include:

▶ instances where a suspect has been held on bail for many weeks and has not been brought to trial. News media have the right to ask why no action has been taken in such cases.

▶ instances in which suspects have been arrested many times and have been repeatedly released on bail, only to go out and apparently commit the same offense without being brought to trial on the original charges.

▶ suspicion of secret arrests, cover-ups within the ranks of police, prosecutors, or others in government.

▶ uncovering of new evidence (such as in "Watergate" and other cases in the history of "Free Press versus Fair Trial") which would justifiably reverse or widen the course of some court proceedings.

▶ definite service to public where safety is concerned (such as a killer on the loose: see Richard Speck case, earlier in this chapter).

In any event, you must be sure that you are on pretty firm ground before you venture outside the rules. This is not something a beginner should attempt. If you are not a seasoned veteran who can document his case carefully (perhaps with the aid of the station's own lawyer to be sure you do not leave yourself open to contempt or libel action), then you had better turn the matter over to someone who has the expertise to handle it. For every case in which a reporter has managed to uncover meaningful evidence and bring about "true justice," there are probably two or three cases in which newsmen have managed to *thwart* justice by printing or broadcasting unfounded speculation.

Most common among the abuses of which many are guilty are the cases in which a reporter has several other stories to cover besides the current court case—so he rushes in for a moment, takes a quick look at the trial, rushes out to cover something else, comes back and catches a few glimpses of testimony, and then files his stories based on this limited view of the trial. Judges and lawyers not only have the right to question such spotty coverage, but some of them have been ordering the doors to the courtrooms closed while the trial is in session, meaning that you must sit through several hours of testimony and get the *whole* story, or not be admitted at all. Even this tactic has failed to shut off all the abuses. Defense Attorney F. Lee Bailey is quoted in a Bar Association speech as saying that on the last day of the Carl Coppolino murder case in Florida, a reporter from *Time* magazine came to town and caught a few bits and pieces of summations in the case, then filed a story which Bailey claimed was "pontifically written with the usual expertise." Despite the article, which was not very flattering to Mr. Bailey's client, there was no conviction in the case, and Attorney Bailey pointed out to the Bar Association gathering that the reporter "did most of his research, because I was there, in the bar of the . . . Buckaneer Motel." It is not the first time, and it will not be the last, in which the news media have been accused of aiding a potential *miscarriage* of justice rather than serving its noblest causes.

There is one more important aspect we should cover regarding the topic of crime news and "Free Press versus Fair Trial." You may not find it in any standard set of guidelines on this kind of coverage, but there is another force at work upon the newsman. At far too many stations, management is unfortunately not noted for its courage when it comes to controversy. Many station managers have gained their positions without ever working in a newsroom and are simply not prepared to handle some of the tight situations involving news. They have a tendency to "panic" when a lawyer calls up or some public official complains. You must find out in advance just how well-versed the management is in the principles of broadcast journalism.

*Will the management back you up?* That is the main question—guidelines or no guidelines. You could be 100-percent right and the caller be 100-percent wrong when he complains to your station manager about a news story, but there are times when being right is not enough. You "rocked the boat," and that is enough in some managers' eyes to fire you! Check this angle out *first;* it is worth knowing about. If you find that the manager at your station is not too well-versed in news, then "play it safe," at least until you can get a better job. In small stations, you are better off not "rocking the boat" when controversies arise. Rather than risk contempt citations, subpoenas, and jail sentences by becoming some kind of journalistic martyr for a station that is only paying you "peanuts" and would not even bail you out, much less defend you, it is better to wait for the day when you can work for an outfit where the people in the front office can stand the pressure.

For example, in the case where local police covered up a a murder story while claiming they had no jurisdiction (as mentioned earlier in this chapter), the newsman ran not only the murder story but a story about the "cover-up" attempt and the station manager nearly had a heart attack for fear of offending local officials.

There was another case in which a mistrial had been declared in city *A* because of prejudicial publicity in the news media about the alleged murder suspect. When the retrial was scheduled in city *B*, a station manager there was so afraid that his own reporters might violate some court ruling that he forbade them to file voice reports from the courthouse. Instead, they filed their stories with the wire service, and the manager felt very comfortable at seeing the newsmen back at the station reading the stories which they tore from the wire service machine. To this day, he probably does not realize from whom the wire service was getting its information.

As Alexander Kendrick puts it in his biography of famed newsman Edward R. Murrow, "there are those in the industry who believe broadcasting can move men, and even some who believe it could move mountains, but they are outnumbered by those who believe all it has to do is move goods." This will be discussed in some detail in a later chapter, "A Word From Your Sponsor—The Outfit That Signs Your Paycheck," but for now, if your station manager seems to have come up through the ranks by moving goods without much attention to news, keep those stories bland and do not go for those journalism awards until you are working for a station that can appreciate the effort.

## INVESTIGATIVE PROJECTS

1. *Education:* More and more of those men who are walking the beat and driving patrol cars have college degrees in Police Science and other similar fields. Probably even the Chief and his top officers are working toward Masters degrees. Find out what the local force is doing and what the incentives are (higher pay, qualifying for promotions, etc.). What has been the effect upon the community? (Court prosecutors, merchants, and businessmen, minority group and civic leaders, and members of the general public may have noticed the effects of more educated policemen over recent years.)

2. *Security:* There is a growing industry that supplies watchdogs, hidden cameras and alarm systems, armed guards, etc. Has this changed the emphasis in local police work, or is it barely keeping up with the increasing crime rate? Do regular police officials see these efforts as helpful, or do some gadgets hinder more than they help?

3. *Careers in police work:* Have the "PR" people at police headquarters keep an eye on the promotion lists for you. When someone is about to be promoted to one of the higher offices in the department (depending on the size of the town and how "urbanized" your area is), have these people help you line up a chat with the individual who is to be promoted. Go over things like:
   - ▶ what it was like when he first started police work,
   - ▶ the changes that have taken place since he has been on the force,
   - ▶ the most interesting, most dangerous, most embarrassing, or most amusing cases,
   - ▶ views on current law enforcement trends, etc.

   Then, on the day the new stripes are officially presented and the promotion is officially announced, release a few short excerpts which you have edited in advance from this conversation.

4. *Repeat crimes:* Yes, their job is just to "enforce" existing laws, but would local officials like to see less leniency in the courts, changes in the bail and/or parole laws, more

rehabilitation in the prisons? What is the trend locally on offenses by ex-cons and parolees? What about juveniles? Could police use some more help with these problems? From whom, and how?

5. *Drugs:* Are violations of the drug laws still on the rise in town? Do they fear there is more to come? What has been the pattern in the past year? What have police been doing to combat the problem? Do they plan any educational programs, or do they have any under way? What kinds of drugs are involved locally? What age groups?

6. *Drug-related crimes:* Is true that addicts would rather burglarize than openly attack someone, or have drugs been linked to a number of muggings, purse-snatches, and other personal attack crimes? How can area residents guard against the "rip-off" or burglary raid by those who are on drugs?

7. *Drug rehabilitation:* How effective are local programs? Are there any "half-way houses" in your area? If residents of these houses do not stay "clean," is there a jail term awaiting them? How do the neighbors react? Are there any real success stories as a result of these programs?

8. *Criminal rehabilitation:* Check with area prisons and correctional institutions to see if there are any inmates who are allowed to leave the grounds to work in the area. How are these programs working? Check with local parole officers: How has their program changed over the past few years? How do police rate these programs? Do they disagree with the progress reports of those who run such programs?

9. *Minorities:* How does the local force relate to minority groups and individuals? What community relations programs are being carried out? Are officers helping with community groups on a paid or volunteer basis? Are some policemen taking foreign language courses in order to better communicate with a local minority group?

See also the investigative projects in the previous chapter which may deal with minorities and police:

9: Truant Officer

12: Pedestrian Safety

13: Predictable Civil Unrest

14. Black Law Enforcers

15: Ambulance and Fire Truck Drivers. (Are police asked to provide escorts to protect these other agencies in some neighborhoods? What is being done to improve relations?

16: Arrests in Disadvantaged Neighborhoods

17: Courtroom Behavior

10. *Long hair:* Has this controversy reached the courtroom in your area? In one state, police were charged with stopping and searching all cars with long-haired or "hippie-looking" occupants while letting all others pass by. In another, parents of a boy ousted from school because of his hair length sued the Board of Education and won. What cases have come up in your town or state, and who has been winning them?

11. *Civil liberties:* Check with the nearest office of the American Civil Liberties Union and see what some of the latest issues have been. Without jeopardizing any specific court case by discussing it while in progress, see if details of several completed cases might reveal a pattern in your area in which certain liberties are threatened.

12. *Courtroom security:* Since the spectacular cases in recent years in which some defendants have disrupted trials and others have had to be removed from the courtroom or bound and gagged, what new measures are in effect in your area to prevent such disruptions? (You may not get *judges* to comment, but perhaps the Bar Association can line up some people who are qualified to discuss this with you.) Are local measures seen as adequate, too severe, or too lenient?

13. *Prosecutor's role:* Spend a day with the prosecutor, or have him over to the station for a panel discussion. (Leave your portable tape recorder behind if you are going into the courtroom with him!) Interview him later in his office about the kinds of cases he handles. He gets a file folder from police with evidence claiming the person named is

guilty, but is it not also his job to occasionally discover flaws in police work and to point out evidence which, in fact, proves the subject's innocence? Has he ever had trouble with the news media concerning the "Free Press versus Fair Trial" issue?

14. *Defense counsel:* Do a project similar to the one above with the prosecutor, only from the opposite viewpoint. Perhaps a "public" defender may have more interesting comments—does there seem to be a connection between economic status and prospects for acquittal? (Be sure not to include mention of any cases that are currently underway.)

15. *Juveniles; family relations:* Use cases that are a few years old to protect the former defendants. What is the effect of broken homes, alcohol, drugs, etc., on these cases? What other factors seem to pervade this area? Do some of the kids seem to come from wealthy homes? What rehabilitation programs are working? Which ones are not?

16. *Rights of juveniles:* What has been the effect of recent Supreme Court rulings applying former "adult" rights of accused persons to juvenile cases, such as the right to be represented by counsel, right to remain silent, inadmissibility of certain confessions, etc.? Have recent changes in the voting age and oher measures changed the definition of a "juvenile" in your state? How?

17. *Police specialties:* There are many policemen who never walk a beat or drive a patrol car. Some of them spend the day in laboratories testing chemicals, paint, blood samples, etc. Others specialize in fingerprinting, photography, sign-painting, etc. Screen through the Division Captains if you have a large police force and see which specialties would make the best topics for discussion. Do not overlook topics like Pedestrian Safety (See previous chapter, Project 9.)

18. *Rights of the accused:* How has police training changed over the years in view of court decisions regarding warnings to suspects about their rights, and regarding release of information to the news media locally? Spend the day

at a police training academy. Attend some courses with policemen; interview instructors. Check libraries. What are the new books telling today's policemen?

19. *Free Press versus Fair Trial:* Although this topic was discussed at length in this chapter, the public-at-large may not fully realize how this issue has affected their lives through changes in local arrest and court procedures. See if local police forces and Bar Associations can help you put together a panel discussion on the topic. Tape it, then edit it for documentary use with narration.

20. *Consumer protection:* Have your local "Ralph Nader" types drop by for a taped discussion of area swindling practices. You can anticipate some of these practices in certain seasons of the year, such as driveway-sealer hoaxes and roof-repair scandals in the spring and gifts and gift-wrapping bargains at Christmas time. Check with the Better Business Bureau in your area for leads, as well as with local consumer organizations.

21. *Flimflam artists:* Have they been active lately? It might be a good idea to go over some of the "old" case histories with policemen who have memories of some of the tactics used, so that your listeners will be more aware of the approaches and recognize them. Point out that elderly people are favorite targets, and that swindlers usually want you to give them cash in an envelope under some pretext, such as a make-believe "bank detective" trying to catch a supposedly embezzling clerk.

22. *K-9 Corps:* Interview police dog trainers and handlers about their interesting aspect of police work. What kinds of cases are they most often used for these days: searches, rescues, crowd control, building security? How long does it take to complete training? What are the costs and methods involved?

23. *Women on the force:* How have they advanced since the original "Meter Maids" of years ago? Are the women on the force in your town still assigned to such "noncombat" duties as handing out parking tickets and serving as crossing guards, or do they have the full status of the men? Are

their numbers on the force significant, or are there just a "token few" in their view? Are they advancing through the ranks as rapidly as the men, or do they feel that promotions are tougher to come by because of their sex?

24. *Police community programs:* Does your local force have a P.A.L. or similar program underway involving youth, senior citizens, minorities, antipoverty groups, or the public at large? How do these work? What are their goals? Do the men participate in these on a paid or volunteer basis?

## IN-CLASS AND HOMEWORK ASSIGNMENTS

1. Obtain the address of your state or local Bar Association and write a letter to them, asking for their latest literature on "Free Press versus Fair Trial." Write a similar letter to your state broadcasters' association (whose address you can get from any nearby radio or TV station) and compare their answers. Who seems to have the upper hand in your state on this issue, and why? Is there a set of voluntary guidelines in effect? Compare it with the "model" guidelines in this chapter and note the differences.

2. In the library, find some articles about arrests and/or trials. Quoting from these articles to support your viewpoint, tell whether you think anything in the articles violated the rights of the accused to a fair trial. (Older newspapers, published prior to some of the more recent Supreme Court decisions on this issue, may contain more examples of violations.)

3. It is 7:25 a.m., and the desk sergeant at a local police station has just told you over the phone that it was a pretty quiet night last night—no arrests. You tune in to hear the 7:30 newscast on another station and they have a story about a holdup at an all-night gas station in town where the attendant was wounded and several hundred dollars in cash was taken. You call the police again, and the fellow who told you it was a "pretty quiet night" before insists that he has no information on it, and repeats that there are "no arrests on the blotter." He suggests that you call the Detective Bureau around 9:00 or 9:30 (after the other station has had the story on the air for a couple of hours dur-

ing your important morning drive-time newscasts) and see if they have anything on it. No, there is no one else at headquarters you can talk to right now. You would like to believe what the desk sergeant is telling you, but this is about the tenth time this has happened this year. What would you do about this? Outline several steps and some alternatives.

4. The police radio from a certain state police barracks is unusually busy tonight (at around 11:15 p.m.). Many coded calls give you the impression that something important has happened. There seem to be several patrol cars working on it. The trooper who answers at the barracks says he just came on duty and that there's "nothing in the pile of news releases" about it. You know very well that he knows what is going on, because his voice is the one on the police radio answering all those calls from the outlying cars. What would you do? Outline the steps you would take to handle the situation just for "tonight," and then outline what you would do in the long run to be sure this does not reoccur.

5. Not all of the trials mentioned in this chapter involved abuses of the Sixth Amendment ("Fair Trial") by the news media. In fact, some were outstanding examples of how the First Amendment ("Freedom of the Press") can help the cause of justice. Make a list of these trials and tell why each one was helpful to the concept of press freedom.

# Chapter 6

# Relationships With Hospitals

There is one cardinal rule you will always have to keep in mind when you are checking out a story at a hospital. That rule is as follows:

*Their primary responsibility is preserving human lives.*

That is just their *primary* responsibility. Running a close second to that is the alleviation of suffering and the treatment of injuries and illnesses where, although the patients' lives may not be threatened, cure and relief are certainly necessary and desirable. Finally, the smooth operation of the hospital for the benefit of *all* the patients (not just the one or two you may be interested in) is a priority which ranks, in their minds, far ahead of any thought of helping out the news media.

## CONTACTS WITH HOSPITALS

Any difficulties you may find in getting a story from a hospital may be the result of these humane and necessary priorities. Hopefully, many of the people at the hospital with whom you speak will realize that you have got a job to do as a newsman and that you have some deadlines to meet, but many of them consider their jobs more important than yours for the reasons that were just listed and rightfully feel that their priorities are more urgent than yours.

**173**

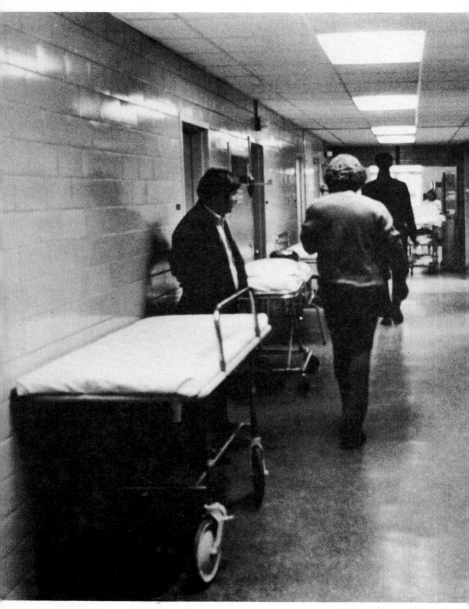

Photo by Chip Hires.

Dealing with people like this, who have different priorities and who are "marching to a different drummer," takes a lot of tact and diplomacy. If you call up with an arrogant "drop-everything-and-tell-me-all-you-know-right-now" attitude, they will quickly learn some of the evasive tactics we outlined in our police chapter, such as not having the authority, jurisdiction, or proper clearance to release something, not being able to locate an authorized spokesman for you, just coming on duty and not knowing anything, or a favorite one in some hospitals—plugging you into a phone extension in an empty office, letting it ring for awhile, and telling you that "Sorry, no one answers." You can avoid all this if you develop an awareness and understanding of *their* problems and *their* methods of operation. You will have to know when to be patient and sympathetic with that nurse who has just worked a heck of a shift with phones ringing and patients buzzing for attention. You will have to sense when it would be better to call back, not to push for too many details, etc.

*Some* people with whom you will be dealing in the news like to develop an awareness of your operations, your methods and your deadlines, and to "think along with you," anticipating your needs so as to gain your good will and perhaps some favorable news coverage from time to time. Politicians and public relations men are particularly good at this, as will be discussed at further length in later chapters. This is not so with hospitals; they are not running for election and they have nothing to "sell." (A few will occasionally ask for help with a fund-raising drive, but the point being made is that *you* need *them* more than *they* need *you*!) Instead of expecting them to think along with you, as with the politicians, you will get a lot more out of hospitals if *you* learn to think along with *them.*

## SOME GENERAL PRINCIPLES
### Timing vs. Priorities
No newsman can or should expect a complete and automatic briefing the first time he calls on the heels of an emergency. First of all, many of the points of information sought will

not be officially confirmed. Most of the information not ready for release must await careful examination by a physician. Others are simply not authorized to make certain judgments about a patient or his condition. After a hospital physician has his say, there are also the patient's relatives, lawyer, family doctor, police, and others to be notified and consulted before certain things can be released to the news media. Of course, all this takes time.

### Confidential Information

In addition to a patient's physical care, a hospital is also responsible for protecting his good name and reputation. In much the same way that a doctor, swearing to uphold the Hippocratic Oath, will not discuss the ailments of his patients, a hospital considers its medical records as confidential documents. By the same token, you are not dealing with "secrecy in government versus the public's right to know" here; you are dealing with an individual. You may recall that the RTNDA Code of Broadcast Ethics (presented in the first chapter) says that: "Broadcast newsmen shall at all times display humane respect for the dignity, privacy, and the well-being of persons with whom the news deals."

### Legal and Other Restrictions

Many people other than those who are running a hospital have a say in what can be released about a patient. The patient himself has some control over the matter if he is in any condition to communicate. If he is suing someone, or being sued, police and the lawyers for both sides may restrict information to protect their own cases and to protect defendants' rights in court as discussed in the previous chapter. Relatives, family doctors, and others will often come before newsmen for various reasons.

### Accredited Spokesmen

Almost all hospitals have official spokesmen who are qualified and authorized to make statements to the news media. It is unfair to "badger" a switchboard operator, nurse's aide, or other employee into giving out information. Maybe the official source is the Admitting Office, the Nursing Supervisor, or some administrator. Quite frequently the official source will change, depending on whether you call during regular office hours, at night, or during a weekend or holiday. You would do well to have a chart of these times and sources for each hospital in your area. In fact, you should know the *names* of the people involved, not just their titles, and they should know *your* name. This helps to keep the contact warm and to eliminate many possibilities for misunderstanding. Knowing their names and how their system works is one way of "thinking *their* way"—a point which was made earlier.

## Emergencies

Trying to reach the Emergency Room itself when the ambulance has hardly arrived will not only jeopardize the welfare of the patient involved, it will jeopardize your ability and that of other newsmen to get information from that particular hospital for a long time to come. This is no time to pressure them; they are "uptight" as it is. You should try to leave a message with that "accredited spokesman" who was mentioned above, or at least leave the message with someone who is not directly connected with patient care, specifying the information you want. Then call back later when this person has had a chance to get the information for you without interfering with the emergency procedures.

## Disasters

For things like plane crashes, train wrecks, hurricanes, etc. (see next chapter), many of the normal rules and procedures for gaining information will change. First of all, in bringing in large numbers of people, the employees who usually talk to newsmen will probably be "drafted" for other duties. Secondly, the Federal Aviation Agency or some other authority may become involved, taking jurisdiction over all news releases. The timing of releasable information and the channels you normally go through to get such information may all be disrupted. If the situation warrants, you may have to assign extra reporters to conduct a "vigil" at the hospital in order to get whatever scraps of information become available while someone else from your station covers the crash scene. Just how helpful these other staff members from your station may be depends upon whether or not they are getting paid for it and upon other arrangements made *in advance.* (See Chapter 11, "A Word From Your Sponsor," about the roles played by other station employees.)

## RELEASABLE INFORMATION

Each hospital will have its own policy about what kinds of information can be given out to the news media, but even that policy can change from time to time without notice. For one thing, disasters and other emergencies (just mentioned above) will drastically change normal routines for the hospital people and affect their ability to deal with newsmen. For another, the consent of various other parties such as the patient's relatives may be involved. The patient's lawyer, doctor, or the police may all have authority to withhold certain items from you. It may just depend on the time of day; the nurse on a particular floor may have only limited time and authority to talk about her patients during the night, while the Public Relations Director has both the time and the authority to tell you a lot more during office hours.

Here is a *general* list of what is normally released, but do not get angry if your local hospital falls short on some items:

(a) *Admission:* Acknowledgment that a patient has been admitted.

(b) *General Condition:* (Satisfactory, fair, poor, critical.)

(c) *Births:* Parents' names, address. Child's sex, weight, name, and time of birth.

(d) *Deaths: Only* following notification of next of kin. Name, address, and time of death or "D.O.A." *(Dead On Arrival* at the hospital). The *cause* of death can only be given if it has officially been determined by a physician or medical examiner. (Remember from the first chapter that you *repeat the name* of the deceased as a double-check for your protection, and that you get the name of the person who gave you this information.)

(e) *Police and accident cases:* Name, address, marital status, sex, age, occupation, and employer of patient.

(1) *Nature of accident:* If it has been verified by police, employer, or other reliable witness who can be quoted.

(2) *Burns:* Statement that a patient is burned, degrees, and area of body burned. (*Cause* might be withheld for a number of reasons.)

(3) *Fractures:* (Except in head.) What part of the body is involved and whether the fracture is simple or compound.

(4) *Head injuries:* Only a simple statement that there has been a head injury. Do not expect any elaboration.

(5) *Internal injuries:* Only a simple statement that there are such injuries. Again, no elaboration.

(6) *Intoxication:* Do not expect a hospital to confirm or deny this. Most likely they will refer you to police or another agency involved.

(7) *Poisoning: Perhaps* there may be some admission of accidental child-poisoning or of food poisoning where a number of people have been eating at the same place, but this implies an accusation. Most hospitals will make no statement about this. They will refer you to police.

(8) *Rapes and moral crimes:* No statement. Refer to police. (Even police will limit themselves to words like "attacked" or "assaulted" without any sexual connotation, because they are not medical authorities. Physicians will release this only to police.)

(9) *Shootings, stabbings:* They might admit that the patient has a "penetrating" wound or "puncture" wound, but do not be surprised if they stop there. If that is where *they* stop, be sure that is where *you* stop when you rewrite the story. To assume any more, even if it seems obvious, puts you in the position of making an accusation or affecting pretrial evidence.

(10) *Unconsciousness:* Only a statement that a patient was that way on arrival, but not how he got that way. The hospital may possibly refuse comment about consciousness later on, and will go to the standard condition terms such as, "fair," "poor," "critical," and so on.

## PROTECTING YOURSELF: SOME GOOD TIPS

### Name of Spokesman

You may remember the example given at the beginning of this book where the lady tells you the patient died. That actually happened to the writer once, and after the newscast the phone rang. A voice at the other end asked, "He's dead, huh?"

"That's right," the writer answered.

"He's right here," said the caller, "I'll let you talk to him!" Then the writer got to talk with the "dead" man himself.

As soon as the writer had hung up from what undoubtedly was one of the most embarrassing phone calls of his entire career, he called the hospital in a complete rage to find out who would give out such misleading information. You guessed it: nobody at the hospital knew anything about it, and they were quite annoyed that we would dare imply anything like that about their institution.

*Always* get the name of the hospital spokesman, even if there is no death or serious detail involved. Make it a habit. You may run into some reluctance on this when you first institute the practice in a town where they have not been doing it, but you can assure them that their names are for reference only—that you do not intend to use their names on the air. If they still will not give their names at first, you may be able to get by with the title, department, and time of the call for less serious cases. Remember, this is only *at first,* but it is still not good enough for deaths or for cases where criminal charges or controversy is involved, and it is a sign that you have some "missionary work" ahead of you. You should drop by for a chat at the Public Relations Office at the hospital and explain that this is your way of preventing misunderstandings and misinformation. You may also tell them that this is your way of verifying the fact that you are talking with an accredited spokesman and that you are actually helping them to protect the hospital's reputation and integrity.

## Understand Functions

You may want to make your own small "organization chart" for each hospital, because the lines of authority will differ from one to another. The Public Relations Office may not even be in the chain of command when it comes to releasing medical statements, but may simply confine itself to news about fund-raising, new buildings, staff promotions, and the like. Taking the time to study your area hospitals saves you the aggravation of being transferred from one anonymous phone extension to another when you are back in the newsroom working on a story under pressure.

## Blood Donor Appeals

Occasionally a newsroom will receive a phone call from a friend or relative of someone who is undergoing an operation. The friend will ask you to put an announcement on the air asking for donors to go to the hospital and donate a certain type of blood. *Do not do it!* This is an area that can become subject to great confusion or even to "hoax" calls, just like school closings. If there is no written policy in effect for your area, then you will at least have to satisfy yourself that such an appeal is coming only from a physician or from an authorized hospital spokesman. Even this precaution should only be a temporary step: You must contact your area Red Cross, Medical Society and hospitals, asking them to come to some written agreement on how to handle such calls.

## Allergy and Pollen Counts

Watch out for some controversy between weathermen and medical men. Before you broadcast someone's "Pollen Count," be sure that medical authorities in your area agree that he is qualified to make such a count. A "Pollen Count" implies that people who are allergic to pollens are likely to suffer some symptoms, and many doctors feel that weathermen are not qualified to make this kind of judgment. Do not assume that the pollen count for a nearby town is "good enough" for your area, because you may be at a different elevation above sea level, there may be different allergy-producing plants growing in your area, and the presence or absence of other pollutants in the air may have an effect on the pollens. Do not get caught in the middle; let these factions agree among themselves first.

### Alcoholism, Drugs, Mental Disorders

While you are checking with your area Medical Society about the other issues which have been raised, you might include these last few topics in your discussion and see if there have been any problems involving the news media and the treatment of such stories. See if there is a Mental Health Association, a Drug Education Council, and an Alcoholism Organization for your area. Get in touch with these people and see if they have any guidelines to offer about news coverage. Do not wait until you (or some other area news outlets) make some kind of error and issue some kind of offensive story. Open up your communication with these people *in advance* for your own protection.

### Funeral Homes

Is there a written policy at your station, or are you "playing it by ear?" Agree with management on just how detailed any death notices should be and under just what circumstances they should be broadcast. Set up a way of preventing any possible hoax calls. Determine whether there are any special community needs (such as Orthodox Jewish, where burial is required before sundown on the day after a death occurs, and the newspapers in your area may not be able to carry the announcement in time to notify friends and relatives). Some stations carry obituary stories only when the deceased person's prominence would make such stories "newsworthy," while other stations carry them as a local community service but with less detail than the newspapers. In any case, get a policy written down (with management approval) so that you will have something to point to when someone questions your fairness or when you must decline a request for such a story.

**Evasive or Misleading Tactics**

If you feel that you are not getting all the information to which you are entitled, you may want to read again the section on evasive spokesmen from our chapter on police stories. Many of these same principles apply in your relationships with hospitals and other medical organizations, and some of the solutions proposed to problems in getting information from police sources are applicable here.

# INVESTIGATIVE PROJECTS

1. *Walk-in services:* Many hospitals are now staffing clinics around the clock where people can stop by for the kind of treatment that used to be administered by the old-fashioned "country doctor" or general practitioner. Other groups of doctors have formed their own medical centers for group practice, frequently near larger hospitals. How are these arrangements in your area? What are the advantages and disadvantages? Ask doctors, patients and administrators.

2. *General practitioners:* What is the role of the G.P. in your area? Is he slowly disappearing in favor of group practice arrangements or other forms of medical service such as the walk-in clinics mentioned above? What is the trend in your area, the present status, and how do people feel about it? Are there some towns that no longer have a doctor in your area?

3. *Survey:* In connection with the role of the G.P. (above), ask the medical staff at an area hospital or group practice center—especially those who are not general practitioners—if they would advocate laws or regulations requiring doctors to be general practitioners before they can specialize, and the reasons for their answers. Ask the G.P.'s the same question and compare their answers.

4.  *Hospital volunteers:* These people enjoy the opportunity to do something for others. Who are they? Teens after school, senior citizens, housewives, etc.? What are their duties? What is their training, their schedule, and their relation to patients and medical personnel? Can the hospital use some more of these people? How can your listeners get more information?

5.  *Birth control and abortions:* Get an update on the philosophy and the existing laws for your area. Is there a hospital policy or a legally mandated policy on abortions and birth control matters? Is it administered pragmatically with population problems in mind or just in response to patients' demands? If your state has not legalized abortions, would this hospital be able to handle such cases if they suddenly changed the laws? If the state has already liberalized such laws, what has been the effect?

6.  *Communicable diseases:* What diseases have been of concern in the community lately, and which ones are expected to return? Have there been any real epidemics in recent years, and are any expected? What about children's diseases, like chicken pox, diphtheria, etc.? Do the schools have immunization programs? How do they reach adults in the community with immunization programs when such programs become advisable or necessary?

7.  *Drug abuse:* This is an increasingly complex problem for hospital personnel. Nurses and doctors who several years ago had mostly to receive emergency patients with broken limbs, cuts, and other ailments must now quickly recognize what kind of "trip" an incoming patient may be taking if he is on drugs. They do not just look at the arm for needle marks anymore, but in such places as behind the knee, under the tongue, and between the toes. Arrange to discuss with hospital personnel whose job it is to handle such cases and just what they are doing to stem the tide. Administrators or Chief Physicians may be willing to discuss the special training involved in ths area.

8.  *Drug rehabilitation programs:* Are they really working? (See similar projects on this topic in the previous chapter.)

What rehabilitation facilities are located in your area, and what is their role in relation to medical and law enforcement agencies?

9. *Specialized services:* Many hospitals have gone to a great deal of effort and expense to raise funds and acquire special equipment and to hire specialized personnel for such things as heart and lung ailments, prenatal care, treatment of epilepsy or nervous diseases, etc. If your local hospital has such a specialization, they would most likely be quite happy to talk about it with you, both to inform the public and to gain further support for their project. (At least one radio station has won a national award for a documentary on prenatal care entitled "Care of the Unborn.")

10. *Blood donations:* This has also been the subject of award-winning programs in which a radio station follows a pint of blood from the donor to the operating table. Interviews with bloodmobile personnel, donors, blood bank officials, hospital administrators, surgeons, and patients highlight the value of blood donation programs.

11. *Infant mortality:* This is frequently a measure of a community's general health status. Although it is a grim statistic, its rise or decline shows the need for better health care in a particular city or points to the progress being made by local health authorities. Baby deaths are generally on the decline throughout the nation, but in some underprivileged and other areas they may be on the rise. What is the situation locally, and what are the reasons for improvement or concern?

12. *Venereal disease:* Just when everybody thought the V.D. problem had been brought under control in recent years, there has been a sharp turnaround in many parts of the country. Many states and urban areas are reporting a rise in V.D. cases after many years of decline or inactivity. What is being done to handle stepped-up treatment demands? Is there an educational program underway to combat it? *Should* there be one? (Watch out for controversy on this one—many factions believe that talking about

these matters on the radio will only increase local promiscuity.) Where should such an educational program be conducted: in the schools, in the newspapers, in public forums, on the radio? For whom: teenagers, parents, the general adult public? (Hospital people can put you in touch with municipal, county, and state health authorities who may have more complete statistics on this.)

13. *Child poisoning and children's accidents:* What seems to be the most common reason to rush a child to the local hospital lately? Are many of them swallowing things carelessly left within their reach by adults? (Birth control pills swallowed by children are a new phenomenon. What are the effects?) Are children involved in more accidents with power mowers and other power tools lately? Which ones? What else might bring them in for stitches, casts, stomach-pumping, and X-rays lately?

14. *Dietitian:* What is it like to cook for such a large group with such specialized needs? What popular foods in homes and restaurants must be avoided in hospital menus? Are there any great changes in the menu according to the makeup of the patient population? What extra precautions must be taken when serving hospital patients? Does the medical staff have a say in menu planning? How?

15. *School nurse:* What have been the major medical problems in the past school year or two? What is the school's relationship with the hospital? Is the ambulance at a local school more than once a month? Is the budget for bandaids higher in elementary schools? What are the current problems in the senior high schools: drugs, pregnancies, athletic injuries?

16. *School psychologist:* Do the problems of guidance differ with age levels when it comes to mental health? What are the effects of broken families, alcoholism, economic levels, etc.? Perhaps these same questions can be related to the community at large if there is a mental health facility willing to discuss them, and to discuss the possible solutions for such problems.

# IN-CLASS AND HOMEWORK ASSIGNMENTS

1. Prepare a list of hospitals and medical services within a ten-mile radius of your school, their phone numbers, and chief spokesmen. Include such organizations as the Red Cross, local medical societies, city-county-state health offices, drug rehabilitation and treatment centers, ambulance squads (if separate from hospitals), mental health, alcoholism, allergy, and other specialized groups. Be ready to defend each listing if called upon to do so, and to tell something about the function of each group (other than the hospitals themselves) and its relation to local hospitals and the community.

2. Evaluate the performance of the stations in your area with regard to hospital and medical stories. Select several specific stories for discussion and match them against the guidelines found in this chapter. (You may have to tape record or "monitor" a local station for this purpose, or request copies of particular stories from the stations involved.) Over a period of several days, see if you can determine whether any station in your area is flagrantly violating the principles outlined in this chapter. Be ready to document your claims.

3. Choose a topic from the investigative projects for this chapter and write an imaginary transcript which includes:

   a) 10-15 second introduction by newsman or disc jockey.

   b) Taped narration by investigative reporter, before and after.

   c) Excerpt of interview with doctor, hospital administrator, patient, or medical authority talking about the topic called for in the project.

   Total reading for items a, b, and c above should not exceed 60 seconds.

4. This chapter mentioned that a radio station had won an award for a documentary entitled "A Pint of Blood," in which they followed the donated pint of blood from the donor to the operating table. Assuming that you will have half an hour to stage a documentary program, outline another situation in which sequential order can be used to dramatize an

issue or a procedure. You may select from the investigative projects if you wish, but indicate your starting and finishing points and describe the subtopics you will explore and the people you will interview along the way.

5. With one or more classmates as members of your "team," select a topic from Project 4 (above) which has been approved by your instructor and put together a half-hour documentary on tape. Allow several weeks for completion of the project, including editing of excerpts from the various interviews and the writing of a narration which will "tie" the parts of the story together.

*Chapter* **7**

# Searches, Rescues, and Disasters

The scene: a busy newsroom. Phones are ringing, the clock on the studio wall advances mercilessly toward that newscast deadline, the on-the-air monitor and the police radio compete with the teletype machine in a symphony of bedlam. Among the many little stories you have rewritten for the "steenth" time is that one about a light plane missing and believed "down" somewhere, only this time you have shortened it a bit and you just say it is believed to have crashed. What's the difference? You are in a hurry.

Plenty. The phone rings after the newscast, and it is the wife of one of those men aboard the plane, believing she is probably a widow by now. You try to console her, promising to keep in touch if there is any word on the fate of the missing aircraft. Trouble is, someone else gets in touch with her first— her husband. He calls from another airport where they landed to avoid the storm, and you suddenly discover when the boss calls you into his office that a plane that is "down" is not always a plane that has "crashed."

One word can be pretty powerful at times, can it not? This is almost like covering civil disorders, and many of the lessons from that chapter apply here, but there are some distinct

Photo by Chip Hires.

(Mock disaster scene)

differences. For one thing, your words will not affect the final outcome. Whatever has happened, has happened without your help. A few people might hear your story and volunteer to join the search and rescue efforts as a result, but your words will not be "inflammatory," as they might be in a civil disorder. Your story can give rise to other emotions, though—panic, fear, and grief among the family and friends of the supposed victims. Unlike the civil disorder situation, the general public will most likely go about its normal business, but for the people whose friends and relatives are involved in your story the feelings will be very intense.

Exaggerated reports are a major pitfall in this kind of story. Remember the example in the chapter on the "basics" about someone who calls to say that a fire is "out of control?" That is likely to happen here. Most laymen are very poor news reporters. You may use their phone calls as "tips" and proceed on your own to check out the details, but never accept their reports as "gospel truth" until you have some confirmation from competent authorities. Radio Station WNEW in New York City tells about a man who called them and said he had seen a plane crash into Jamaica Bay. It turned out that he really *had* seen it, and when they checked it out they had a really big "scoop" over their competitors. Notice that *they checked it out.* What if the caller had claimed there was a mid-air explosion, or a collision? What if he had named a certain airline? Even experienced newsmen have been known to write that a plane from X airlines exploded in mid-air, only to have a Civil Aeronautics Board investigation reveal that there had been no explosion at all, not even a flash fire.

Some years ago, a group known as the Aviation-Space Writers' Association came out with a booklet entitled "The Newsman and Air Accidents." Its purpose, as you might guess, was to prevent some of the inaccurate and misleading coverage that seemed to go along with accidents in the aviation industry. Some of the guidelines which were suggested in their booklet seem to be quite applicable to news coverage of other types of accidents, such as those involving trains, buses, and the like, and also to those situations where emergency forces are mobilized, and fast but accurate response is necessary from the broadcast news media. This chapter will cover such events, including natural disasters such as hurricanes, tornadoes, floods and earthquakes, and also major fires, collapsed buildings, and other phenomena in which Civil Defense and medical personnel may be present at the scene along with policemen and firemen.

## WHO IS IN CHARGE HERE?

One of the first things you may notice when a plane crashes or even when a bank gets held up in your area is that your old friend the desk sergeant at local police headquarters may not seem as cooperative as usual. This is not something personal, but it simply happens because a federal agency has stepped into the picture and taken jurisdiction over the case. Local officials may have been told to simply seal the area off and keep quiet, tending only to emergency medical needs until federal authorities reach the scene. If you hear a detailed story "break" on another station first, it is not because the local police are holding out on you, but it is most likely because your competitor knows which federal or state agencies to contact first. The other station most likely has not only kept a list of the right phone numbers handy, but has also kept the contacts warm with the people at the various agencies involved long before any such plane crash (or whatever it is) has occurred.

A familiar complaint from many of these agencies is that no one talks to them until they are too busy. The Federal Aviation Agency (FAA), the Civil Aeronautics Board (CAB), aircraft manufacturers, airlines, and others would be more than happy to show you the complete operation of an airport, including the control tower and air traffic control centers. They do not expect you to go back and do a news story on them right away, but they hope that your knowledge and understanding will give you the background you need when an emergency arises. State Police, the Coast Guard, the F.B.I., and other agencies hold luncheons, open houses, press conferences, and similar events at least once or twice a year. It is up to you to take advantage of these sessions and try to keep in touch with these people throughout the year.

One good way to keep in touch with a great many "emergency" agencies is to sign up for some training with local hospitals or civil defense units. These groups stage "mock disasters" for their volunteer members every year or two, and they might consider allowing personnel from your station to train with them for communications needs. The mock disasters are intended primarily to train "EMT's," or Emergency Medical Technicians. By the time such an event is staged, most of the trainees have had many hours of classroom preparation. For you to sign up with them as an EMT trainee would be somewhat misleading, because you would be expected to perform a medical function at the scene of a mock or even real disaster.

Another good reason to investigate the possibilities of such training is to see, in advance, just how much backing the station management is going to give you once a real disaster occurs. The writer has known some stations where a "Disaster Plan" is always standing by, including phone charts and overtime pay arrangements for secretaries, salesmen, and others to come under the jurisdiction of the news department for the duration of the emergency, and the writer has known (and worked for) other stations where the one lone employee who is at the station when a disaster occurs is "stuck" with all the coverage.

If you are just coming into a new station, find out if they have:

1) A "Disaster List" of phone contacts and names, so you do not fumble or bother the wrong people when a story of this type occurs, and

2) A "Staff Mobilization Plan" for your station, so you will know whether or not you will get stuck with the duties of extra coverage (perhaps without extra pay) when such a story breaks.

One excellent reference book that should be in your newsroom if you plan to be ready for developments in the field of aviation, not only of the major passenger carriers but of the smaller private and industrial planes, is the annual AOPA Airport Directory. (AOPA is the Aircraft Owners and Pilots Association, Washington, D.C. 20014). It looks like the average telephone book from the outside, but inside there are more than ten thousand aircraft landing places listed in much the same way that motels are listed in the directories put out by each major motel chain. Phone numbers and names of those who operate these facilities, along with such information as scheduled airlines and nearby lodging and ground transportation facilities, are little items of information that could suddenly "come alive" when you need them in a hurry. The directory is published every year, and sells for $10-12 (a little less for AOPA members).

Perhaps you are not sure whether to call the control tower, the FAA, or some other agency for information about an air accident. Although the FAA is quite well known, it usually does *not* investigate major air crashes. In fact, it may at times find itself in a defendant role if its own personnel in control towers or weather stations can possibly be associated with the cause of an aircraft accident. Major accidents, and those accidents which involve fatalities, are investigated by the National Transportation Safety Board. The Board occasionally delegates to the FAA the investigation of nonfatal accidents involving smaller aircraft. In order to keep abreast of the latest policies involving such investigations, write to the National Transportation Safety Board, the FAA, and the CAB. They are all located at 800 Independence Avenue S. W., Washington, D.C. 20590.

Even if you have determined which agency is investigating the crash you are trying to cover, you may find it all but impossible to get certain details on the progress of any investigation. This is for several reasons: one, of course, is the distinct possibility that criminal charges or at least large civil lawsuits may come into court as the result of such an accident, and that therefore any discussion of "evidence" would come under the rules discussed at considerable length in the "Police Beat" chapter. Another major reason is that this kind of investigation may take months and months of probing through wreckage and reconstructing practically the whole aircraft in order to determine what went wrong.

Just because the FBI shows up at an air crash, do not assume that they are "in charge" of the investigation or that sabotage or some kind of criminal activity is suspected. It is just that the FBI happens to have a specially trained disaster team which specializes in identifying bodies and other specific items, and they are there at the invitation of the National Transportation Safety Board, which will rule on the *cause* of an air accident. The Board also investigates rail, highway, and other transportation accidents. Write to them for contacts in your area.

As for calling the control tower, you could be getting yourself in deep trouble. Just as the physicians in a hospital emergency room are not to be distracted from their job of saving lives, the people in an aircraft control tower not only must properly direct air traffic but they may possibly, through just such a distraction as your phone call, be suspected of negligence and blamed for the accident. The way to be sure you are not interfering with vital operations is to arrange for a personal visit to the airport and spend a few hours copying down names and phone numbers of the people who will be able to talk to you when you need them. Depending upon the size of the airport, these could range from a central information office to various passenger and freight agents for airlines, and right on down to officials at hangars and flying schools around the perimeter of the airport. If the airport is not in your local area but you think you may be in contact with them from time to time, try a letter or a phone call to the main number, asking who the spokesmen would be in the event of an emergency.

To get acquainted with the CAB and the FAA, drop a line to the "Information Officer" at the following addresses which correspond to your area, and ask if they have any guidelines or other information that would help you to provide responsible news coverage, including names of those to be contacted at their own particular agency.

As for other federal agencies, you should be in touch with the weather bureau regularly in any event, not just "ripping and reading" the forecasts from the wire service. Find out who the

## Civil Aeronautics Board Field Offices

| Area | Bureau of Enforcement | Telephone (FTS) |
|---|---|---|
| Anchorage, Alaska | Paul R. Steinman, III<br>632 Sixth Avenue<br>Anchorage, Alaska 99501 | Call Seattle Operator 8-206-442-0150, ask for Anchorage 907-265-4845 |
| Los Angeles, California | Norman Phillips<br>P.O. Box 92007<br>Los Angeles, Calif. 90009 | 8-213-536-6297 |
| Oakland, California | Donald W. Bright<br>Hillsdale Executive Center<br>2555 Flores St. Suite 450<br>San Mateo, Calif. 94403 | 8-415-876-9051 |
| Miami, Florida | Frederick I. Untiedt<br>Box 592014 AFM Branch<br>Miami, Florida 33159 | 8-305-526-2535 |
| Chicago, Illinois | Dean Witt<br>O'Hare Lake Office Plaza,<br>Room 254<br>2300 East Devon Ave.<br>Des Plaines, Ill. 60018 | 8-312-694-2686 |
| New York, New York | Paul Wallig<br>The Federal Building,<br>Room 219<br>Kennedy International<br>Airport<br>Jamaica, New York 11430 | 8-212-995-3324 |
| Fort Worth, Texas | George L. Myers<br>P.O. Box 1689<br>Fort Worth, Texas 76101 | 8-817-624-6394 |
| Seattle, Washington | John V. Knudson<br>Airport Plaza—19415<br>Pacific Highway South<br>Seattle, Washington 98188 | |
| CAB Main Address: | Civil Aeronautics Board<br>1825 Connecticut Ave. N.W.<br>Washington, D.C. 20428 | (202) 382-6031 |

## Federal Aviation Agency Regional Offices

| | |
|---|---|
| **Alaskan Region:**<br>AL | Hill Building—632 Sixth Ave.<br>Anchorage, Alaska 99501<br>907-272-5561 |
| **Central Region:**<br>IA, KS, MO, NE | 601 East 12th Street<br>Kansas City, Missouri 64106<br>816-374-5626 |
| **Eastern Region:**<br>DE, DC, MD, NJ,<br>NY, PA, VA, WV | Federal Building, JFK International<br>Airport, Jamaica, NY 11430<br>212-995-3333 |
| **Great Lakes Region:**<br>IL, IN, MN, MI,<br>OH, WI | 2300 E. Devon Ave.<br>Des Plaines, Illinois 60018<br>312-694-2291 |
| **New England Region:**<br>CT, ME, MA, NH,<br>RI, VT | 12 New England Executive Park<br>Burlington, Massachusetts 01803<br>617-467-7201 |
| **Northwest Region:**<br>ID, OR, WA | FAA Building, Boeing Field<br>Seattle, Washington 98108<br>206-583-4100 |
| **Pacific-Asia Region:**<br>HI | 1833 Kalakaua Ave. P.O. Box 4009<br>Honolulu, Hawaii 96812<br>808-546-5401 |
| **Rocky Mountain Region:**<br>CO, MT, ND, SD,<br>UT, WY | 10455 E. 25th Ave.<br>Aurora, Colorado 80010<br>303-837-4992 |
| **Southern Region:**<br>AL, FL, GA, KY,<br>MS, NC, SC, TN | 3400 Whipple Street<br>East Point, Georgia 30344<br>404-526-7240 |
| **Southwest Region:**<br>AR, LA, NM, OK, TX | 4400 Blue Mound Rd., P.O. Box 1689<br>Fort Worth, Texas 76101<br>817-624-6221 |
| **Western Region:**<br>AZ, CA, NV | 15000 Aviation Blvd.<br>Hawthorne, California 90261<br>213-536-6207 |

A complete list of FAA Regional, District, and Field Offices and General Aviation District Offices may be obtained by writing: FAA, 800 Independence Ave., S.W., Washington, D.C. 20590.

spokesmen are in your area and set up procedures to be used in case of severe storms, tornadoes, hurricanes, blizzards, floods, etc. Your needs will vary according to the part of the country you are located in, and you may need other agencies at the state or local level to "backstop" for the weather bureau and provide information that is just a bit out of their normal range. For example, West Coast stations will need to keep contacts warm with universities and other organizations which have seismographs and maintain an "earthquake watch." (Four out of five earthquakes in the world occur around the perimeter of the Pacific Ocean.) Stations along the Atlantic and Gulf boasts will want good backing for hurricane information, and newsrooms in other parts of the country should know what kinds of natural disasters occur in their own areas (tornadoes, blizzards, etc.) and keep an up-to-date list of contacts handy. Remember—just the *list* is not good enough! If you have not taken the time to introduce yourself to these people and let them tell you about their procedures, do not expect them to "bend over backwards" for you when you suddenly call up in the middle of a raging storm. In some states, check for state agencies that report on the flooding of rivers, air pollution and pollen counts, forest fire danger, etc. Such information may seem trivial and routine on a day-to-day basis, but these people are extremely valuable when the forces of nature which they are specially trained to forecast and interpret get out of hand.

The Civil Air Patrol, the National Guard, the Red Cross, Civil Defense, and local ambulance and rescue squadrons all belong on your list of contacts to "keep warm." You get the best results when you know them by name and by the jobs they do. Names and phone numbers for all railroads, bus lines, and other "mass transportation" outfits should be on your list. It would be helpful to have more than one spokesman for each of these organizations, and to have both "office" and "home" phone numbers.

If your station is anywhere along one of the coasts or near the Great Lakes, you will want names and numbers for the Coast Guard. Besides saving lives and property through rescue and assistance operations in coastal waters and at sea, it aids aircraft in distress, becomes involved in flood relief operations along the coast, inspects-investigates-enforces matters regarding water safety and boating laws, provides navigational aids ranging from buoys to radar stations and lightships, and acts as a law enforcement agency in areas like smuggling, oil pollution, immigration, etc. Many of these duties performed by the Coast Guard make fascinating stories by themselves, without having to wait for a story that involves some kind of tragedy.

Before ending the section on "Who Is in Charge Here?" there should be a comment on who is *not* in charge. You may recall several points in earlier chapters where it was noted that an excited neighbor is no judge of how big a fire is, or that a fireman is not a medical expert who can tell you what condition an injured person is in, etc. Here, although state troopers, sheriff's offices, and local police are usually among the first agencies to be *notified* of aircraft, boating, and mass transportation accidents, that does not make them experts in whatever field the accident occurred. A major rule would be to *name these sources* in the early stages of coverage. For instance, if local police tell you that an "airliner" has crashed nearby, that implies a large craft carrying passengers. It is not impossible to arrive at the scene, however, and find that it was a cargo plane or some kind of military craft. When your source is not really an "expert" in the field, word the story carefully and *tentatively*, implying enough uncertainty to allow you to revise gracefully without leaving some kind of "credibility gap" for yourself when more accurate information on the event becomes available.

Finally, under "Who Is in Charge," do not forget some of your normally "secondary" sources on your disaster listings chart. School bus fleets in your area should be on there—just in case—as well as major industries and utilities and their spokesmen. Almost all of these outfits have "PR" men who are getting paid to act as official spokesmen when accidents occur involving their personnel or their facilities. You should have the office and *home* numbers of these spokesmen, and keep your listings up to date and the contacts warm.

## DON'T JUMP TO CONCLUSIONS

Since we have talked about experts and *non*experts and about whom to believe, let us talk about *you* as you sit there typing your story, preparing to go on the air. Are there certain things you may be taking for granted? For example, if a plane had crashed at the height of a terrific thunderstorm in your area, would you be likely to attribute the cause of the crash, at least partly, to the storm? If survivors talk about wild movements of the plane just before it hit, saying that a person would have to be crazy to fly like that, would you drop anything into the story to cast suspicion upon the pilot? Well, you would be wrong on both counts if you did either of these things. There have been several cases where all the early evidence seemed to point to severe weather conditions or pilot error which have been traced to other causes such as a bomb aboard the plane or the failure of a vital navigational aid.

At the beginning of this chapter the use of "crashed" as an inappropriate synonym for a plane that is "down" was discussed, and if you think about it for a moment, there are other words that could just as easily pass unnoticed at first for synonyms. A missing boat has not necessarily sunk, a train can "derail" without rolling over or causing any damage or injury whatsoever, and so-called eyewitnesses to these events can tell you in their state of excitement or shock that there was an explosion although careful investigation later reveals that there was no explosion at all.

If a certain type of plane seems to have been in the news a few times recently, it is always a temptation to put several mishaps together, to mention that this kind of plane was involved in each one, and—*voila!*—you have just led your listener to conclude, without even having to say it yourself, that this kind of plane must not be that safe or that well-made. You have just caused damage to a corporation's integrity, credit, or ability to carry on business. This is libel, and you can be sued for it. Passengers might stop riding that kind of plane. Airlines might stop buying it. If an authoritative source such as CAB or the FAA does not draw conclusions about a certain kind of plane, then certainly you had better not do so. If they do "ground" a certain type of aircraft temporarily, pending an investigation, stick close to their quotes. This is no time for embellishment.

In regard to embellishment, it may be well to point out that colorful, spectacular writing may just not be appropriate in most disaster stories. Perhaps if there is a spectacular rescue and a happy ending, then some heavier adjectives may come into play. Otherwise, stories like these should be handled very conservatively. If there is any doubt as to how "serious" the disaster may be, then tentatively go with the more conservative figures and *understate* the situation. There is no sense "crying wolf" when your listeners will already be shaken by what they hear to begin with. If half the town has just been leveled by a tornado, people are not tuning in to hear your magnificent writing style. They just want to know what is going on.

Not only your writing style must change with a story like this, but your behavior at the scene during coverage must also undergo some modification. Here are a few ground rules to keep in mind:

▶ Arrive with the *proper credentials*, obtained in advance from any agencies likely to be involved. (Get those letters in the mail *now* if you are already working for a broadcast news department. It is too late when the disaster has already occurred.)

▶ Do not bring any unqualified "guests" with you. The writer will never forget a fellow who worked as "police stringer" for one station who thought he did not need any credentials because he was so well known by all the local police. He arrived at the scene of a plane crash with his eight-months-pregnant wife and claimed they were both members of the "press." Federal investigators promptly hustled the two of them right out of there.

▶ Do not touch any of the debris—even the tiniest piece! What may seem at first to be a worthless souvenir might actually be a vital piece of evidence, and its *position in the wreckage* might be an important clue for investigators.

▶ Do not expect to have priority on phone booths or even your own mobile radios or walkie-talkies. Under emergency conditions, investigative and rescue officials may have the authority to commandeer your equipment or other nearby facilities for their own communications needs.

▶ Look for an *official* public information officer and avoid hindering investigative and rescue people. These latter people have their rescue and investigative jobs to do. A number of them do not trust newsmen, anyway, because their "tentative" statements in the middle of a rescue or an investigation may have led to inaccuracies and distortion in the past.

▶ Be prepared for the worst working conditions you can imagine. This is not going to be a comfortable press conference down at the hotel ballroom with drinks on the hosts. Have the proper clothing and footwear ready for swamps, heavily wooded areas, snowstorms or rainstorms, extremes of heat, cold, wind, darkness, insects, etc. An emergency pack of the kind of clothing and equipment you will need would be a good item to keep in the trunk of your car. You never know when or where these things are going to happen.

▶ Have a system worked out in advance to keep "tabs" on the body count. Preferably, someone should be back at the station to coordinate the reports from the crash scene, the hospital and morgue, and other sources. Be sure that the victims counted at the crash scene and then sent to the hospital or morgue are not counted twice. Someone should attempt to check the numbers coming from these sources against a passenger list, if the latter is available from the transportation company; or against a street directory, hotel register, etc., if buildings or neighborhoods are involved. (Do not take it upon yourself to identify the dead or injured, or even to speculate on conditions. Leave that to the medical experts.) Although newspapers usually perform the task of printing detailed passenger lists and/or lists of deaths and injuries, you should have someone from your station attempt to compile such a list even if it is just for your own information or to handle phone inquiries. Accounting for each individual by name may have an effect on the numbers you use in your broadcast stories, providing a greater measure of accuracy.

## BE SURE YOU ARE COVERED

Have you ever seen elementary school kids play "kickball"? The rules are very similar to those in baseball, only the game is played with a large, very soft rubber ball about the size of a basketball so these young people can catch it more easily and so they will not get hurt. Since not all of them can catch very well, it is legal to throw the ball right at the runner and if you hit him he is "out." Quite often on one of these teams there is a little fellow who imagines himself as the big star. He usually wants to be the pitcher, but when the ball is kicked (instead of batted) this same youngster wants to play all the fielding positions at once. He grabs the ball somewhere in the infield and tries to chase the runner between bases, not noticing that other runners are already scoring. Finally, he thinks he is close enough to hit the runner and gives the ball a mighty heave, missing his target by a country mile. The ball goes 'way outfield, allowing everybody to run home safely, or if aimed toward home it goes nowhere near the little kid who is catcher. The frustrated little star gets called every name in the book by his teammates, but ends up blaming everybody but himself. After all, why did they not help out? (Their answer: because *he* had the ball the whole time!)

Many "eager-beaver," small-station newsmen do this all the time. They jump into the car and race out to the scene of some crash, forgetting that "home base" is not even covered. Excitedly, they cover the story at the scene. Then, almost invariably, they call the station and expect salesmen, secretaries, and other nonnews people to drop everything and receive the story for immediate broadcast with the efficiency of a big "network" newsroom. You will see them at drownings, train crashes—you name it—tying up the only phone booth for miles around while they curse and scream at the people who they blame for fumbling back at the station. If they could only step out of the picture for a moment, they would see who is *really* doing the fumbling. They are no different from this little kid in the kickball game we talked about, and many of them even go around with the title "News Director."

You may recall another part of Chapter 2, "On the Scene," where one of the points made was to "know who will be receiving your material." You were asked to see that these people are *"advised"* that you will call, so that you would not have to spend time in the phone booth while they play records with one hand and try to find some tape and take-up reels with the other. Now, for the kind of coverage discussed in this chapter, these people should not just be advised, they should be *trained* at some length to provide some depth in your station's news operation. If you are not the News Director, you will want to clarify with whoever holds that job just what is expected of you in "disaster" situations. Unless they can give you a good accounting of who will be handling your story when you go to the scene, you will be better off staying right there and doing it by phone.

This brings us to another point: Who said that disaster coverage involves just *one* newsman going to *one* scene? Think again. Whether it is plane, train, bus, car, or boat, the "accident" scene is likely to be a long way from the hospital, the morgue, the headquarters for whatever agency is investigating the mishap, and the office of whatever firm owns the vehicle involved. Just as in the story of the little kids in the kickball game, one newsman trying to be at all of these places at once is likely to accomplish very little. If you tune in your competitor and hear that he has reporters at the scene of the accident, at the hospital, or at any of these other locations, it is most likely because he has someone back at his station's newsroom competent to receive the reports. Once again (it can't be said too often) if you are new with the news operation at your station and you find that they have no "disaster" plan to mobilize their staff members, *find out exactly what they would expect you to do* in the event of a "Searches, Rescues, and Disasters" situation such as described in this chapter. Chances are, they would prefer to see you stay at the station and handle it by phone than to go out there and try to be a "hero" like that little kid in the kickball game.

## SOME BASES TO TOUCH

Just "straight" news coverage of disaster stories is not good enough. Your vocabulary must reflect an awareness of certain basic terms used for each situation, (weather, aviation, etc.) and the possibility that your station's *advertising* may be affected by its news coverage are some examples of areas that cannot be overlooked:

► *Commercial policies:* If you have an airline that sponsors a newscast, do you think they would enjoy hearing their commercial played right next to a story about one of their planes crashing? Hardly. Most airlines suspend their advertising for at least several hours, some for several days, in the wake of a major airline crash. Some apply this only to their own airline, others to all major domestic carriers, and others to just about any major air accident around the world. Check with your traffic and sales departments, and be sure that you have a copy of the specific instructions to be followed for *each* airline that ever does any advertising with your station, whether their ads are currently running or not. Do this for bus lines, sightseeing and fishing cruises, and any other transportation or utility companies where accidents involving their facilities may warrant suspension of advertising.

► *Vocabulary:* The difference between "down" and "crashed" was mentioned at the beginning of this chapter, but do not stop there. Just because the general public calls any big snowstorm a "blizzard" does not give you the right to do so. If you are not sure of the difference between a "near gale" and a "strong gale," or between a "storm" and a "violent storm," or between a "heavy snowstorm" and a "blizzard," then your listeners will be even *less* sure when you carelessly start throwing the wrong adjectives around. The National Weather Service issues these and other definitions periodically on the wire services, and they will be glad to provide you with a copy if you write or phone them. There is also a difference between "emergency," "precautionary," and "unscheduled" landings of aircraft. You only use the term "emergency" if the safety of the aircraft was threatened and a crash was likely if the plane had not landed immediately. "Precautionary" is used when the pilot feels that repairs are advisable but there has been no serious threat to safety, and "unscheduled" landings occur when babies are born in flight or passengers get sick, etc. If the vehicle in your story is a train or a bus, that still does not give you the right to throw in the word "emergency" carelessly. Use the airline definitions above, and you will not risk building a "credibility gap" with your listeners.

▶ *Next-of-kin:* Do not get so wrapped up in your coverage at the scene of a disaster that you forget the rules from our "hospitals" chapter on clearances for medical information. If and when your station trains nonnews employees for coverage of disasters or civil disorders, all the "hospital" rules should be part of the training. Do not broadcast the names of any deceased victims unless you are sure of the arrangements for next-of-kin notification.

▶ *Hijacking:* Again, remember the guidelines from the chapter on police and the courts. Be sure that your story uses only charges that can be specifically attributed to some police officer or airline official *by name.* If, in your haste to rewrite the story for the "umpteenth" newscast, you make it sound as though *you are* accusing the suspect, you can start running into problems involving pretrial publicity, libel, etc.

▶ *Rewriting:* "Rip and read" stations can sometimes drive you up the wall by saying every half hour on their little "capsule news headlines" (or whatever they call them) that a plane or train has "crashed." Just because it may have come off the wire that way, do not feel that you must have the plane *crash* every hour or half-hour. Look for fresh angles such as the rescue efforts, the investigation, the words of hospital spokesmen or airline/railroad officials, etc., updating developments as they occur.

# INVESTIGATIVE PROJECTS

*Note:* Not all of the agencies listed in these projects will be located in your area. Obviously, an area not near the coastline or one of the Great Lakes is not likely to have the Coast Guard as one of its prominent search-and-rescue agencies. If there are few airports of any significant size in your area, you are not likely to find personnel from the CAB, the FAA, or the Civil Air Patrol. You will have to adjust these projects to fit local needs and conditions.

1. *Train wrecks:* What agencies spring into action when there is a major *train derailment* involving passenger injuries in your area? Do a survey of area Red Cross, Civil Defense, Ambulance Services, Fire Departments and/or Rescue Squads, hospitals, and railroads likely to be involved. Are there readiness plans in effect? How many people are involved, and what are some of their jobs? Who would coordinate such an effort? Are there special equipment stockpiles? Training programs? When was the last time these people were called out for a real or "mock" emergency? Could they use more people? What are the qualifications for joining their ranks, and with whom do you get in touch?

2. *Natural disasters:* What natural phenomena have caused disruption, or are *likely* to cause disruption in your area? Earthquakes? (Are you in a "fault" zone?) Tornadoes? Floods from rivers or seacoasts? Severe snowstorms, thunderstorms, flash floods in normally arid regions, hurricanes, dangerous atmospheric inversions from air pollution? What are some of the chief concerns at Red Cross and/or Civil Defense headquarters when such a problem occurs: housing for evacuees, ambulances, medical services, food and uncontaminated water? Do a survey of the kinds of natural disasters that could hit your area and their likelihood of

occurring. What agencies would become involved and what is their plan of action? Arrange to visit some of these agencies at their meetings or training sessions and get some taped sounds for radio or videotaped scenes for TV such as training activities, interviews with instructors and organization officials, etc.

3. *Air traffic:* Ask local airline and airport officials, pilots, etc., about their situation. Have there been more "near-misses" lately? Should the smaller, private aircraft laws and regulations be tightened up, or do the larger commercial aircraft seem to be having and/or causing most of the problems? What would happen if there were an air crash locally? Who would be called into action? What about a smaller plane getting lost? Would different people be involved in a search than those involved in a crash? What would be their roles? When was the last time these people were called out for a real or "mock" emergency, and what happened?

4. *Boating:* Check with the Coast Guard or with the Harbor Master: What is it like on a typical summer weekend? How many rescues do you make during the year, and when do most of these occur? Do the weekend "amateurs" have more mishaps than commercial vessel operators? Are "pleasure craft" and water-skiers more likely to have accidents than fishing boats, barges-tugs-tankers, etc? What are the various kinds of problems: motor breakdowns, capsizing, drowning, getting lost, beached, stealing, etc.?

5. *School buses:* Check with fleet operators and school officials: How many bus routes cross railroad tracks? What kind of warning devices are at each of these crossings? Ask bus drivers: What are some of the hazards along your routes that could use some attention? Do a survey of other organizations in your area which operate buses, such as churches, private schools and camps, etc. Are their drivers trained and licensed the way school bus drivers are? Must their vehicles meet the same inspection standards? Is there a "loophole" in state laws that allows these groups to operate with little or no inspection and with drivers who hold nothing more than a regular automobile license?

Should some legislation be proposed to correct this situation?

## IN-CLASS AND HOMEWORK ASSIGNMENTS

1. Pretend you are on the phone, checking on a reported plane crash:

   "Sheriff's Office, Deputy Blough speaking."

   "Hi. This is (your name). We've got a report from a listener that some kind of plane crashed out near Highway 109. Have you got anything on it?"

   "Yes, sir. From what we can tell, it's an airliner from Frontier Airlines. Most of the rescue squads and the General Hospital are sending ambulances over there. It's out by the fairgrounds. Looks like the pilot was having trouble with the thunderstorm or something. The say he was trying to make it to the racetrack at the fairgrounds, but he came right down into that power line that crosses Route 109 and flipped right over."

   "Who told you about it?"

   "We had a call from a Mr. Haney just up the road from there. He says the whole thing just exploded and burned right there on the ground. There probably aren't any survivors."

   a) What are some of the things that are "wrong" with the deputy's description?

   b) Write a sample of the bulletin you are going to put on the air.

   c) List several things you are going to do next, including your contacts with other sources and with other station personnel, and tell what you are going to ask and/or tell these various people.

2. Pretend you are the News Director at a local station.

   a) Make an "Emergency Mobilization" chart for your station, assuming a staff of:

   2 other news reporters besides yourself
   4 disc jockeys, including the Program Director
   3 salesmen, including the General Manager
   2 secretaries
   1 transmitter engineer
   1 cleaning lady or custodian
   1 accountant/bookkeeper

3 spouses of regular employees above, who have volunteered for such emergency duties.

Counting yourself, that is 18 people. Assume that the station is on the air throughout the emergency coverage. Also assume that these people have been trained according to a station disaster plan and define each person's role in a way that would "fit" various kinds of mishaps from natural disasters to major transportation accidents.

b) Make a "Searches, Rescues, and Disasters" chart of all the government, volunteer, transportation, utility, medical, and other public and private agencies that would become involved in the various kinds of natural and other disasters that could occur in your area. Be sure that your chart accurately reflects the urban or rural character of your community and your geographic location within the country.

For this chart, look up as many numbers as you can in the phone book for these organizations, but *do not call them* for names or other information unless assigned to do so by your instructor. (If every student compiling this chart were to call each of the emergency organizations involved, it would create an unbearable nuisance upon these agencies and might even jeopardize their emergency operations or harm their relations with legitimate news media in your area.) You may have to leave "blanks" for the names and job titles of spokesmen for the various agencies on this chart, or perhaps use fictitious names just for the purpose of this assignment, depending upon the directions given you by your instructor.

# Chapter 8

# Government and Politics

The phone rings in the mayor's office. His secretary answers it, and there is a newsman on the other end:

"This is W--- in Boondock. Any news for us today?"

"Nope. Sorry, not today."

"Well, okay. Thank you very much. Bye-bye, now."

. . . and the fearless newsman goes to the next phone number on the list, probably repeating the conversation with the secretary of the next mayor in the next town. Occasionally, a small town official may "use" the unsuspecting newsman for a little free exposure, giving him a worthless story about some "pet" project he is involved in. Usually the "big announcement" is about some routine road work or something that some town department does year in and year out without much fanfare. The newsman takes it all down just the way the mayor says it, perhaps even tape recording the comments so that he can use it later as an "actuality." He never asks questions. He would not know *what* to ask, and he would not know *whom* to ask, other than the mayor or the mayor's secretary.

## REPORTING THE BUSINESS AT CITY HALL

Maybe the scene described above is not typical. Maybe, outside of the networks and the 10- to 50-kilowatt stations on

Photo by George Kochaniec, Jr.

the AM dial and the big-city VHF operations in television, there *are* a few stations which have highly qualified reporters who regularly cover government and politics full-time and in person, but they appear to be few in number compared to those who consider such news sources as "just another phone number" on the list. This scene, we suspect, is repeated throughout the land. In many cases, it is imitated by newsmen who call such high-ranking state and federal officials and governors and congressmen. Fortunately, there are those who have done their homework as newsmen and who know *what* to ask, *whom* to ask, *how* to ask, and *when* to ask. (The writer stresses "when," because the best time to get good stories of this type is not necessarily at a press conference, nor is it necessarily with a tape recorder turned on or even a notepad in hand.)

Gone are the days when even a newspaper can get by with just a "city hall reporter" and a good wire service to cover the political scene. In-depth reporting and documentaries have gone far beyond the daily "walk-through" of city halls, legislatures, and political headquarters. The old process of waiting for the "pseudo events" to happen at the mayor's office in bits and pieces and to just take them all down in whatever order they occurred has pretty much disappeared in recent years, but it still hangs on in small markets where stations have one-man news operations. In these outfits the newsman hardly has the time to leave his phone and typewriter long enough to go to the bathroom before it is time for another newscast. In towns like these, the "news" is whatever the mayor *says* it is, and vital local issues like zoning changes and school bonds can go all but unnoticed unless there is a newspaper to cover them. The broadcast media are just not up to the challenge—a situation that is not necessarily the fault of individual newsmen.

Thousands of dollars are likely to come and go in stories about urban renewal, planning and zoning, schools, taxes, etc. Plans for racial balancing through busing or construction of low-rent or low-income housing in an affluent suburb will fill up an auditorium quite easily and draw more community attention than the election of a congressman or senator. Intense pressures build up over the quality of education, the cost of housing and the kind of neighbors you will have, and the ability of municipalities and other governmental units to raise taxes and to keep up with the services demanded of them. If you are going to cover these things adequately, you cannot just sit at your typewriter and knock out newscasts for six to eight hours and then go home. *Somebody* from your outfit has to not only attend these public meetings but study the issues in advance so as to fully understand what is going on.

There is the problem: fully understanding what is going on. The writer has seen News Directors who hire a "stringer" to go over to City Hall and attend council meetings. The individual takes a cassette tape recorder and a notepad and sits there in the auditorium waiting for the show to begin. In come the councilmen, the mayor, the city clerk, and a few other officials, and motions-and-seconds to pass or accept this-or-that start whizzing by at a dizzying speed. Councilmen get up to make proposals and someone says that these are "first readings" of bills but all you hear are titles. What many an inexperienced stringer does not know before he is sent out to cover such a meeting is that many of these issues have been discussed among the councilmen for several weeks, if not months, and in some towns they have been discussed behind closed doors right up to the very moment they come out onto the council floor in abbreviated form. What the stringer also probably does not know is that bills introduced for "first reading" in many town councils are not subject to debate. Even for measures that have advanced to final debate and passage or defeat, the councilmen are using a sort of "jargon" or "shorthand" language which, for their purposes, saves time and repetition among themselves but leaves the average onlooker with his head spinning.

In some cities, these councilmen have actually *rehearsed* the whole meeting at someone's home or private office in a session that is politely referred to as a "caucus." (The writer has even attended such meetings in mayors' offices on the day before the real council meeting.) Very often, the only invited guests are those of the majority party, and the motions and seconds for the next day's council meeting are all set up like football plays in order to get measures passed quickly before the minority party can gather any strength to defeat them. It is no wonder, then, that the poor stringer attending for the first time from the local station has not the foggiest idea what is going on. Although some states have now passed anti-secrecy laws forbidding secret meetings of governing bodies, it is still fairly easy for a "few old friends" to get together and talk over some items of mutual interest. Disappointed, the stringer returns to the station all but empty-handed, and the News Director, expecting some decent stories, decides it is "not worth it" to try to cover City Hall. He will just go back to doing it by phone, covering only the key personalities and major issues as they come into the open.

A variation of this "caucus" routine is the "run-around" defense used by public officials who do not want the press prying into their business. All department heads and minor officials

Photo by Chip Hires.

are told not to talk to newsmen; everything must "clear" through the mayor's office. This procedure becomes a very convenient bottleneck through which very little news of any real significance is likely to leak. (As we shall see in a later section of this chapter, it does not always work. It worked for Richard Nixon until Watergate, and it worked for Lyndon Johnson until the press coined the term, "credibility gap," and led him toward his decision not to run for reelection. These two presidents, and many other governmental leaders throughout our country's history, have run into Abe Lincoln's maxim about fooling "all of the people all of the time." You can believe that some alert and inquisitive news reporters have helped this process along.)

Suppose that you have been hired as that "stringer" to cover city hall for a local station. How are you going to get by some of the problems already discussed? Well, for one thing, you must know these people *in person* and find out just what makes them tick. This is not done overnight, and it is not done with a daily phone call to someone's secretary. Your number one goal is visibility—yours and theirs. Within a few weeks, you should be able to name at least six officials at City Hall besides the mayor, and to point them out by name and title in any crowd. You should know the majority and minority leaders on the city council, and you should be sure that they know you. The contacts with all of these officials should be warmed up over a period so that when you greet one of these people by name (not necessarily their first name), they will respond by greeting you by name, and most likely by your first name. None of this will be very easy. It is pretty frustrating to be stopped by a secretary who always says her boss is out or that he is very busy, ". . . but I'll tell him you stopped by." If this starts happening to you, do not "just stop by." See if you can line up an appointment for an interview about the functions of this person's department. Find out where else this official shows up besides his office, so you can arrange to show up at some of the same places. Get hold of the official schedule of appointments. Set up some questions that can be answered only by this person, not just by a secretary who can look up the answer in a file cabinet. Keep smiling—some people take quite awhile to come around.

Stop in at the city clerk's office. This one official usually has the agenda for council meetings, as well as reports, budget proposals, bills for proposed ordinances, etc. He should also have copies of the city charter, outlining the powers and duties of each official, and a directory of boards, commissions, and all city officials. Determine, if you do not already know, whether your municipality is governed by a "strong mayor" franchise (one in which the mayor appoints all members of major boards and commissions) or a "weak mayor" setup in which members of boards are elected. Study other variations, such as City Manager, Metropolitan Council, etc.

The city clerk should also have a schedule of all board meetings in the city government. This should help you to anticipate all such meetings by calling a day or two in advance to chairmen and other key members in order to get an idea of what is coming up. Municipal governments must also put out "bid notices," asking for interested firms to compete for contracts on anything from school cafeteria operations to road and sewer construction. Many of these major items in a town's budget are newsworthy by themselves.

As you have gathered, a lot of this is meticulous, painstaking work. If you can pursue it full-time, it will only take a few weeks to get it "off the ground." If they only let you out of the newsroom for an hour or so every day, it will take you much, much longer. At this point many stations give up. There are some advantages, however, of "hanging in there" a little longer—for one thing, you will find that after awhile you are able to catch things in the debate that goes on at council or even board meetings that used to get by you. Where your competitor might report only that certain items were "passed" at last night's meeting, you pick up implications "between the lines" that reveal *why* some items on the agenda meet defeat. Some of the people proposing these things may just be trying to gain favors for their friends, and if you are careful to quote them properly or use taped actualities skillfully, their own words will do the job for you. This is something you will never get by just having someone jot down what was "passed" and what was not passed at some meeting.

Another distinct advantage of the momentum you build by "hanging in there" at City Hall can be measured in terms of *nice, warm contacts.* These contacts not only give you material for stories between meetings, but they give you a sharper insight into what is *really* going on as you sit there watching the meetings themselves. If your competitor does not have these contacts, he has to wait for the meetings themselves and try to outdo you in tape-recorded "actualities." You can walk up to these officials on the street, bump into them at local gatherings, even call them at home if it is a big story or a close relationship. You know what questions to ask; you know what stories to *anticipate* even before they happen. All this gives you a big head start in any coverage involving these officials and their activities.

A small town once had a lady who had been covering local politics as a "stringer" for a newspaper in a nearby city for many years. She knew where all the local politicians went on their coffee breaks, and she knew just who came and went in various town hall offices during the day. For some reason, she suddenly stopped working for that newspaper and started writing for several papers in more distant cities. A "sweet young thing" (probably just out of journalism school) was sent in to replace the lady who had switched papers. The new gal was a hard worker and a good writer, but when you picked up that paper for a few months after the changeover, you could tell what was missing: *nice, warm contacts!* On some nights, it almost looked as though that town had dropped off the map.

"Now," you may be tempted to say to yourself, "that's a good way to get even with my old boss. I'll just keep my contacts to myself and take that phone list with me when I leave." Unfortunately, that only works in the short run. Within a few weeks, your replacement is likely to start building those contacts again for himself, and within a few months the audience will notice little or no difference in the coverage. The long-range effect of such "burning-your-bridges-behind-you" tactics will be to leave the lasting impression that you were pretty childish and unprofessional. That will not help you when a future employer wants to check your references and past employment record. More on this is given in the chapters "A Word From Your Sponsor—the Outfit That Signs Your Paycheck" and "The Industry and the Profession."

## "NOBODY HERE BUT US CHICKENS"

No doubt you have heard that old story about the farmer who goes out to the henhouse carrying a shotgun in the middle of the night and yells out: "Who's in there?" Back comes a frightened voice: "Nobody but us chickens!" You can easily imagine that the farmer has some doubts at that point, and you can just as easily imagine the mood of the press for a long time during the Watergate period when President Nixon and his aides refused to acknowledge that anyone in the White House had any connection whatsoever with the growing scandal. Just when it began to appear that the news media would reveal such connections anyway, with convincing evidence to back them up, Mr. Nixon held a brief news conference and claimed that there had been some new, major developments. He announced that he would not allow anyone in the Executive branch to claim immunity from prosecution and said that he would suspend anyone indicted in the case.

Reporters, hot on the trail of many of Mr. Nixon's associates and suspecting even the President's own involvement, were in an ugly mood. As Nixon suddenly left the room without answering any questions, they turned on Press Secretary Ronald Zeigler, demanding a clear explanation of the apparent contradiction between earlier White House denials and this sudden claim that "new information" had come to the President's attention. Squirming under the barrage of intensive questioning, Zeigler attempted to wrap it up by simply pronouncing the current presidential statement as "operative" and ruling that everything which had been said prior to that time was "inoperative." Nobody laughed then (they were too stunned), but for months afterward there was an enormous backlash of cartoons, editorials, jokes, ridicule, and other harsh criticism of Zeigler's "inoperative" statement.

At that point even the White House had joined the ranks of the lowest-level political hacks throughout the land in the use of dishonest, blatantly cheap tactics with the news media. Now that everyone fully realizes that these less-than-honest ways of dealing with newsmen can range to just about any level of government, here is a handy checklist of some of these maneuvers so that you can easily identify them and deal with them when you attempt any political or governmental coverage:

▶ *Concealment:* Silence, of course, is in the best political traditions. It is an old rule never to answer charges made by an opponent in an election campaign, and politicians can just as easily apply this to newsmen. Like that set of three little monkeys which is sold in souvenir shops ("see no evil, hear no evil, speak no evil") it is easy just to pretend to be unaware of anything wrong.

▶ *Limited access:* By creating a "bottleneck" situation, one can discourage many reporters from hanging around. It just will not be worthwhile, especially for broadcast stations, to wait in someone's office for several hours just to ask a couple of routine questions. It is easy to complicate the process by which reporters must obtain information, such as requiring all City Hall employees to "clear" everything with the mayor's office or by having all reporters get their information from a secretary, a "PR" man, or some intermediary who can "screen" it.

▶ *Denial of access:* Although many states now forbid secret meetings of governmental bodies, there are still many activities which may take place behind closed doors or away from the office. A good way to evade newsmen is to carry on one's shadiest political activities at a time and place where one does not want to be seen. Another is to come and go by the back door, letting newsmen sit outside in the reception office never really knowing if he is there or not. The Washington *Post* was denied access to White House parties when articles about Watergate became too embarrassing for the administration. By this same process, some local political party can just "forget" to invite you, the newsman, to their barbecue.

► *Roadblocks and smokescreens:* One good tactic used by some governmental sources is to "bury" you in an avalanche of irrelevant information. As you wade through this quagmire of material, the hope is that you will become discouraged in your search for the truth. The Nixon Transcripts were an example of this tactic: Only the major news organizations, with dozens of reporters reading throught the night, were able to make any sense out of the massive documents. Even then, as the House Judiciary Committee learned when it listened to the actual tape recordings upon which the transcripts were supposedly based, there were discrepancies and missing portions. The smaller the news organization—say a one-man news department from a daytime radio station—the sooner it is likely to quit.

► *Deceit:* This is a wide-ranging term and will have to be broken down even further. Deceit can be carried out with just words, with actions, and by manipulation of certain people, events, and objects. To define it first: *deceit* is the act (or the attempt) to mislead, misinform, or bewilder you. It can be done by simply lying, it can be done by distorting or "stretching" the truth, or it can be done by "throwing you off the scent." At whatever level, it involves some form of "throwing a little sand in your eyes" by imposing ideas or beliefs that will contribute to your bewilderment or confusion, or that will impair your ability to distinguish between what is true and what is false.

Now that it is defined, here is how you, as a politician, can do it:

1. *With words:*

   ►► Deny, misstate, or falsify key information. Usually flat-out lying is pretty hard to do under press scrutiny, so you will most likely never come upon a whole story that you can claim is an absolute falsehood. You have to look for *small parts* that are wrong, skillfully woven into larger statements that are basically true.

▶▶ "Distort" or "stretch" by using euphemisms and misleading labels for what you are doing. Also, omit little things that might be embarrassing. This was done extensively in the Watergate affair during the Nixon administration, with many clandestine operations made to appear as though they involved national security.

▶▶ "Dupe" the press by providing some distraction to obscure the story or to lead them away from what they are really after. Announce a new program, criticize, or launch a verbal attack upon someone, or dream up an "emergency" and deal with it effectively. If all members of the news media will not swallow your story "hook, line, and sinker," at least many will "rise to the bait" by doing a story on your distraction, focusing public attention away from the issue that was causing you some problems.

2. *With people:*

▶▶ Use "front men" and intermediaries such as press secretaries and PR men, and channel all your information, nice and clean, through them. This saves you the embarrassment of being asked direct questions by the media, and gives you time to dream up clever answers when you get a few tough questions. It gives your "front man" time to stall, claiming that he must check with you for an answer and hoping that the reporter will forget about it.

▶▶ Give people nice-sounding job titles that do not describe what they are *really* doing. Have some of your activities carried out in second-hand fashion by anonymous persons in cloak-and-dagger underworld style. Hire some people as "decoys" to answer questions for the news media while others who appear to be in harmless subordinate roles are engaged in activities you would rather not publicize.

▶▶ Conduct your business behind-the-scenes in smoky back rooms; rehearse it, caucus it, make sure that all the deals are worked out in advance so that when your people go "out in the open," there is no debate, no discussion of the issues, just a little parliamentary sleight-of-hand ("now you see it, now you don't") and have your PR people snow the press with slick handouts to lubricate the process.

3. *With objects and events:*

▶▶ Press releases and handouts are a good vehicle for carrying your version of the truth the way you would like to see it written. Hire a "Madison Avenue Man" to tailor everything you are going to say publicly and to explain everything you do in your terms.

▶▶ "Stage" some events, Barnum-and-Bailey style, to attract a crowd. You may be accomplishing very little, but always put on a dazzling presentation so it gets good coverage from the news media. (Like the militant organization that called TV stations in New York, asking them when it would be convenient for them to come over and film the burning of a Russian flag in front of the U.N. Building.)

▶▶ Have expressions of support voiced at key times and in strategic places (such as the Committee to Reelect the President sending thousands of telegrams to the White House supporting their own man's position on certain issues during the Watergate months.)

▶▶ Conduct your own surveys, perhaps with a phantom organization that looks impartial, and announce the favorable outcome. (Journalists are starting to catch on to this one, though, especially during elections.)

▶▶ Throw a heck of a party. This way, you can beguile reporters and maybe even blur their journalistic vision a little with some drinks and some friendly people. Invite newsmen to dinner; it is pretty hard for many of them to sit there eating a meal that may be costing the party faithful $25-$50-$100 a plate and then go back and "chop" you when they sit down to their typewriters.

▶ *Acting hurt:* Besides the various forms of deceit and concealment just explained, there are other ways to manipulate news coverage. One favorite way of many politicians is to act the role of a victim. At the top national level this is often referred to as "wrapping one's self in the flag," but at local levels they would look silly claiming national security as a reason for nondisclosure. Instead, you are likely to get hints that your coverage is "not in the public interest," or that they are not telling you something because it is "not in the best interests of the town" (or the state or county) for you to probe into a certain area. Politicians using this tactic will exaggerate their own embarrassment to imply to all observers that you are out to get them. There may be implications that your coverage is in poor taste, that you are aggravating a sensitive situation that ought to be left alone, or that you are overstating your case or sensationalizing it. (Remember that Ron Zeigler referred to the Watergate break-in as nothing more than a "third-rate burglary" and refused to comment further on those grounds.) They can accuse you of creating a "tempest in a teapot" or claim that your inquiry is "absurd" for some reason, like the third-rate burglary which was too absurd to comment upon. An old tactic is to claim that the news media are misquoting you or taking your remarks out of context. In all of these "acting hurt" situations, the message is that you are getting too nosy about a delicate situation which they would rather not have you pry into.

▶ *Counterattack:* Finally, when concealing, limiting, or bending the truth does not work, and they have not managed to get you to back off by acting hurt and implying that your coverage is too roughshod and unprofessional, then some politicians can become like cornered animals —they start fighting back. One of the easiest ways to do this in small towns is to call up the reporter's boss. If the station manager is afraid to offend local politicians or the chamber of commerce, and if his hands tremble when he gets a call from the mayor, the superintendent of schools or any local businessman, that is the weak link in your journalistic chain right there. All the politician has to do is carry his "wounded" act (the one described above under "acting hurt") to your station manager, and that could be the end of your story. Right here, you are being put on the defensive, which is just what the politician wanted. First of all, your own boss has suddenly become an additional obstacle. You have to defend your story against the "complaint" he has just received. Then, you must convince him that it is worth the hassle, in *his* terms of potential loss-of-income to his struggling business, before you can proceed. Obviously, you will have to weigh your highest principles of journalism and honesty against your own instinct for survival. Is this little station paying you enough, and would they back you strongly enough when you needed it or would they just abandon you in their own selfish interests, to make it *really* worth your "nailing" a small-time politician? Is there somewhere else you can look for support, like the wire service or reporters from other news media? The decision, when something like this happens, is all yours.

Of course, not all stations are small and not all managers are timid. The writer cited the previous example because he has worked for a few outfits that are like that. The larger the station and the broader its advertising base, the less vulnerable management will be to such tactics. It is then that a wounded politician will have to escalate his tactics and start applying pressures through certain influential advertisers, discredit you and/ or your station with a number of his friends in business and government, or force you into some kind of "squeeze play" to get you off his back. Such tactics can range through leaking stories to your competitors, shutting off some of your contacts and news sources, and getting advertisers to "drop out."

Just to give you an idea of how rough the going can get, consider this eye-opening passage from Carl Bernstein and Bob Woodward's best-seller, *All the President's Men:*

> Around this time, the White House began excluding the *Post* from covering social events at the Executive Mansion—first, a large Republican dinner; then, a dinner for past, present, and newly designated Cabinet officers; then, a Sunday worship service; finally, a Christmas party for the children of foreign diplomats. The immediate target was *Post* reporter Dorothy McCardle, a gentle, 68-year-old grandmotherly fixture of the Washington press corps, who had covered White House social events for five administrations.

> On the same day Mrs. McCardle was barred from the prayer meeting at the White House, Bernstein had dinner with friends, among them a reporter from the *Washington Star.*

> The *Star* reporter told him an interesting story about a conversation he'd had with Colson a few days before November 7:

> "As soon as the election is behind us, we're going to really shove it to the *Post,*" he quoted Colson as saying. "All the details haven't been worked out yet, but the basic decisions have been made—at a meeting with the President." Colson advised the *Star* reporter to "start coming around with a breadbasket" because "we're going to fill it up with news" that would make reading the *Star* indispensable, while freezing out the *Post.* "And that's only the beginning. After that, we're really going to get rough. They're

going to wish on L Street (location of the *Post*) that they'd never heard of Watergate."

Soon, challenges against the *Post's* ownership of two television stations in Florida were filed with the Federal Communications Commission. The price of *Post* stock on the American Exchange dropped by almost 50 percent. Among the challengers—forming the organizations of "citizens" who proposed to become the new FCC licensees—were several persons long associated with the President.

Of course, just because here are listed some of the tactics that *can* be used by governmental and political people does not mean that they *are* used "every day in every way" by all the people you are going to run into at City Hall or at higher levels of government. While you have to be on your guard, you definitely cannot go around with a frown on your face and a chip on your shoulder as though every politician were a liar. As Associate Editor Paul Weaver of *The Public Interest* puts it, "The relationship between newsmen and source, between press and government, is one of structured interdependence and bartering within an atmosphere of amiable suspiciousness. Each side knows its role." This book is attempting to help you know that role—by knowing "how to play the game."

Earlier in this chapter, things like dropping in at the city clerk's office and building nice, warm contacts were discussed. Mr. Weaver, who was just quoted, goes one step further and comments on our *relationship* with those contacts:

The press can make its contribution to the system only by maintaining close access—a closer access than can ever be provided by law. The price of such access is some degree of cooperation and sympathy for government—not a slavish adulation, as it is sometimes said, but a decent respect for authority, a willingness to see government and persons in government given the opportunity to do their job.

Since this "degree of cooperation and sympathy" is part of the ballgame, it involves subtle ground rules about which you have no doubt heard before. Prominent among these are the "off the record" and "background" situations. These are necessary even if they appear to be less than the whole truth and nothing-but-the-truth arrangements. No one can expect every public official or even every businessman or other news source to stop what he is doing and make a complete statement to justify his every action if, in so doing, he is going to disrupt his office to the point where he will have to spend all his time on the phone defending himself.

Usually, the understanding is that the newsman would like to know what is happening in general terms so that he can report it clearly to his audience and not make a fool of himself on the air by guessing at possible outcomes. In exchange for an explanation that will help him to understand what is going on, he agrees to such things as not quoting and perhaps not even naming the person who gave him the information. Thus, by quoting a "City Hall spokesman," you are sparing the Public Works Director a direct confrontation with the people in your audience who will not like the story later today about the street paving program. If his office is flooded with angry phone calls, he can also say he heard your story on the air and modify it a little bit by saying that no final decision has been made. This takes some of the "sting" out of it for him personally, and gives him time to rework his paving plans a bit to suit the occasion because no one can pin him down as the source for your story. This example just used is normally referred to as a "background" story. You do not quote anyone exactly word for word, and you disguise the source sufficiently so the public cannot be sure whether it was a paving crew foreman, a secretary, a councilman, a commissioner, the Public Works Director, or even the mayor.

In *deep background,* you not only drop the quote but you completely drop any hint of a source. Instead of attributing your knowledge to a "City Hall spokesman" as you did in the background situation, you more or less become the source yourself. ("W--- News has learned that such-and-such *may* happen . . .") Always put such stories in a way that they can be changed or denied if your hidden source is getting too much flak from the public. Yes, you *do* get stuck protecting your source and holding the bag if the story backfires. If you think it is going to be a sensitive story, then you have several choices. One—do not run it. Two—get one or two other reliable sources to confirm for you (for your records only) that the story is true (a method used extensively by Bernstein and Woodward in their Washington *Post* Watergate coverage). Three—get some documentation or evidence *other* than a spokesman which will prove the truth of your story if it is challenged. (In the "Public Works" example, it could be that the paving machines are already parked in the neighborhood earmarked for the project, or that some contracting firm has an order in writing which specifies where the blacktop is to be delivered tomorrow morning.)

*"Informed sources"* is a level somewhere between *background* and *deep background*. Instead of saying they are "City Hall" sources, you are removing it from City Hall and just saying that "someone" told you. It is almost the same as saying you learned it yourself, as in the *deep background* situation.

*Off the record* means that you are allowed to *know* what is going on but you are not allowed to *use* it in broadcast or print. This is used for a number of wide-ranging situations. For example, when socializing and relaxing, governmental people want some degree of privacy—the kind you would expect when you get home from a hard day's work and kick off your shoes—and they do not want to see what they are saying to their friends come out in print or over the airwaves the next day. A big sign on the wall in a dining room used by legislators at one state capitol simply says, "OFF THE RECORD." Any newsman who joins a state senator or representative for lunch is not expected to run right out and do a story on it. If he does, it is the last time he will ever be invited.

At the other end of the spectrum, *off-the-record* classification is used for sensitive projects where it is believed that advance publicity may damage the outcome. For example, when it appears that the city council is about to hire a new city manager, they may tell you that they have narrowed it down to a certain candidate but that he must be allowed to give proper notice of resignation at his present job. In addition, although most of his credentials and references indicate that he is probably the one they are going to hire, not all of his references are in yet, and there is always that possibility that something may turn up at the last minute. It would be particularly embarrassing for the news media to prematurely release news of his appointment and cause problems at both ends. What this *off-the-record* information does allow you to do is to anticipate the story and get it all ready. It also keeps you from running stories on other candidates who were vying for the post which would lead to speculation they might be chosen.

There are obvious weaknesses in this little system of "backgrounding" stories and speaking off the record. It allows these people who are giving such stories out to control the material you are getting and the manner in which you may release it. When the practice was so sorely abused by the Nixon administration, leading to deception of the public and putting newsmen into a position where they were helpless, there was a "truth backlash." Many reporters stopped showing up at press briefings; others just went out and investigated on their own, and still others took everything with a grain of salt, checked it out with other sources, and released it anyway under their own terms.

In a local area, your councilmen and commissioners might not even know what "background" and "deep background" mean, much less any modifications of them such as "informed sources." Before you assume anything, check around and see what the ground rules are. Ask other reporters from competing media; you are not stealing any stories from them, you are trying to find out what the rules are so you do not make a fool of yourself and get thrown out of your first press conference or something. In some parts of the country, they have weird little ground rules of their own, maybe because some member of the news media really caused some embarrassment years ago, and local politicians are still living with the fear that it could happen again.

In Connecticut, for example, the writer heard the story going around that when the New York Stock Exchange feared it would be taxed for stock transactions it threatened to move to Greenwich, just across the state line. This caused New York City officials to think twice about imposing any such tax, but at the height of the controversy (so the story goes) a bunch of newsmen rushed up to the Governor of Connecticut and asked him what he would do to encourage the Stock Exchange to make the move. Trying to gather his thoughts and ad-lib at the same time, the governor said something like:

"Well, gentlemen, . . . . ah, first . . . . ah, before I could make any recommendations to the legislature at all, . . . ah, . . . I would have to be sure that, . . . ah, . . . the stock market is definitely going to come to Connecticut."

This story itself is "on background," which is to say that a friend told the writer about it, so he will not name his source or the station allegedly involved, but he was told that one station went back and put the Governor's voice on the air, saying:

". . . the stock market is definitely going to come to Connecticut."

The writer never did get to check on the accuracy of his friend's story, but somehow all were feeling the effects of it at the state capitol. That Governor never let the broadcast people get near him with their cameras and tape recorders again, except for prepared statements on things like Girl Scout cookies. He did manage to get pretty good exposure on radio and TV, but only on the stations *he* picked. For anyone wanting to "tape" the Governor, the message was always, "Don't call us; we'll call you."

Finally, in learning how to "play the game" with politicians, there is the practice known as the *advance* or the *embargo.* Stories marked *"hold for release"* at such-and-such a time have been given to you in advance, and there is an embargo (an order prohibiting their use) until the specified time of release. Sometimes the exact hour of the release is printed right on the first page of the material, usually timed to assure fairness to the various competing news media in a given area. On the wire service, you will often see stories written about the speech the governor or the president is going to give, asking you to hold them until the time of the speech itself. On other occasions, a famous world or national leader may be seriously ill and near death and the wire service will "advance" the story of his life, carefully marking it with an embargo until the death has been confirmed. Sometimes such stories will remain tacked up on the wall near the wire service machine for several days. Embargoes have been abused too, for example the case of a governor who had signed hundreds of bills passed by his state legislature but who had his press secretary release only a few a day so that he could keep his name in the news. Not only has the press challenged these "phony" embargoes in recent years, but the immediacy of videotape and the instantaneous transmission of live material by the broadcast media and the "Photofax" and "Unifax" transmission of pictures for the print media have cut down the elaborate advance preparations needed for broadcast and publication in just about all of the media.

Even when you receive an advance copy of a speech, you have to be very careful that it matches what the speaker actually says later. It is not uncommon for prominent people whose speeches have been drafted by speechwriters to depart from their prepared texts and "tuck in" a few remarks of their own. While you can use the advance copy for analysis and for stories which summarize what was supposedly said, be sure you term it "prepared for delivery" if you have not double-checked to see if that is what actually was said. This protects you if, for some reason, the speaker does not get around to saying whatever it was you are doing a story on.

## YOUR PROFESSIONAL CONDUCT IS SHOWING

A little earlier, some tactics used by politicians who are "cornered" and start to fight back were mentioned. That does not mean to imply for one moment that any governmental, business, or political leader who calls your boss is necessarily "cornered." It could be exactly the other way around. In this kind of news coverage, from City Hall to Capitol Hill, the people in your stories are more likely to "talk back" than in most other areas. You normally do not go up and introduce yourself to a burglary suspect or a crash victim; you get his name from a police blotter or a hospital admissions list. Even people involved in civil disorders will rarely offer any rebuttal to an individual newsman. They may be upset at the station or the news media in general, but the chances are slim that they will even remember your name, much less call up your boss. With mayors, councilmen, state legislators, and so on up the line, it is a different story. They can, and often do, comment on the performance of reporters assigned to cover them.

It was never assumed in this book that your first assignment is going to be the White House. Some textbooks on "how to do it" will show you photos of the author or some well-known network newsman from bygone decades interviewing a President, almost as though they expected you to go right out and do that the very next day. (In their chapters on crashes, they like to put photos of how NBC covered the crash of the Hindenburg in 1937.) This is all very nice if you bought the book wanting to know the history of broadcasting, but this is not 1937 and you will not be covering the Hindenburg crash tomorrow, much less the White House or even the Governor's Office.

What you will want to know, as a starter, is how to get along well with the people you *are* covering and *will be* covering in the near future. Assume that your local reporting duties will take you through City Hall and perhaps a county building of some sort. Maybe several communities in your area have teamed up in a "regional" or "metropolitan" government for schools, transportation, or other services. You may see state legislators here and there, and maybe the governor or a U.S. Senator will swing through about once every year or two, but that is about all. Perhaps a Congressman from your district will be the highest-ranking official you will see all year. Suppose, for the moment, that these are the people you will be dealing with. Here are some "tips" that may help you warm up the contacts with them and at the same time gain respect as a professional:

### If You Can't Hold Your Liquor, Stick to Ginger Ale

There is nothing more revolting than to watch a young kid from a small radio station laughing uproariously and slapping the majority leader of the state senate on the back as though they were old buddies. They are not. The senator has a good law practice, about three or four terms in the senate and several terms as a representative, looks about fiftyish, and is wearing a $150-$200 suit. The kid must be all of 20 to 23, wearing a $15 sports jacket from a discount house, flunked out of college, and has too many drinks in him. Everybody in the room hears the laughter and knows exactly what is wrong. The kid's boss may or may not hear about it through the grapevine. That station will probably not be on the guest list for awhile, and some of the sources the station had for news will dry up.

### Parties Are Frequently Off the Record

If you are not sure about the ground rules, it is better to sound stupid for a moment while you ask someone than to get yourself in hot water by just going on the air with it. The writer once did a story about a "snowbound" party where some legislators had been stranded at the state capitol by a heavy snowstorm. He knew automatically that no one was to be quoted on anything, but he thought it would be harmless to say that the Speaker of the House had cooked some really good spaghetti and meatballs. He was furious! He had told his wife a different story about being stranded along the road or something, and the *existence of the party itself* was off the record. After that, the writer always made it a practice to ask the hosts if it was all right to do a story on the party, even if it was a fund-raising affair and it appeared as though they were *seeking* the coverage.

### Your Name Is Not Eric Sevareid

Nor is it Walter Cronkite, John Chancellor, or Harry Reasoner. The writer has seen many a newsman become all wrapped up in his own self-importance simply because governors, presidents, and astronauts will answer his questions when he is holding a microphone toward them or because he sits behind a beautiful-looking set under all those lights and everybody is paying attention to him when he reads those little paragraphs he has prepared for the news show. More than one Program Director has told how they have had to take a newsman or even a News Director and "ease him out of the picture" because he was getting too big for his own britches. The trap of self-importance is one that is very easy to fall into. Joe Barbarette, who served as News Director for a couple of Hartford stations, tells about the difficult task of taking over as Press Secretary for the late Senator Thomas Dodd, just after the Senator had been censured by the Senate for irregularities in campaign fund-raising. Joe says that there were many newsmen who had the arrogance to call up and ask the Senator to reply on the spot to some charges made against him by a critic or political enemy, as though a United States Senator had nothing better to do than to go around defending himself all day. These reporters did not seem to want to hear about it when the Senator wanted to make an announcement on his own, and many of them had no idea what committees Dodd was on or what activities he was normally involved in, but when somebody hurled any kind of accusation at the Senator they were right there on the phone demanding an answer. A variation of this, said Joe, was the assumption by some reporters that a Senator is some kind of walking encyclopedia. They would ask questions that seemed to come "right off the wall" about topics with which Dodd was unfamiliar, and then they would act just a bit indignant when he did not have a glib answer ready. This is where that quote from earlier in the chapter about "a degree of cooperation" and a "decent respect" comes in. If the Senator you are talking to is on, say, the Foreign Relations Committee, you are being unfair by expecting him to know right off the top of his head (while your tape is rolling) detailed answers for issues confronting the Agriculture Committee.

## "Rip and Call" Can Be Worse Than "Rip and Read"

When a story from a leading newspaper was quoted on the wire services to the effect that a certain politician may have done some arm-twisting to get a big government contract for a few of his friends, many stations around the state grabbed the phone and dialed the man's office number with their tape recorders rolling. They were all looking for a 20- to 30-second denial to put on a cartridge. If you think this is really heavy investigative journalism, think again! It is nothing more than cheap bandwagon-jumping to be the umpteenth station to call after your state AP or UPI radio wire has done a rewrite on some newspaper's original story. Some of these stations stooped even lower by crossing out the name of the newspaper in their wire service copy and running it as though they had dug up the story themselves. A few then added insult to injury by not running the politician's denial when he explained that the source who had leaked the accusation to the newspaper was a disappointed contractor who had lost out in the bidding. Why did not these stations run the denial? Because their big local newscast at noon was supposed to be a shower of dazzling audio cuts (tape-recorded voices and sounds in every story) and they wanted this man's denial in his own voice on their tape. If he would not perform, they would not run the story.

### If You Are Not Qualified to Analyze or Editorialize, Do Not Do It

Although Spiro T. Agnew resigned in disgrace as Vice President of the United States, he did manage to send some shivers through the broadcast industry (especially the TV networks) with his charges of "instant analysis" by what he termed a "tiny, enclosed fraternity of privileged men elected by no one . . ." Network *news* presidents, and presidents of *entire* networks themselves were able to rebut the Vice President's charges in various ways, but most of those rebuttals were based on a strong premise that the people commenting in any way upon speeches made by President Nixon or by Vice President Agnew himself were professional journalists with impeccable credentials. Said ABC News President Elmer Lower, ". . . I could not have arrived at my present post without two score of news executives having made individual and independent judgments about me along the way. And I might add that none of these men ever asked me about my personal opinions . . . Had I ever violated their trust, I would not have been in their employ the following day." If you lack the credentials of a network news president or even those of a reknowned commentator, then you must build *some* kind of a base from which to direct any kind of analysis or criticism. First, you have to have a consistently reliable reputation for reporting just the facts. If any of your stories in recent years have come under question for reasons of accuracy, even for being overstated or exaggerated, then you are vulnerable. All they have to do is point out that you have been wrong before. Although Senator Edmund Muskie of Maine disagreed with Mr. Agnew and his attacks on the news media, he did concede that "no matter how honest the purposes of any political administration, it does have a vested interest in making the facts fit its policies." This is important, and it fits a point made in the first chapter on the basics where it said that "being first is not as important as being right." As Spiro Agnew put it:

Just as a politician's words—wise and foolish—are dutifully recorded by press and television to be thrown up at him at the appropriate time, so their words should be likewise recorded and likewise recalled.

When they go beyond fair comment and criticism they will be called upon to defend their statements and their positions just as we must defend ours.

The whole point here is not that you should be afraid to editorialize or analyze, but that you should do your homework and know what you are talking about first. "People in glass houses shouldn't throw stones," as the saying goes, and although Mr. Agnew himself has dropped out of the political picture, his attitude that the media "will be called upon to defend their statements" will live on for some time to come.

## IN THE HALLS OF THE CAPITOL BUILDING

It has happened in several state capitols by now: The legislature is in session and there is a corps of individuals who see themselves as "God's gift to journalism" following each other up and down the hallways. Whenever a crowd seems to be going into some room, they think it must be a news conference, so in they go with tape recorders or notepads in hand, waiting for whoever it is to make his statement and for that ever-present mimeographed handout called a "release." Then, when the session breaks up, they all scurry for the phones and file what amounts to little more than "carbon copies" of each other's stories.

Even here, with dozens of legislators to choose from, and with hundreds of others such as lobbyists, citizens testifying before committees, state officials who have to explain their departmental policies, county, municipal, and other government officials from around the state, and a host of other sources, it is disappointing to see that many newsmen are still "event-oriented" in their coverage. There has to be that news conference, that handout, that actual testimony or debate, before many of them will write a story. In a way, these people qualify more than anyone else as that "little fraternity" . . . with ". . . similar social and political views" that Spiro Agnew criticized, operating with that "pack mentality" which *Time* magazine ascribed to the Washington, D.C., press corps.

Fortunately, if you keep your eyes open, you may spot a softspoken fellow who does not appear to be following the pack, at least not all of the time. After a while, you may also notice that this is the fellow whose stories everyone else is clipping out and saving so that they all might have an idea of what is really going on. This fellow who appears to be the "loner" is the *real* investigative reporter in the group. Rather than sit around with the guys in the press room waiting for something to happen, he slips out and sees a few people on his own. He knows not only *who* and *what* to ask, but *how* to ask the right questions. Quite often, it is over a cup of coffee across the street from the capitol, and without a notepad in his hands. He has done his homework, he has made a business of knowing these legislators and government officials personally over the years, and he can *anticipate* stories before they happen because he knows all the "symptoms" of a building story. For example, he knows the sponsors of all the bills and the chairmen of all the committees well enough to stop them in the hallways or even on the floor of the house or senate and chat about their *"pet"* projects and problems. He has a rapport with these people which relaxes them. He does not put them on the defensive by shoving a microphone in their faces or approaching with pencil and pad in hand.

Obviously, this "model" reporter did not accomplish this level of operation overnight. He probably did not even do it in one or two sessions of the legislature. Using procedures very much like those outlined earlier in the chapter, he painstakingly built up those "nice, warm contacts." This time, however, just the warmth of the contact is not enough. The atmosphere is more politically charged but in a more subtle, sophisticated way. The stakes are higher, because these people are legislating the criminal laws, laws on commerce and industry, institutions, education, and a wide range of topics that will affect your life style and that of everyone else who lives in that state. These are not just the municipal "housekeeping" services that you see in city council meetings, such as how much to pay policemen and financing of road and sewer projects.

If it is your "freshman" term for legislative coverage, you may have to "follow the pack" for a while before you can start going out on your own. In the first few weeks, you just have to get to know your way around the building (many of the older state capitols are architectural nightmares) and who the key people are in each party and in each "house" of the legislature. Attend the press conferences and hearings, get to know who the committee chairmen are, and gradually pick up the "rhythm" of the place. Your stories will probably not be Pulitzer Prize material, but you can "customize" them by approaching the legislators from your station's local area. Usually, they will appreciate the coverage. It is not given them by the media from elsewhere in the state. It will be more interesting back home, too, because, after all, your listeners are their constituents.

State capitols are far better than city halls when it comes to printed material for the information of the public and the press. Here are some of the helpful guides, directories, schedules, and other documents that are commonly available in most capitols:

### Legislative Directory

Many states have a pocket-sized directory which lists each member of the state House of Representatives and state Senate by name, district number, seat number, etc. These directories also contain lists of committees and the majority and minority leadership positions. Often members are listed alphabetically as well as by district number, with indication of party affiliation. In some states the guide is free, either at government expense or provided by some state-wide business association as a public service. In other states, you must purchase your copy from a private firm which has been given the concession to print this and other legislative documents. This is probably the most important item on your list of necessary reference materials. It is usually given out in such offices as the House Clerk, Senate Clerk, or Secretary of State, but other reporters in the Press Room or elsewhere around the capitol can tell you where this and other materials are obtained if these offices mentioned do not seem to apply in your state.

Other items to look for are as follows.

### Hearing Schedule

The times and room numbers where various legislative committees will hear from various groups and individuals on their views of pending bills. Very often, the testimony is very colorful and makes good actualities for both TV and radio if legislative rules allow such sessions to be recorded in your state.

### Bill Index

A listing of the titles of all the bills filed for consideration by the legislature. Usually "HB" means they were originated in the House, and "SB" indicates Senate origin. Most states list these under categories which pretty much match the names of the committees that will hold hearings on them, along with one-sentence definitions of the purpose of each bill. Browsing through this index, you can mark the bills that you think would make interesting coverage for your area, then look them up by number, or request copies by number, in the "bill room."

## Copies of Bills

Rarely would you want to read the complete text of every bill from top to bottom. In some states, any legislator can file a bill on any topic at any time, and bills in these states can run into the thousands. In other states, each party "screens" the bills to be filed by its members, combining the best features of competing proposals. Often members of a particular party must "clear" bills with others from their own party who are on the committee that will hold hearings on the bill. Even in states where bills are screened or "prefiled" like this, the amount of reading you would need to do would be prohibitive even if you were reporting on nothing but the legislature full time. Perhaps a few major newspapers and the wire services will request copies of *all* bills and set up their own "reference library" during a legislative session, but as a lone reporter you would be far better off requesting bills by number from the index. Besides the overwhelming amount of reading you would have to do if you had individual copies of all bills, there is an expense in some states. In one state, the writer simply requested a box number in the bill room and the box was filled up for him every day. In another state, the firm doing the printing wanted a few hundred dollars for the "subscription."

## House and Senate Calendars

These one- or two-page documents are usually issued daily, and indicate which bills have "made it" through the hearing stage and are out on the floor of each chamber for debate. This does not necessarily mean there will be a debate. It took the writer a few weeks in his first legislative session to discover that the leaders of opposing parties get together and line up days when there will be no debate. The list of bills on such days is usually quite long, none of them are major pieces of legislation and none of them are considered controversial. A bare quorum sits there and sleepily votes approval on just about all of these bills. If any bill is challenged at all, they have usually agreed in advance that it will be dropped for the time being and rescheduled for a time when debate is going on. If you are sitting there recording everything during one of these sessions, chances are you are missing some big stories that are developing elsewhere in the building. The way to save yourself some wasted time is to drop in at the Majority Leader's and Minority Leader's offices and ask them if they expect any controversy on the bills scheduled for floor action. The Democrats will tell you which Republican bills they dislike, and the Republicans will tell you which Democratic bills they will oppose, but do not expect either party to tell you which of its *own* bills is liable to be controversial. After all, they would like to get their own stuff passed without rousing any opposition at all if they can do it. (Of course, an exception to all this can occur when someone is mounting "surprise" opposition to some measure. The strategy is to catch your opponents out to lunch and defeat their measure before they can gather their forces.) Generally, though, you can tell by checking with party leaders and with your friends in the legislature where the "quiet" spots are and where the "hot" spots are going to be. Then you mark the bills on your House or Senate Calendar and get ready.

### Press Room Bulletin Board

In most states, there is something that passes for a Press Room, but the variations are wild. Try to see if there is a place where all the invitations to parties, press conferences, etc., are posted. If you are going to be there full time, see if local "ground rules" permit you a desk. Sometimes the phones are all WATS lines covering the whole state and the calls are on the taxpayers at a package rate for the whole building. Other times you will find that each individual news organization has had to install its own phone and probably even locks it. At any rate, you will have to do some hanging around in the Press Room at the start and ask veteran reporters from various media if there are any other materials normally available to the press other than the ones mentioned here. Usually, you will find the others who work in the Press Room fairly cooperative on general information like this; it is just a noncompetitive courtesy. Some of them, unless you are directly competing with them in the same town or broadcast area back home, will swap tips with you and "backstop" for you when you make friends over a period. One good example of this is when the House and the Senate have hot debates going on at the same time. You cannot be in both places at once, so you take notes in one chamber while a buddy does the same for you in the other room. Several committee meetings scheduled at the same hour can also be covered in this fashion.

## Limitations

In some states, just get dressed up and carry a tape recorder and they will let you sit in the Press Section. In others, a sergeant-at-arms at the door will want to see your "Press" pass as you enter. Major newspapers, broadcast outlets, and wire services may have reserved seats in the Press Section. You have to check. Also, there are known legislatures where anyone at all—press or not—can just sit in the balcony with a cassette tape recorder microphone hanging over the rail near the P.A. speaker. In other states, such recording is prohibited except on special ceremonial occasions or when the Governor is going to give his "State-of-the-State" address. Again, you have to check.

## Phone Directories and Audio Hotlines

You are not always going to be at the capitol building whenever a story breaks about state government. The legislature may not be in session (some legislatures meet once or twice a week year-round, others meet every day for a period of two or three months in a round-the-clock orgy of bill passing), or the source of your story may be in some government agency in a building nowhere near the capitol. One way or another, you will eventually want to get your hands on a phone book that lists the numbers of all the departments and agencies in the state government. The writer's experience has been that these are pretty hard to come by. They are usually given out once a year to those reporters who have become fulltime fixtures at the capitol, and to the wire services. The book can be worth its weight in gold if you are sitting at your typewriter in the newsroom back at the station and you want some information from a specific government official or office. Rather than run up long-distance charges by calling the capitol switchboard, or rather than driving to the capitol (which is impossible in most cases, unless your station is located in the same city or one of its immediate suburbs), you can just pick up this little book, dial the right number, and finish typing up your story within a few minutes.

As for the "Hotlines," these come in several variations, but they are good to know about. If you are calling from a TV newsroom, they will not help your visual product, but they may have some information you will want to use in your own rewrite or to send a film crew out to cover. The best ones, of course, are the ones that you can call free; your boss will not have to get nervous about all those toll charges to the state capitol. On the other hand, you sometimes "get what you pay for." If it is a canned, prerecorded announcement, the temptation for many small stations is to run it regardless of its value as a news story. They think this "audio" gives their audience the impression that their news department has good contacts in state government, but the days are long gone when the public is that naïve. Listeners will conclude by themselves over the long run that you are just taking advantage of the "freebees." There is much greater value to one of these free phone numbers if a real, live person answers the phone when you call and you can ask questions. (Congressmen and federal agencies have started these phone services, too. Get hold of the numbers if you do not already have them, because they can save your station a bundle of money.)

### Your Own "Issues File"

Many stations keep a "futures file" on event-oriented stories, but the weakness in having this as your *only* system is that you are tied to scheduled happenings. What you want for legislative and government coverage is a set of *topics* that will precipitate stories *when you want them,* not when some legislator wants to beat his own drum by telling only about the bills that he himself has filed. As you read *Time* or *Newsweek* at home, tear out articles that would make good stories in your own area if you asked some of the same questions. For example, another state may have an innovation or "pioneer" piece of legislation in a field such as motor vehicle laws, education, medicine (like the abortion issue or fluoridation of public water supplies, etc.) or may have experienced a public "backlash" as the result of some neglect, loophole, or abuse of its laws. Keep up with editorials in various newspapers: Read one at home as well as those which may be lying around in your newsroom. The better your understanding of basic issues is, the better your questions may be. Some of the issues you read about today will come back to you as questions months or even years from now, and they will put you far ahead of the "pack" that must wander around the halls of the capitol waiting for handouts and press conferences.

## Stringers From Other Stations

Your station may not be able to afford to keep a reporter on full-time or even part-time at the capitol. In cases like this, it is usually not hard to find a newsman who works for a station in or near the capital city itself who would be willing to send you big stories on a "per story" basis. Often, it is a reporter who has the morning newsroom shift at his own station and then hops over to the capitol in the afternoon. His boss does not mind a bit, because quite likely his own station is getting the coverage free. Even if they are paying for it, they do not mind their own guys making a little "bread" on the side as long as they get the stories first and as long as their man is not calling stations close enough to be considered competitors. You might even find newspaper people here and there who can at least give you "voiced" correspondent reports if not taped actualities. As the telephone company says, "it's the next best thing to being there."

The "capitol" building referred to is at the state level, but many of the ideas presented here are applicable to the county building in your area and even to some aspects of congressional and other federal coverage. The United States as a nation has more than 150,000 more-or-less "local" units of government, ranging from more than 3,000 counties to somewhere around 40,000 municipalities, towns, townships, or whatever they may be called in your area. Along with these are over 100,000 school districts and more than 10,000 districts for such purposes as flood control, sewage, agriculture, etc. To try to describe your needs as a newsman in anticipation of all of these governmental units would be an impossible task. Obviously, this book has left some questions unanswered and it has answered some that you will probably never need. From here, you just have to fit the "basic" points to the form of government in your area.

Now here is how to approach the *federal* establishment.

### Congressional Staff Directory

One of the most valuable reference books in any newsroom is the *Congressional Staff Directory* put out every year by Charles Brownson, a former Congressman himself. The volume is not only found in many newspaper and broadcast newsrooms across the country, but is on the desk of most Congressmen, Senators, and their own staff members. It is as basic as a dictionary to anyone who has more than the slightest casual reason to get in touch with any office in Congress or the Executive Branch of the federal government. It has the names and job titles of all staff members of every Congressman, including those who run offices in the state capital and other cities back in the Congressman's home state. It has all their phone numbers and extensions, and even biographical sketches of key people like Press Secretaries, so you can find what stations or newspapers they have worked for in your state and can get to know them better. It has all the committees and subcommittees on which any member of Congress serves, and a list of all the cities and towns (over 1500 population) he represents. For the Executive Branch, it lists all departments and agencies, along with their liason and information officers and their room numbers and phone extensions. If the price seems a bit "steep" to your boss, then just get it every *other* year, after Congressional elections. Drop a line to: Congressional Staff Directory, 300 New Jersey Avenue, S.E., Washington, D.C., 20003, and they will send you their latest prices and information.

## Regional "Public Information Officer" Directories

Pick out any federal agency whose address and phone number you may already have, and see if you can get in touch with the *Public Information Officer* for the *region*. He could be in Boston for the six New England states, or New York City for that state and several others nearby, etc. You may have to probe around a bit before you find him. When you reach him (or her), ask if you may have a directory with the names and phone extensions of *all* the spokesmen for *all* the federal agencies in your region. Usually, these PR people have professional associations or groups of their own, and very often such groups put out very handy guides listing all the correct *office* and *home* phone numbers of all the Public Information people in their agencies. Such guides are usually free, and if you ever need to contact anyone from the Internal Revenue Service to the Food and Drug Administration, or even the authorities at a nearby military base, you have specific numbers, names, and job titles for all of them. If you are at a station in Alabama, for example, the spokesman you want may be in Atlanta, Georgia, or in Tallahassee, Florida, and you would be wasting a phone call by calling Washington, D.C.

In major cities, there may be societies of these PR people, who represent *all* levels of government, not just federal. If you are within 100 miles or so of a major metropolitan area, ask specifically if such a PR organization exists and if you can get a copy of their directory. As you browse through the directory, even the titles of the agencies will give you ideas for stories on "slow" days—consumer affairs, environmental protection, harness racing, labor, landmarks, liquor, and so on.

## Public Employee Organizations

Concerning directories, there is one available in New York City from the Office of Collective Bargaining entitled *Public Employee Organizations.* In other areas, you may have to look for such an office under "Labor" or "Unions." The booklet lists the officials and spokesmen for the "locals" and "parent organizations" for each union that does business with the government, from architects and boilermakers to transport workers, upholsterers, and wardens. It is a handy directory to have for labor stories.

### Congressional Quarterly ("CQ")

This is a subscription service used by major network news operations and others who have a "Washington Bureau." If your station is getting its Washington coverage from a network, most likely the correspondents are doing a good enough job and you would not need a reference service of this caliber. This is, essentially, a package of all the items mentioned under "state" capitol coverage, such as hearing schedules, House and Senate calendars, etc. Unless you have a reporter covering these sessions, such detailed information would be of little use to you. In addition to the "agenda" and "directory" type items, CQ puts out things like a "scoreboard" indicating the progress of major bills as they make their way through hearings and floor votes in each house, and does analysis pieces on major issues shaping up. Unless you are working for a 50,000-watt all-news station, you can probably do just as well with network and/or wire service coverage, backed up by regular phone contacts with your state's Senators and the Congressmen from districts in your coverage area.

## YOU ARE ALSO ACCESSIBLE

Now that you are lined up with some hints on access to the various news sources in state and federal government, here is a warning about some people who will want access to *you*. There are many legitimate "concerned citizens" who show up to testify in committee hearings and who deserve to be heard whether their views are popular or not. There are, however, slick lobbyists for special-interest groups and self-appointed gadflies who represent extremist viewpoints. The lobbyists may want to take you out to lunch or to give you tickets to a show or ballgame, or even send a case of liquor to your newsroom around Christmas. They may not ask for any favors when they give these gifts, and some of them will never dare to hint at any reciprocation on your part—they just want you to enjoy the "glow" of their friendly approach and stop right there. Others, though, may be around in a few months trying to push a certain viewpoint. Do not get yourself in a position with *anyone* where they would be able to come back and say you owe them the favor. If what they are doing for you or giving you is so big that a simple "thank you" will not take care of it, better decline.

The gadflies, on the other hand, are those who frequently use a "kooky" approach to gain attention. They will storm the hearing room, picket, hand out leaflets in the hallway, scream obscenities, berate the chairman, etc. In one state capitol where the writer attended a hearing on a bill to fluoridate municipal water supplies, some physicians and others who sincerely opposed the bill and were trying to present their case in a responsible manner suddenly saw their whole argument sunk by a noisy crowd of extremists who disrupted the meeting, grabbed the microphone and screamed into it, accusing the legislators of a "conspiracy to poison us all." It is true that people like this are very colorful and controversial, but if you give them another "soap box" to stand on and play that back on your newscast as though that were the whole story of the hearing, moderates on both sides of an issue may be cool toward you in the future, and all the kooks will know you are an easy target.

## POLITICS AND ELECTION CAMPAIGNS

What is a politician? Normally, he (or she) is someone who wants a job in the government at some level, by election or appointment, and all the power, prestige, and other "fringe benefits" that go with that job. Here and there are politicians who want a little more power, or a few more "fringe benefits," than the job really deserves, and who will use underhanded means to get what they want. This, basically, was the story of Watergate in the Nixon administration, but it has been the story in too many other cases since the nation began. As a result, people sometimes tend to regard anyone who runs for office as being somewhat tainted with some inordinate form of greed in a "guilt-by-association" way of reckoning. A citizen who runs for office can be just as honest as anyone else, but because getting elected requires a certain amount of shrewdness and certain adherence to party obligations, people often suspect such an individual of wanting *something* for his personal aggrandizement, or else, we ask ourselves, "Why else would he be running?"

Throughout the U.S. the public has become accustomed to seeing a basically two-party system in operation. In special cases, reform groups and splinter parties may mobilize to support or defeat certain issues, but these are rarely permanent. There is usually a party that is in power (called the "majority" party), and its opposition (called the "minority" party). At the core of any party organization are the "professionals," or those elected and appointed officials whose jobs pretty much depend on getting elected and/or reelected. Next to them are private citizens who have something to gain or lose by their party activity, ranging from acceptance of their viewpoints on how the government shall be run to flat-out favors such as jobs for themselves and their relatives or help in dealing with some office of the government. Finally, there are the less articulate party members who may never be seen at a campaign headquarters, and who are somewhat confused by all the intricacies of government but who feel that voting for, and maybe even putting on a "bumper sticker" for, a certain party or candidate will somehow help them in the long run.

In the "good old days" before radio and TV came along, strong party organizations (called "machines" in many parts of the country) won their votes with all kinds of favors for the people who lived within their domains. Everything from free picnics and outings to bags of coal and extra police protection would obligate the local citizenry to a certain political machine. Occasionally, powerful new ideas, sectionalism ("us" against "them") or special-interest groups could disrupt these party organizations, but for decades they were the dominant factor in the country's political makeup.

Along came the 1960's and 1970's and all that changed, save perhaps for some of the very lowest-level races in the most "localized" situations. The book *The Selling of the President,* written by Joe McGinness, described how candidates who could get together great fortunes could "sell" themselves to the voters. Not only did Richard Nixon spend $12 million on broadcasting alone to beat Hubert Humphrey in 1968, but Nelson Rockefeller spent $12.6 million for a total compaign budget (with at least $2 million going to radio and TV) just to get reelected as Governor of New York two years later.

Where does today's broadcast *news* reporter fit into all of this? It used to be the function of journalists to examine the qualifications and investigate the behavior of all candidates, and to report on their findings to the electorate, so that the voters could choose intelligently. Today, obviously, not many of the voters are paying attention to the journalists; they are watching the spot announcements. As *Congressional Quarterly* put it, "men of great wealth . . ." (can win elections by) ". . . presenting their politics to the voters on television and spending their way from obscurity to success in a matter of weeks." There is legislation being introduced and considered at various levels in an attempt to control this "selling" of candidates, but as of this writing none of it has been too successful. In the meantime, it was said that you cannot expect your first assignment to be the White House, so this book will assume that you are dealing with city, county, and perhaps an occasional state official, plus one or two Congressmen at the most. It will also assume that their spending is not at such a level that it completely obliterates any need for good news coverage. This means, for the sake of discussion, that pressures will be building upon you and that you will be a target for propaganda from opposing sides.

Primaries, of course, are the runoffs among the people who want their party nomination. In some states, party conventions nominate candidates, and primaries only become applicable if a defeated candidate at the party convention wants to challenge the convention choice. If the challenger gets a certain percentage of the registered party members to sign a petition, there will be a runoff. If not, the convention choice stands. In other states, however, primaries are a free-swinging affair with a multitude of candidates all vying for their party's nomination on a rather large ballot.

The temptation, if you are new at this, is to get right down to the nitty-gritty and really "get relevant" about all the issues. You may interview a candidate or two—really putting them through their paces—and you may even write a special documentary report on one or two issues. The trouble is, if you have bothered to tune in to your own station lately, that the disc jockeys have been playing four or five commercials in a row between each record, and most of these are paid political announcements featuring the voice of every candidate for every office right down to dogcatcher. The audience is at the saturation point, and for you to turn around and give them more of the same thing will just drive them all to their 8-track stereo cartridges. In the "primaries" stage of any election campaign, the trick is knowing what to *leave out.* To run every statement offered by every candidate will not help to inform your audience. It will simply make a "blur" out of the whole business. At this stage, you must *select* just the few *major* issues that seem to be common to most primary races in your area. Just because a candidate comes out with a statement on some topic, it is not an "issue." He would like to make it one, yes, but you—not the candidates—should control your own newscasts.

Once the primaries are over, in whatever form, a week or two may go by for intraparty fence-mending, closing-of-ranks, and all that, and then they will get back to you. You will be invited to the big grand opening of their headquarters, and they pass the word that some big party dignitary (maybe the Governor or a U.S. Senator) will drop by. Do not be taken in. These are usually local folks, volunteers, and not slick, professional politicians for the most part, unless you are in a large city. They are very friendly and they offer you cups of coffee and a button with the candidate's name, but they regretfully announce that Governor what's-his-name had to cancel his appearance at the last moment because of some other pressing business. What they have just done is gotten you into their headquarters with your cassette recorder, and you are too nice a guy to walk out on them without getting a few of their candidate's words on tape—perhaps giving a pep talk to the campaign workers—and the popping of the balloons, etc. Yes, they *are* nice folks and they *are* sincere and friendly and all that, but if opening a campaign headquarters is a big story for you, my friend, you must *really* be in the boondocks! Do you think it will run as front-page stuff in tomorrow's paper? It may be worth a passing mention, say about one line, in a larger political story, but is it worth running that interview you did with the candidate?

From here on in, it is all invitations, handouts and freebees, especially from the underdogs. You and your spouse, if you are married, can get yourselves invited to some pretty elegant affairs at hotel ballrooms. "No-no, that's all right, the drinks are on them." For an incumbent government official to do this would be a little unethical, but for rank-and-file volunteer party workers to do it is all part of the game as long as *you* know where to get off the bandwagon. If they buy you drink after drink all night, and you dance your shoes off and end up having such a fantastically good time that you "close the place" and go on from there to someone else's place for a few more drinks afterward, you may have already compromised your so-called objectivity. If the opposition has offered you nothing but a mimeographed release in the mail the next day, how much weight are you going to give it with memories of last night's party dancing in your head? Use the party to *your* advantage, building up some of those "nice, warm contacts" already talked about and meeting some new and interesting people, but do not be so overwhelmed by the whole thing that you end up being just a PR man in reporter's clothing for them. The whole point here is: *you*, not they, must control the overall situation.

Another approach is the offer of free "audio" cuts to radio stations and free film footage to TV stations, with portions of staged "interviews" with their candidate. Some campaign radio-TV managers have been really good at this in recent years, sending out these edited "answers" and providing you with a script so that you can ask the "questions" just as though you had done the interview yourself. The point here is that you *did not* do the interview yourself! *They* wrote the questions, *they* wrote the nicely worded answers just the way they wanted them to come out, and *they* are controlling the situation! This is not saying that the whole thing is evil and that you should not run a single word of it, but that you should *consider the source,* not swallow it whole.

Considering sources, there is the matter of public opinion polls. As the old saying goes, "there are lies, damned lies, and statistics!" If a candidate releases a poll or survey, what do you *think* it is going to show? Right! No candidate ever releases a poll that says he is losing. If a so-called impartial survey organization calls up or mails you the results of a survey showing some candidate in the lead, question the source. Who ever heard of this impartial survey outfit before? Are they well-known nationally? How long have they been in business? What is their rating with Dun & Bradstreet? Who asked them to call you? If their answer is a coy, "We just thought you'd be interested because you're the local station in that area," ask them who paid for the survey. Just identifying the source is not good enough in some political stories; the *motivation behind the source* must be clear. Even if their facts are correct as far as you can tell, why are they telling you this? Would this same outfit have called you and reported the outcome of their survey if the results had been favorable to the *other* candidate rather than the one who appears to be the front-runner? Think about it.

You are likely to get the chance to interview some candidates. This is your function. You are the journalist, and you are performing your task here so that the public will know what these candidates are all about—on *your* terms, not on those of the candidate. It would be unfair for you to take advantage of this sudden "power" that you have and force Candidate *A* to answer all the charges that Candidate *B* has dreamed up. After all, that is Candidate *B's* function: to dream up as many charges as he can. In fact, you can assure Candidate *A's* campaign manager that that is *not* what you are going to do. You are not going to be "used" by either side. You are going to ask your own questions. This does not mean that *none* of Candidate *B's* charges will be brought up during the interview. It just means that anything selected at all will be as a result of your best news judgment.

There have actually been cases where campaign managers, in setting up an interview appointment, will have the nerve to ask for a list of questions in advance. No way. This borders on censorship, and gives them control of the interview. You can give this campaign manager one or two very general topics that you would like to explore, but tell him quite frankly that you want the interview to be spontaneous and that you reserve the right to cover other topics you feel are relevant. (Your message is implicitly that *you* control the interview and he does not!)

As your campaign season approaches, you will want to have a number of reference materials handy to help sort out all the confusing information with which you are going to be bombarded. First, go down to the store and pick up some poster cardboards and some "Magic Markers" and do some charts on the races you will be covering locally. You will not need them for state-wide offices, such as Governor or Secretary of State, or even for U.S. Senator, because the wire services do a good job on them and you need only to embellish this if one of the candidates comes to town or there is some "local" angle involved. On the others, though, the name of the job with its district number and the present incumbent in that office is very handy. Maybe you can indicate by color-coding or some symbol whether the incumbent is stepping down or running for reelection. Many of the releases you get will go out of their way not to mention opponents by name, and you will often find yourself having to fix up candidate Smith's release by adding that "Al Smith is running against Bob Jones for the seat now held by John Kirk in the 34th District, which comprises the western half of the county." Smith does not know it, but you may be helping him this way. Listeners may have heard his spot announcements going by at the rate of six or more per day, but they have not meant anything. Suddenly, mentioning the district by number and location, and pointing out that old John Kirk is coming to the end of his term up there in the legislature awakens some listeners to the fact that they will have to choose someone else. As a result, Smith's spots will no longer go in one ear and out the other, and neither will those of his opponent. On top of that, some people may want to know about Jones so they can know who *not* to vote for. On the basis of some of the advertising, plus some of the articles in the paper and some of the gossip around town, and, yes, my friend, some of your newscasts, they will feel well-informed and decide that they do not like Jones so Smith will get their vote as the lesser of two evils! In other words, you have done Smith a favor by putting his opponent's name and the incumbent's name back into the story, even though they were both from the opposition party.

Also, after the primaries, you will want to set up file folders on each candidate, with color-coding and symbols to indicate the party affiliation, district number, and what they are running for. Releases you never think you will need and those you have already used should go into these folders. When it looks like you may get a chance to interview either or both candidates in a race, pull out the folders and make some notes that will help you to develop questions. Just remember not to use *all* of Candidate *B*'s charges as questions for Candidate *A*. Make up a few questions based on the candidate's own releases so you can get the interview rolling by having him talk about the things he is familiar with, and then drop in some questions you have made up yourself. These need not be controversial issues. They can just be sort of "daydreaming" about some of the creative opportunities that will face such a candidate when (and if) he is elected. Just pick out an area, for example, Zero Population Growth, and without getting into the abortion controversy, see what your candidate will do about such things as the closing of maternity wards and unneeded school buildings and the increase in the percentage of senior citizens in his district. The question may seem insignificant in the context of the interview you are doing at the moment, but what you do not have to tell your candidate is that later in the week you are going to pick out his answer and that of his opponent and put them side by side so that your listeners or viewers may compare. In fact, if it is a sit-down studio interview of any considerable length, you may plant several of these "sleeper" questions into it.

If an angry campaign manager complains later that you were unfair in using questions that his candidate "wasn't prepared" for, you may point out that:

1) His opponent "wasn't prepared" for it, either.
2) If he gets into office, there will be a great many things coming up that he will not be prepared for.
3) It is your job as a journalist to see if a candidate can talk intelligently about topics *other* than those he grinds out in his campaign propaganda.

The only thing they might be able to get you for, so you should be warned about it again, is that business of not asking someone who is running for Congress a question that should be answered by someone who is running for city council. Know what things these people are expected to handle when they are elected, and stick to those issues.

Not only should *you* stick to those issues, but so should your candidate. A favorite trick of some candidates is to seize upon an issue which can never be resolved by the office for which they are running. They may get very angry and flustered when you point that out to them right in the middle of an interview, but that is part of your job. For example, a candidate for City Council was going around one year campaigning on a "fear" issue: motorcycle clubs riding through certain residential neighborhoods en masse. He was promising changes in laws about wearing helmets, in state legislation about vehicle inspection and drivers' licenses, and a whole range of things that were clearly in the domain of state legislators, not city councilmen. When the writer pointed this out to him, he blustered around it, saying that he was going to go up to the state capitol and "raise hell" about it, muttering all his favorite campaign phrases about how something should be done about all these "hippies." Unfortunately for him, he was being interviewed by a panel on a live, one-hour show where the audience could call in and participate. The panel climbed all over him, asking him specifically what he meant by "raise hell," and why he was not running for the state House of Representatives, and what, if anything, would he really do as a city councilman in certain specific areas. Be on the lookout for "fakers" like this.

Often, a candidate for higher office with a pretty good advertising staff will create a catchy issue, and others will try to "ride" the wave of this new idea that is sweeping the country (or at least part of it) and speak out on issues that they will never deal with if they are elected. It is your job to spot this and bring them back to discussion of the duties involved in the post they are running for.

Offices like the City Clerk, County Clerk, and Secretary of State usually have an "elections" division which provides statistical information to the news media. Among the things you should expect from them are calendars which list all the deadlines for filing candidacy petitions, holding nominating conventions, reporting on campaign funds, etc. If you are not on the mailing list for these things, call up and request that they include you. After all, you are performing a service for them by publicizing all of these dates so that the voters, party organizations, and candidates may comply with the election laws and regulations. Also available should be statistics telling how many of each party are registered in each district. Drop in at these offices and see what other items they have which may or may not be mailed out, such as maps of district boundaries. Also, if you are just being added to the mailing list, see if there is anything you may have missed during the past year or so that other newsrooms might already have hanging on the  wall.

When the campaign gets underway, certain documents filed by the candidates become public information. Just because the deadline is Friday at 5 p.m. for the filing of disclosure-of-income forms does not mean that some candidate will not quietly bring his form in at 11 a.m. on Tuesday. You will have to watch these offices like a hawk. In many states, government secretaries and other civil service employees are forbidden to call the news media. In still others, they just are not known for their warmth and will "play dumb," giving you a poker face and/or the run-around, saying that only some other official is authorized to release the information you are seeking. In recent years, this practice has generally been known as "stonewalling." If you do not want to run into that stonewall during campaign season, spend some time a month or two in advance dropping in for a friendly chat with the person who is authorized to release such information in your city, county, state and whatever other governments you will be dealing with. Find out whom to contact when that "authorized" person is out of the office. Jot down the phone extensions. Explain very carefully just what you will be wanting, and who else from your station may be calling or dropping by. Set the whole thing up carefully, so that you do not hit them "cold" and wind up emptyhanded while your competitor has the whole story on the air.

Finally, while you are seeking these people, find out what arrangements they are making for election night. Whom should you see about "reading" the figures from the backs of voting machines after the polls close—or will it be easier to go to their elections office at the city hall or capitol building? (Will their office even be *open* that night? In some areas, only the campaign headquarters of each party have unofficial totals, and the official report just waits until the next morning or runs hours behind the party and news media figures.) Find out whether it is even worth it to deal with these people at all on Election Night, or whether their function will only be to confirm what everybody already will have known for several hours.

## ELECTION NIGHT—A DIFFERENT ANIMAL

Other than what you see on the major TV networks and hear on their radio counterparts, it is hard to describe a "typical" election night in an individual broadcast station. Some stations bring in a cast of extras and put on a performance that would do credit to Cecil B. DeMille or Barnum and Bailey. The "extras" can range from local Jaycees and their wives to whole dormitories full of college kids, or even to the entire staffs of newspapers with whom the broadcast station has worked out a deal. Others provide coverage similar to that described in our "disaster" chapter, with salesmen, secretaries, and the boss's wife all pitching in. There are stations where just the regular newsmen make a little overtime, other stations where an all-music format demands just token coverage mumbled softly with the regular news headlines, and of course there are the "daytimers" who are off the air and whose news people can go out in the field and enjoy all those parties, collecting material for broadcast the next day. At one poverty-stricken UHF television station where the hoped-for sponsor did not sign up for the planned coverage, a novel solution was to have an unidentified staffer go out and throw rocks at the transformer on a utility pole, knocking the station off the air for a night. Then, blaming the vandalism on the neighborhood kids, they could tell all those extras not to bother showing up and give all the regulars the night off, saving what would have been a rather sizeable payroll for the evening, not to mention the costs that would have been involved in running lights, cameras, projectors, and an unbelievably "thirsty" transmitter.

To add to this kaleidioscopic variety of presentations, you will find that some stations believe in having a large staff at the studio and just phoning all the precincts, while others will put just one or two "editor" types in the newsroom and send an army of reporters out to polling places and political headquarters. Still others will do a little of each of these things, depending on their budget, their format, and very often on whether or not the evening's coverage has been sold to a sponsor. Some stations will work out of phone booths, while others will go "first class" and order up "remote lines," sometimes moving practically their whole operation to some hotel ballroom. Of course, another major factor is the kind of election you are covering: If it is a big November presidential job and your governor, a U.S. senator, all your congressmen and state legislators, mayor and city councilmen are running, you've got a big night ahead. If it is mid-May and the election is for the Village Board of Selectmen and a few constables, that is something else. The whole point here is to let you know right at the start that there is no *"one"* way to cover an election, and anybody who tells you so is grossly misinformed.

Do not tell your boss that. You may be a bright "eager beaver" just out of journalism or broadcasting school and you have learned about all the really neat ways to do this, but that does not mean he is ready for you. At his station, maybe there *is* just "one" way to do it (the way they did it last year, and the year before . . .) and you will just do what you are told and that is that. All through this book it was assumed you are a beginner at this, and that assumption still stands.

However, "beginner" and "News Director" are often one and the same at more stations in this country than one would care to admit. Very often, the one-man news staff is just simply given the title of "News Director" because there is no one else to wear it. This young fellow, or gal, supervises no one at all. He reads most of the newscasts, makes all the phone calls, and goes around town introducing himself as the News Director, and no one ever challenges it. If this is the situation you find yourself in, you may suddenly discover as you approach election night that you are not *all* the "News Director" you thought you were. In fact, this happens even at larger stations where the News Director is used to supervising one or two full-time news staffers and a few stringers. Suddenly, the General Manager walks in and just sort of "takes over" the News Department, or a large chunk of it. Do not be hurt: Just be ready. There are many reasons for this, and some of them are as follows:

First of all, if your news coverage for Election Night is anything more ambitious than your normal, day-to-day coverage, there are probably some additional expenditures involved. Payroll is one of these. On the station's normal organization chart, you do not usually have authority over copywriters, salesmen, secretaries, disc jockeys, and other nonnews personnel. It is entirely in the General Manager's domain to tell them when to show up and how much overtime they are going to be paid. Some of them may be "thin-skinned" for various reasons: the jocks see themselves as stars, the salesmen see themselves as somewhat independent adults with their own initiative and are not used to the discipline of journalism, and others may consider themselves higher up than you or at least equal to you in the station's hierarchy and will somewhat resent the reversal of roles even for one evening. One way or another, they are just not accustomed to taking orders from you, so the man they usually obey steps into the picture.

In Election Night coverage, there are often extra phones or remote lines to install, facilities to rent at hotels, transportation, meals, and other costs. If it is local TV, you have a great many sets and charts to build to give those figures a good visual backing. All the regular programming and commercials that normally run that evening have to be rescheduled around the election coverage, and a big enough sponsor has to be "sold" on all these extra expenses if the program is going to get off the ground, because few local stations can afford to just mount one of these productions and absorb all the extra costs. If the boss has stepped into your newsroom, he is worried about all this and more. After all, *your* job is done when the elections have been successfully covered, but he has paychecks to get out and other bills to pay long after the night is finished.

As said earlier, there is no "one" way this is done. You may be blessed with a boss who stays out of the newsroom and goes to bed early, hoping perhaps that the whole thing will blow over. You may be blessed with a boss who stays out of the newsroom and goes to bed early, hoping that the whole thing will blow over quickly, that his candidate will win, and that he can pay for all of this. Even if that seems to be the case early in the game, keep checking to be sure. Election Night has an effect on some people that a full moon has on others. The writer had an elderly General Manager one time who had been used to running a nice, quiet FM wall-to-wall music station for many years. Suddenly, his AM license came through for a 1-kW daytimer. Several weeks were spent on the daytimer announcing that there was going to be really big coverage on the FM on election night, and that the station wanted everyone to listen. Apparently he was totally unaware of all this promotion, and as he put on his hat and coat to leave late in the afternoon on Election Day he said, "Now I don't want to hear any of that 'election business.' You understand?"

"But sir," the writer protested.

"No-no-no. I just want music. Just play nice music, and those who want election results can watch TV. Good night."

And out he went, leaving the writer to call up about twenty people he had asked to come up for the evening and to tell them that it was all off. The writer just played music, and he was so embarrassed that he left all the phones off the hook. It was a good lesson. The twenty people would have shown up "free," because several staff members had planned to stage it as a party, with wives helping out with phone calls and refreshments and the rest more or less donating some time just to show the local competitors that the station had something they did not. But he did not even want that.

The moral of the story is this: *check with the boss.* Many of them just become "weird" about Election Night coverage for reasons you will never guess. Give him lists of the people you plan to bring in, the exact details of the kind of programming you would like to have on the air, whether it will be continuous or just a number of "inserts" into the regular programming, and all the details you can think of from charts and adding machines to hotel rooms and remote lines. Then get ready for him to knock half of it down. It may be very uncomfortable for you to keep going into his office and to constantly see your beautiful ideas being "shot down" but by the time Election Night arrives, your understanding of what's going to happen will pretty much match his understanding, and you can concentrate on putting your very best journalistic abilities into what is left of your coverage plans.

Now that you have checked with the boss, what about the actual physical arrangements for the night itself? Well, considering all the modifications and approaches already discussed, here is a generalized "checklist" based on the writers' own Election Night experiences at a number of stations over a period of several years.

## Personnel

You may not have enough people to assign one per job for each of the jobs listed below, but these are some of the things you may want done.

*Producer*—Someone with "News Director" and "Program Director" abilities who is *not* tied to any particular room, microphone, typewriter, or any job or piece of equipment. He can just "rove" and direct things, backstop, switch people from one task to another, and keep things running smoothly from an overall viewpoint.

*Director*—One who is responsible for the overall station sound (and/or picture) for the night itself. Gives the marching orders for the disc jockey to cut out of his music and pick up the network or the news studio. Makes sure newsroom or remote people are "standing by" before switching to them. Gives "wrap-up" signals to one source before cutting away to go to another.

*Anchor Man*—Obvious term. Does not try to give all the details himself, but acts as an M.C., calling on others to present their information. "Presides" over the newscasting and reporting, tying it all together and filling in between individual reports to allow for switching.

*Switching*—TV stations already have engineers who do this but at a radio station a disc jockey can do this. If you are bringing in reports from numerous sources such as network, newsroom, studio, remote, phones, cartridges for commercials and other nonnews sounds, etc., he will have his hands full.

*Wire-Service Editor*—Someone who makes all the trips to the wire machine and sorts out the copy, giving the anchor man and others who will be taking *only what they need* and keeping irrelevant material out of the way.

*Network Monitor*—Someone who holds the advanced schedule put out by whatever network or audio service you subscribe to, checks the cues and the timing, listens for closed-circuit advisories, and works out a signal system with the Director for picking up network feeds. If TV, include remote crew feeds.

*Tape Editor*—A person who is fast with tape machines and cartridges (and a razor blade if necessary). For TV, use him for VTR (Video Tape Recorder) work.

*Film Editor*—Someone who does nothing but receive incoming films (from whatever source, developed or undeveloped) and has them ready with cues and timing for broadcast at the appropriate time. Provides Producer and Director with "menu" of these films, and they, in turn, decide what they want mounted for showing and give the cues to the anchor man. (Obviously, this is for TV only.)

*Recap and Rewrite People*—Occasionally, the anchor man will want to call on someone to tell us where we stand and summarize what has been going on. One or two such people going back and forth between their typewriters and a microphone should be able to handle this. They can get their "source" material from the wire service man, charts in the studio, phone people, etc.

*Phones*—Secretaries with adding machines are good at this. They can take down totals from stringers and total them up if necessary, then pass the phone to the "Tape Editor" (above). If the stringer should call with something big that should go right on the air, "live," then these secretaries should be trained to signal a director. Even though the report is going on the air right from the phone booth, these secretaries should still jot down what the caller is saying. Otherwise, it may be lost the minute he hangs up.

*Public Information*—It is annoying, but people keep calling up the station to ask for information on specific races. If some of your on-the-air people try to handle all of these calls, they may get distracted and the quality of what is going out over the air will suffer. Bring in a couple of workers who would be willing to just look things up for people who are calling in. (Try to arrange for your stringers to call a number other than that used by the general public.)

*Swap Man*—One station very obligingly gave out free "voicers" and audio to other stations around the state who called, but somehow never did manage to get anything from them in return. The station people had simply taken time out from "on-the-air" duties to do these feeds. Set up someone who does not have to worry about going on the air, but who can just sit there and not only give out feeds to other stations but also *receive* a few in return.

*Live-Remote Anchor Man*—If this is a big night for you locally, or if your station covers county or state election races, you may be planning to go on the air "live" from campaign headquarters of the leading candidates. You will need good, articulate newsmen who can work under pressure, not just some ordinary stringer.

*Remote Engineers*—Larger stations have these anyway, but if you are a small operation in which the guy on the air is the guy who is pushing all the buttons, it will not work very well on a night like this. Send a disc jockey along with that newsman who can worry about connecting microphones, riding gain, getting cues over the phone, and all the technical details. This will leave the newsman to concentrate on getting the story straight.

*Stringers*—As said before, there is no "one" way to cover an election, and the number of stringers as well as their qualifications for whatever they are doing is entirely up to you. Usually, they phone in from such places as voting precincts and campaign headquarters, but you will have to fit them to your own situation. Some will be qualified to give voicers or live on-the-air reports right over the phone that last usually from 20 seconds to just under a minute. Others will simply give their information to somebody who writes it down and passes it to the "on-the-air" personnel.

*Studio Engineer*—If you are working at one of these places where disc jockeys with Third-Class FCC Licenses get up while their records are spinning and walk out into the transmitter room to take readings, this would be a good night *not* to do that. Bring in the guy who has the First-Class License and is handy with pliers and a soldering iron if something breaks down. He can be busy checking out remote lines and plugging in extra mikes for studio interviews, etc., a couple of hours before you go on with this extravaganza. If he does not do much else the rest of the night, it is nice to know he is there anyway.

*Political Analysts*—Perhaps there is a former mayor or former congressman around who would not mind coming over to the studio and helping your anchorman with the meaning of the figures as they accumulate. Ask each party to recommend a few "elder statesmen" to you, and give them a call. A panel of two such individuals, one from each major party, would be a valuable addition to your coverage. They know the territory and can spot trends very quickly. They add "believe-ability" to your broadcast because they are the *real thing,* and listeners and voters who elected them to the offices they held a few years back will respect their views.

*Overnight Crew*—If it has been a big election and your regular news team has not only covered their regular shifts for the day but has stayed on to do this Election Night, they will be dragging a bit when they come back in the morning. A couple of college kids who work for a campus station nearby (maybe even one or two of those who worked as "stringers" for you while the "live" election coverage was on the air) can come back into the newsroom, clean the place up, rewrite all the stories with fresh leads for morning, and get all the victory and concession statements mounted and ready with intro's. You will sound so much better in the morning. This crew can also save you a lot of aggravation the next morning by typing up charts of all the results in carbon copies so you can have them next to all the phones. As a matter of fact, one of them might even work something like a 1 a.m. to 9 a.m. shift so that he can answer phones until the secretaries get in at 9 and keep callers off the backs of the newsman and disc jockeys.

*Victory Spotter*—If you have many races going, you might want to have someone who is fast with a phone and a tape recorder and who can chase those victory and concession statements in "hot pursuit," getting them on the phone from candidates, stringers, and other sources, and organizing them on cartridges with cue-sheets and labels so they can be run both for Election Night and the following morning's newscasts.

*Chartmakers and Statisticians*—Whether you are TV or radio, you will want some kind of graphic information on display one way or another. For television, the level of the artwork has to be much more sophisticated. The writer cannot guess how big your TV station is, and whether or not it has an art department. If it does have an art department, and they spend most of their time on commercials, this is one night where their expertise would be helpful. For radio, your anchorman and political analysts, recap and public information people will all want at least a blackboard-and-chalk display of the figures so they will not have to shuffle through piles of wire copy and other papers to recall figures that were broadcast 5 or 10 minutes ago.

Now, you may sit there laughing, wondering if the writer is out of his head for suggesting what appears to be an extravaganza. Your boss may not think you are serious if you suggest some of the job titles to him. Just observe that these jobs are the result of more than a decade of presidential and off-year election coverage with at least half a dozen stations in four states, and that many of the jobs were created at these "morning after" sessions in the boss's office when the station people were wishing they had invented such jobs the night before. You should understand that you will have to suit your own needs by condensing or expanding this job list, adding jobs of your own and eliminating a few of ours. That is why it was said, right at the start, that Election Night is "a different animal."

## Equipment

Again, the size of your station, the size of the election, and all that, will necessitate your own modifications for this list, but here are a few ideas:

*Remote Lines*—Order them early, and even if it costs a few extra dollars, set up a "rehearsal" time a few hours before your coverage so that someone can actually go over to that campaign headquarters and check them out. There is no use of you waiting until 15 minutes before air time to find out that the remote-line operation does not work the way that you thought it would.

*TV Sets and AM-FM Receivers*—In several stations, quite a bit of money was saved by swapping permissions with other stations to tape "off the air." When the Governor appeared to give his victory statement on a TV station in the state capital, the radio station was allowed to tape the audio and use it immediately. This radio station reciprocated by assigning its "Swap Man" to make sure that the TV station got returns from the radio station's city before anyone else. Elsewhere in the congressional district, stations in other towns were coming up with totals much faster than the wire service could ever handle them. The station had an agreement with these stations to just use each other's figures.

*Adding Machines and Calculators*—Maybe a "trade-out" with an office equipment company will yield a dozen or so of these devices to help you keep up with the totals. The writer favors the ones that give a printout of the results on paper, but the little portable calculators will save you a lot of time, too. Sometimes it is handy to have one machine labelled "Republicans" and the other one labelled "Democrats," and switch from machine to machine as the precinct totals come in over the phone from stringers. Then all you have to do is push the "total" button on each machine as the stringer finishes reading. Otherwise, you would have to add up all the precincts for one candidate, clear the machine, and add up all the precincts for the other. You may want to sit down in the studio with your secretaries or with whoever is going to do this, and stage a little "dry run" so they get the hang of operating these mathematical devices before you go on the air. Just to bring the calculators in "cold" on Election Night may result in some fumbling and frustration.

*Portable Radios for Stringers*—Advise all stringers to get hold of a transistor portable with an earphone on it. It makes it so much easier to "cue" people right over the air whenever this is possible. Do not just assume that it is possible, though. Have the person who is going to do the reporting go to the actual location and check the reception right there in the phone booth. Also, be sure he checks it when your station is on low power if you are going to be on low power during the Election Night coverage.

*Cassette Tape Recorders*—Maybe your station has one or two of these for normal news coverage, but there are some sources where you can get a few for one-night coverage like this. Have you ever considered approaching the public schools? You can promise them that you will check and clean all their machines and put fresh batteries in them, etc., or you can just pay a flat rental fee, but probably they have quite a few of these machines that would be sitting idle in classrooms that night. Maybe an area electronics store would be willing to work out a deal that would put a recorder in the hands of each of your stringers for the night.

*Alligator Clips, Phone Rings, etc.*—Long before Election Night itself rolls around, you should check all the attachments and accessories on every recorder that is going to be out in the field for your coverage. In some phone booths, you can unscrew the cap from the mouthpiece. In others, you need one of those "induction coil" rings. You would be wise to have your stringers take their recorders to their Election Night locations and try to feed you some material from the cassettes in advance, just to see if it will work when the real thing is underway.

*Extra Tape and Take-up Reels*—Have your newsroom and control room well stocked with "back-up" supplies in case of breakdowns. There is nothing more frustrating than to see your coverage fall through just because a tape broke.

*Chart Materials, Grease Pencils, etc.*—As you type up new returns or tear a new item from the wire, you will want to mark the time on it, so the anchorman and others can see at a glance which piece of copy has the latest figures. You may want a plastic or formica surface for your charts so that you can use eraseable grease pencils for filling in your numbers. "Magic Markers" are all right for setting up the titles and chart outlines, but they tend to run dry during a show because you are reaching "up" to do your writing, and they do not allow for corrections when reports from precincts prove inaccurate.

## Training

The writer has seen some well-planned Election Nights fizzle simply because all these people who are thrown together for the evening either do not know how to work with the equipment, with each other, or both. Here are some hints to avoid this:

*Everybody-Out-of-Newsroom Training*—Make it clear that anyone who does not show up for some "dry-run" training ahead of the Election Night itself is to simply stay *out of the way* when the night itself comes along. Well-meaning individuals can (like the boss's wife, for example) show up and try to be "helpful" and end up asking on-the-air reporters to please look up figures for some little old lady who is on the phone. She is completely unaware of who is supposed to be doing what, and sort of stumbles through the evening sweetly asking everybody to do the wrong thing at the wrong time. If you have any possible candidates for this role, see if you can anticipate the problem by diplomatically making your needs known several times over a period of a few weeks before Election Night. Then you will not be faced with having to throw them out of the studio in the heat of tension that goes with such productions.

*On-the-Scene Training*—With your stringers, go over that chapter in this book which deals with all the little things that can go wrong with on-the-scene coverage. Then fill them in on your specific needs. Have each one (on his own time, if possible) drop by the place where he will be reporting from and "check it out," as already described.

*"What-if-It-Breaks" Session With Engineer*—There has been more than one Election Night fouled up by last-minute technical failures which could have been circumvented by simply plugging in some alternate equipment. Trouble is, there are certain engineers who want to take the whole console apart and lie there on the control room floor with a soldering iron and all kinds of little transistors and small parts all over the place five minutes before you go on the air. If your station has a "production room," or if the facilities in the newsroom could be used in the event of a failure in the control room, or vice versa, talk over all these alternatives with your station's electronics wizard a few weeks in advance. Go through a "dry run" with a few of your key people on this alternate equipment, so they will be able to switch to it if needed. It could be that something as simple as giving the stringers an alternate phone number to call would solve the problem; or it could be that an unorthodox use of a few patchcords would do it. One station which had a "mobile studio" van which it normally used for county fairs would have it all turned on and all equipment in a state of readiness on Election Night. TV stations often "bypass" the control room by beaming their microwave programs to the transmitter location on some hilltop when they are doing a remote broadcast. See if you can discuss these "bypass" options with your engineer in a calm, reasoned manner ahead of time. This will eliminate the urge to "do him in" with his

soldering gun if he pulls one of these "parts-all-over-the-place" scenes on Election Night.

*Secretaries and Statisticians*—Under "Equipment," it was mentioned that it would be best to do a run-through with the adding machines, and the like. You may want to do this with just the adding-machine personnel, or you may want to bring them into the all-inclusive rehearsal (below).

*"Battle Stations" Rehearsal for Studio Personnel*—Not counting your stringers, who will be out on the road for Election Night, you will want to sit with your complete production cast and go over a "Mock Election Night" rehearsal a few weeks ahead of the real thing. A few weeks are necessary because if anything goes wrong in a "day-before" rehearsal there is usually very little you can do to make appropriate changes. Not only that, but people who are not used to participating in your news operation will have some questions come to their minds a day or two later as their anticipated role "sinks in," or they may be too shy to ask you in front of everybody else at the rehearsal but they will let you know that they are confused later on. It may be just a matter of bringing in some little stationery-equipment item, or of turning a table around in a studio, but a rehearsal a few weeks in advance will pay off in terms of working out all the bugs.

### Post Mortem

The day after it is all over, get up the courage to ask everyone how it went, and mark down all of the things you will want to do better the next time. The writer has always been grateful to News Directors who have done this at stations where he joined the staff a few years later. It certainly gives insight into the local station's own specific needs and saves you from having to fumble all around and "start from scratch" with each new election.

## FCC REGULATIONS AND THE NEWSROOM

Over the years, regulations and policies have developed which prohibit broadcasters from excluding or even limiting certain viewpoints from the airwaves. These include:

► *The Fairness Doctrine,* an FCC policy which originated when broadcasters were allowed to editorialize in
1949. It requires radio and TV stations to afford reasonable
opportunity for the presentation of contrasting viewpoints on
controversial issues of public importance. (Keep in mind
that this policy deals with *issues,* not necessarily with individuals.) When you hear a station inviting replies to its editorials, or when you hear such replies being broadcast, this
is the Fairness Doctrine in operation.

► *Section 315* (of the Communications Act of 1934)
obliges broadcasters to give absolutely equal opportunities
to all legally qualified candidates for any public office.
Stations may not discriminate in advertising rates nor provide free or paid time to any candidate which is restricted
or denied to his opponents. (They need not give time to *any*
candidate if they so choose—just so all candidates are
treated equally.)

(Technically, news programs are exempt from Section 315,
but disgruntled candidates who feel that you are giving unfair
advantage to their opponents in your newscasts may claim that
you are editorializing and challenge you on "Fairness Doctrine"
or other grounds. Section 315 and the Fairness Doctrine are
somewhat related, but they are not exactly the same thing.
Unless you have had some experience involving one or both of
them, it will simply require some memorizing to tell which one
deals with editorializing and issues and which one deals with
political candidates.)

► *Ascertainment:* In order to obtain or renew a broadcast license, a station must conduct studies to "ascertain"
the needs and interests of the town for which it is licensed
as well as for adjacent communities within its listening or
viewing area. The FCC requires such things as a demo-
graphic study of a station's service area, identification of
and consultation with community leaders, and opinion surveys taken from the general public—all to ascertain community needs. Proposals to upgrade and revise these studies
are constantly before Congress and the FCC. Some radio
and TV stations in recent years have found their licenses
challenged (especially at renewal time or when a station is

about to be sold) by groups who feel that their needs have been overlooked. The groups range from racial minorities to parents, equal rights advocates, environmentalists, and others. They challenge stations on issues which include hiring practices, children's programming, and commercial policies, but they have been known to challenge news coverage in a number of cases.

All of these regulatory devices hang over broadcast newsrooms, although you may not feel their presence on a daily basis. As political columnist William F. Buckley once put it, ". . . what you have is a legislative-administrative-judicial thundercloud that now and then looses a bolt of lightning against this tiny little radio station or that mastodonic television network, in punishment for inadequately complying . . ." In broadcast news, then, you *must:*

(1) be aware of how these regulations have affected the station you are working for, and how they may possibly affect it in the future, and

(2) keep yourself up-to-date with current developments in broadcast regulation which may affect your news operation. Read trade journals like *Broadcasting* magazine, *Billboard, Television/Radio Age,* etc.

## INVESTIGATIVE PROJECTS

Just as it was very hard for the writer to predict what kind of election coverage you will face, so it becomes quite difficult to be all that accurate in suggesting *appropriate* questions for politicians and government officials in your area. Some of the reasons are obvious:

▶ Issues come and go in different parts of the country. Problems which were resolved years ago in one town may be the "wave of the future" in another. As you glance at this list, you will find questions which seem so outdated that people in your town would be amused if you were to go around asking them. On the other hand, you may find a few issues here that have not even come up yet in your town, or some which, with a little rewording, can be brought up to date. Cable TV and use of computers by municipal governments are just two examples. Some towns have had both for years, others will take years to get around to either one.

▶ Not all states grant the same powers to their municipalities. In one state, a city council may pass ordinances on weights and measures while in the very next state this power is reserved for the county or the state government. Services which may be provided by towns in one state are provided only by counties in another. You will have to be sure the questions fit the level of government that you are dealing with, according to the ground rules in your own state.

▶ There is always the "rural-versus-urban" problem. Questions aimed at a county agricultural agent may seem amusing to you if you are working in a big city newsroom, and questions about the fine points of city traffic engineering or zoning for industry may be equally "oddball" if you are not near a city of any significant size.

▶ Life styles which predominate in one part of the country are ignored, ridiculed, or frowned-upon elsewhere. Some of these queries will be just too "corny" or "homespun" in your part of the country, while others may be just too sophisticated and will go right over the heads of most of your listeners or the officials you will be interviewing.

With these limitations in mind, then, here is a list in which the questions are broken down into a number of categories:

(A) *Services* normally provided by a municipality.

(B) *Personnel:* the lives of people in government and politics.

(C) *Economy:* the economic forces at work in a community and how the government attempts to deal with them.

(D) *Proposed legislation:* questions mostly applicable to city ordinances, but which in your area may be more appropriate for county or state legislators.

(E) *Courts:* effects of noncriminal court activity on the community, such as probate, divorce, etc.

(F) *Regulatory powers:* Where ordinances or laws are already on the books, are they being properly enforced?

(G) *Opinion:* what the public thinks about its government. Many of these questions are also applicable for use with legislators under the "proposed legislation" category.

(H) *Politics:* questions dealing with political parties, candidates, and elections.

(I) *State and Federal:* questions which seem least applicable to municipal and county situations.

## (A) Services

1. What new services does your community provide which were not called for in the town budgets of five, ten, or twenty years ago? What led to their inclusion? What new functions can the local government expect to assume in the future?

2. How has technology helped local government? Are there computers at city hall where there were none a decade ago? Are the schools, the police station, or other agencies using closed-circuit TV?

3. Has the town's library kept pace with the times? Do they have microfilm, microfiche, or other microtext materials? Photocopy machines? Can you borrow records, cassette tape recorders, video tape recorders, or 8-track stereo cartridges? What are some of their problems? Recent accomplishments? Plans?

4. How are textbooks selected in local schools? Does the state mandate or recommend certain texts? What criteria do local board members use when evaluating proposed purchases of new books? Has there ever been a book-banning controversy locally? Are there ground rules for avoiding such controversies?

5. Are food stamps equitably distributed in your area? Do you ever hear claims of abuses, and, if you do, how many of them are proven?

6. How is the municipal water supply? Have you heard any comments about service, rates, quality of the water, etc.? Are there plans for expansion?

7. Is the city keeping up with the removal of dead and diseased trees, or do some of these pose a threat to pedestrians and traffic passing by them?

8. What are some of the activities of the local park superintendent in connection with the city's lawns and shrubs? Has he any tips for homeowners on the subject? Does the park superintendent or highway department have any program to clear weeds that may cause widespread allergy problems in the area? What new conservation laws have changed methods used by local governments in dealing with tree removal, dredging or rerouting of streams, filling-in of swamps, etc.?

9. In the City Clerk's office, you can possibly find an expert who can tell you some of the new trends in "vital statistics" locally. Have there been any significant changes in the local birth rates, death rates, marriages, etc.? Can this person make any population projections for your town ten years from now? How will these figures affect the local job market? School construction?

10. Would a regularly scheduled discussion of upcoming "agenda" items for the city council be helpful to your listeners? Perhaps you can schedule councilmen on a rotating basis to comment on their views of proposals before the council.

11. What is the role of city-owned cars in your town? Are they only to be taken for certain purposes, or are they assigned to individuals for whatever needs they may have? Do there seem to be any abuses of the system?

12. How up-to-date is traffic engineering in your city? Are the traffic lights computer-programmed to take a large crowd quickly away from a stadium after a ballgame, or to handle differing patterns as commuters come into town in the morning and leave at night? Do motorists find themselves waiting for a red light just outside an empty shopping center on a Sunday or in the wee hours of the morning? Are regulatory and warning signs up to the latest national standards, or are they the same ones that were erected twenty years ago? Are there special turning lanes at in-

tersections, or do bottlenecks develop? Does your city have a professional traffic engineer, or is this function simply handled by some member of the police force?

13. How reliable are roads and bridges in your area? Is there a testing program regularly carried out to prevent bridges from collapsing through neglect? What are the criteria for making up the road repair schedule? Any areas the public feels are neglected? How effective is local government in filling "potholes" after winter freeze-and-thaw damage? (In some stations, the "Pothole Patrol" keeps local highway crews on the go.)

14. Has local government kept pace with the needs for land-acquisition for schools, parks and public buildings? Who's the real estate "expert" in local government, and what are his qualifications? How have acreage costs gone up in your area over the years? What, if anything, are local officials doing to anticipate future needs? Any applications filed with state or federal governments for "open space" land? If not, why not?

15. Does a school bond issue usually cause controversy in your town? Does the Board of Education just come up with plans building-by-building when the pressure of over-crowding gets to be too much to ignore, or do they have a master plan based on long-range projections? Have these long-range projections changed recently as the national birth rate declines and some communities find themselves selling unwanted schools?

16. What "incentive" plans, if any, do local government agencies have for their employees to contribute ideas that will cut costs or improve services? Are there cash awards, or are town employees better off keeping their mouths shut? Do the mayor, the school superintendent, and other key administrators encourage suggestions, or is there a "paranoid" reaction when somebody tries to tell them what to do? (*Document* any accusations and *use quotes* carefully. This can be a sensitive area, and an administrator who does not want to hear from his subordinates will not want to hear from *you,* either!)

17. What is the role of "consultants" in local government? Are the people being hired legitimate specialists providing services which the town must "import" or are they just undercover operators who cannot stand the glare of public scrutiny as regular employees? Exactly what have they done for your town lately? Is there some qualified and un-biased source who can evaluate these services for you? Do retired City Hall employees manage to stay on the pay-roll as consultants, and if so, is the city getting its money's worth or are there indications of "featherbedding"?

18. Is public transportation subsidized in your area? Should it be? Does your town have any arrangements with adjacent towns to share costs of a bus system or subway line? Have they taken advantage of federal transportation grants for this purpose? Are the elderly or the poor stranded in your city where mass transit used to operate but has disappeared?

19. What services are the state and federal governments pro-viding in your area? Are there too many strings attached to these programs? Would more local control improve the programs, or would it simply jeopardize the source of the funds?

20. Should the city become more active in consumer affairs? Is just the Chamber of Commerce or even the Better Busi-ness Bureau enough? If the city or county does have an office of consumer affairs, what have been some of its activities? Do officials there feel that present legislation has enough "teeth" in it, or are there some weak areas?

21. What about the salaries of your local officials? Do a survey of salaries for positions at City Hall and compare them with those in nearby towns of comparable size. Is your town paying too much or too little?

22. Many towns have consolidated such services as schools, sewerage and disposal plants, animal shelters, etc., with other towns. What services in your town might be con-solidated with those of other towns, and what are the ad-vantages and disadvantages?

23. Can we get more mileage out of schools by using them year-around or by scheduling alternate activities in them? For example, would the public be willing to pay for a swimming pool at the high school by opening it for a fee on Sundays, or to pay for TV equipment for closed-circuit instruction by renting studios and equipment to groups who want to produce public programs for the local cable?

24. Are local government buildings and facilities modern and functional, or are they old and obsolete? How old is the city hall, the library, the police station, firehouses, schools, etc.? Have architects given the town a pretty good deal on new buildings lately, or have there been some "bugs" the minute officials move in? (Be careful with accusations!)

25. Is there "duplication" in local government? Do the building and health inspectors seem to be doing the same job twice when they take a look at a new house, a restaurant, or whatever? Are functions of city government too close to those of county government, and is there room for elimination of overlapping jurisdiction?

26. Is the office of "Civil Defense" or "Civilian Preparedness" still strongly supported in your area? When is the last time they were called out to handle a real emergency? Are their numbers dwindling? Are these people volunteers, or are some or all of them on the local payroll?

27. Does the city seem to take advantage of opportunities for summer recreation programs, adult education, etc., or do you often hear the complaint that there is "nothing to do" for youth or for senior citizens or some segment of the population?

#### (B) Personnel

1. *Appointed officials:* How much does the public know about some of the key people in local government who do not run for election to their jobs? Some nice biographical and noncontroversial sketches of these people and their roles in government would be a good long-range educational project. These can be used for those "special reports" and other journalistic projects which are "nonevent"

in nature. Do not wait for some official to become involved in controversy or scandal before you cover him.

2. *People in politics:* Who are the "king-makers" behind the candidates? How about biographical sketches on the people who serve on the Democratic and Republican Town Committees, or whatever local units of each party exist? How do their policy decisions as party leaders affect those of their elected officials?

3. *Interesting jobs:* Who issues the marriage licenses in your town? Does this person have some interesting anecdotes about recent trends, Valentine's Day, etc.?

4. *United Way, Red Cross, and other leading civic groups:* Do the leaders of these groups seem to coincide with the leaders in government, business, political parties, and elsewhere in the community? How do they view themselves and each other? How do others view them? What is the local definition of an "activist?" Is your town oriented toward social services and activities, or are activists considered "radicals" by a conservative-minded town?

5. *Women in government:* Are they occupying key roles now, or are they still confined to secretarial, clerical, and subordinate jobs? Do some offices appear to have a "token" woman? (Be careful; document or quote all accusations.)

6. *Women who work behind bars:* What are some of the stories that female deputy sheriffs, wardens, matrons, and others who work at detention facilities have to tell? Is there an increasing professionalism among their ranks, such as with nurses, or do these people feel they are in "dead-end" jobs compared with their male counterparts?

7. *Moonlighting:* How many city employees are moonlighting? What are the regulations about holding other jobs? Do city employees view these regulations as too restrictive? Do taxpayers view them as too liberal?

8. *Labor and City Hall:* Have there been any problems with any organizations representing government employees lately? What are the issues? (Do you keep a newsroom file on all contract deadlines and watch for the start of bargain-

ing sessions?) Who does the bargaining for each side? Except when negotiations themselves are underway and the strategy is to keep things confidential, can you get someone from each employee group to talk about the *general* professional goals of his organization and what his group does for its members?

9. *Letters to government officials:* This question can be used for councilmen, mayors, . . ., right on up to Congressmen and Senators. What are the people asking for? Do the demands seem to fit the office to which they are addressed, or are there some indications that the public is not familiar with the functions of certain officials? What are the topics covered by most of the requests?

10. *Jaycees, service clubs, and other civic groups:* What is the effect of their activities on government? Do they sometimes act as "sparkplugs" for new programs at City Hall, such as traffic safety, beautification and clean-up programs, etc.? Does local government "pick up" on any of these programs, or do these groups simply continue them as a public service?

11. *Wives of government leaders and political candidates:* What role does the wife play in the life of a leading government official? Is she active in civic affairs, busy raising a family of young children, working in some profession? (Do it the other way around for husbands of women who are prominent in government or politics.)

12. *Hobbies, vacations, and workloads:* Are some of your local officials good golfers, athletes, antique auto buffs, fishermen? Are there some who "skip" vacations to devote time to the public office they hold? Do some of them work 70- to 80-hour weeks, giving up nights, Sundays, and holidays to their jobs? What effect does this workload have on their family lives?

13. *Women in the work force:* Check your local office of the state employment agency. How has the role of women in local commerce and industry changed in recent years? Are there more women professionals in areas *other* than the standard teaching and nursing of years ago? What are

some of them? Can you get interviews with some of the individuals involved?

14. *Patronage jobs:* Does the "victor" still claim the "spoils" at your local city hall, or are most government employees on a civil service or similar basis? What new jobs were added to the payroll when the present administration took office? What hours do these individuals work, and what specific duties do they perform? Which jobs will disappear if the incumbents lose the next election? Who says so, and what evidence does he back it up with?

15. *Governmental representation:* Who is your State Senator? Stand in a shopping center and ask people coming out of the various stores who their State Senators and Representatives are. Many will name Congressmen or United States Senators, others will draw a complete blank. Chances are, very few people in town know who makes up the laws that govern their lives at the state level. A good survey on your part would increase public awareness of this problem.

16. *Press conferences:* Some presidents of the U.S. have held varying numbers of press conferences over the years, but should the mayor or county executive hold them? If he does hold some, should he hold more, or are the present ones just for "show"?

17. *Public service:* Are politicians serving the public or themselves? Perhaps it would be better not to use specific names, but simply to get a "survey" reading on how the public feels about its government officials at local, county, and state levels. See if sentiment indicates that leaders of government in your area are too ambitious, greedy for power, money-hungry, etc., or whether they seem, in the eyes of a significant number of people, to be putting the needs of the public above their own personal desires. If there is a college or professional survey organization nearby, get some help on how to handle the statistics and the questions properly. Sloppy questions and procedures here can invalidate your results and leave *you* with a credibility gap.

## (C) Economy

1. What are the effects of inflation, recession, or other current trends in the national economy upon local businesses, and what is local, county, or state government doing to offset them, if anything? Are the forces upon your local economy the same as those elsewhere in the country, or have you suffered significant setbacks such as the closing of a major plant or store?

2. Go to your nearest office of the State Employment Service and find out what the local jobless rate is. This statistic might be available for just a phone call each month, and could be used as the basis for a story if you want to get reactions from local businessmen and politicians.

3. What special-interest groups have an effect on your local economy, and what role does government play in helping them or restricting them? For example: veterans, tourists, college students, military personnel from nearby bases, welfare cases, etc.

4. How is the homebuilding-and-construction industry lately? Are realtors, lawyers, bankers, and others optimistic? If there are problems, can state, county, or local governments do anything about them without waiting for the federal government to make adjustments in lending rates, etc.? What is the situation compared with last month? Last year?

5. Are there some special facilities in town that bring in a great deal of tax money, such as stadiums, concert halls, and other tourist and spectator attractions? What about that race track just outside of town? Is it contributing to the city's tax base?

6. Are there any "promotors" on the city council looking for a semipro sports team or other attraction to bring to town as an opportunity to bring in more income? Is there close cooperation between the city council and the local chamber of commerce? Would they consider building a stadium or arena to attract such groups? Are cultural endeavors encouraged, or does everyone drive to some other town for entertainment?

7. Check out some of the major economic indicators in your community: welfare caseloads, building permits, personal bankruptcy cases, and other measures recommended by area government and business leaders, and see if your station cannot take some leadership in devising a monthly or even weekly economic "health report" that your listeners would come to depend upon. Work closely with bankers and others who are good at interpreting such figures, and perhaps for the first month or two just "dry run" the figures by taking your story to these experts and see if they would agree with your analysis. Once this measure is established and accepted, you can make up a list of officials at various levels of government who are supposed to be *doing* something about these figures and ask them for their reactions. Be sure you give enough attention to the "positive" side of the story, so that these people will not feel that you are just looking for scandal and sensationalism when you call.

8. Has the local "Grand List" of real estate assessments become outdated? Are homeowners in one part of town being charged unfair rates because of obsolete evaluation figures? When was the last reassessment in town? Have the city's ways of raising income kept up with the times? Are they fair to retired people and others on fixed incomes? Can you suggest any new sources?

9. What do the people feel about the local tax structure? Compare real estate taxes with such things as sales, income, and motor vehicle taxes. Are basic changes in order? At what level: municipal, county, or state?

## (D) Legislative Proposals

1. What local measures are instituted when a fuel shortage comes along for gasoline or heating oil? Does the city council have any say over these matters, or is everything resolved by some agency in the state capital? Has an odd-even numbering system worked in your area? Should such systems be voluntary or mandatory? Who issues the orders in your town? Does he or she expect any problems in the near future? (Work up a list of oil company spokesmen in

your part of the country. Ask around at the gas stations and heating oil distributors in your area, and have names and phone numbers all ready to go when stories like this appear on the horizon.)

2.  Pollution, noise abatement, and zoning: How are the controls in your area? Are there sources of pollution and noise in town which seem to go unregulated? Who can do anything about them? Does your town have outdated "nuisance" or "disturbing the peace" ordinances, or are the noise abatement statutes based on an objective, scientific measurement such as decibels at a certain distance? What devices measure air pollution in your town, and what laws are on the books for dealing with sources of such pollution? If your town has neither the measuring devices nor the laws for either problem, is anyone concerned about these problems? At what level should legislation be introduced? Could it be that the state already has laws on the books permitting towns to control these problems, but your town just has not gotten around to buying any devices for measurement and enforcement? Would zoning changes or city ordinances help?

3.  Is cable television coming to town? What do the city fathers know about dealing with outlets of mass communication, if anything? Will there be a citizens advisory board ready to participate in local regulation of public, educational, and municipal channels, or will the local people leave it all up to the state and the FCC? What is going to be on the municipal channel and on the school channel? Or will these channels remain blank for the first year or two as they have in many communities where cable operations have begun? Are the local councilmen, school board members, and others reluctant to have their meetings televised? Why?

4.  Have electric and other utility rates gone up sharply in recent months? Is this controlled by your municipality, or is it in the hands of a state public utilities commission? When political candidates go around promising to "do something" about it, ask them exactly what they will do.

5. With recent Supreme Court decisions tossing the ball on morality and obscenity into the hands of local government, what guidelines exist in your area to help enforce any kind of regulation of smut and of flesh films? Would a book dealer or movie operator be able to get his conviction easily overturned in your town because local officials have failed to legally define obscenity within Supreme Court guidelines? Who is supposed to bring legislation up to date in your area, and what moves have been made?

6. Are the driving and motor vehicle laws outdated in your area? Should drivers be reexamined with road tests and eye tests, or should they just be allowed to renew licenses by mail? What are the existing statutes in your state? Do they need revision?

7. What about overnight parking in your town? Are there some abuses? Are present ordinances too strict or too liberal?

8. Do "closing hour" laws for liquor stores and bars seem outdated in your area? Are other businesses subject to regulation of their hours or even days to conduct business? What about Sunday "blue" laws? To whom would you go for changes in these laws: the city council or state legislature?

9. Should "new cities" be created by government planning bodies in state or county legislatures? How have such developments worked out in other areas? Would this be preferable to just "random" growth of housing developments in the outskirts of present towns? Have new housing developments and shopping centers outside the city limits had a detrimental effect on government and business inside the city? What can be done about it?

10. City Charter: Is the document that structures your local government more than fifty years old? Is it a crazy quilt of amendments, or has it been replaced recently? How do local officials and the public in general feel about the way it is working? Do they feel there are too many departments and commissions, or not enough? What would it take to get a new charter drawn up and approved? Is there any

sentiment in favor of such a change, or are local folks content to "let it be"?

## (E) Courts

1. Is probation working in your area, or are potentially dangerous criminals being released to roam the streets rather than rehabilitated as they should be? Interview the probation officer at your nearest courthouse and see if present programs are successful or if he would recommend any changes. See how others view the program.

2. Have alimony and child support laws kept up with inflation and other economic factors in your area, or are they excessively low or even too high? What new legislation is needed in this area and in divorce laws in general?

3. How about the probate decisions lately? How much is the average estate worth in your town? Are there any "favorite" charitable or other institutions getting large bequests? Have there been unusual circumstances lately, like large fortunes waiting for missing heirs, no wills, or cats and dogs inheriting estates?

4. Are some of the newer laws "standing up" in court? Check for cases where there may be "loopholes" in recent laws on obscenity (see previous section on legislation), ecology, noise and pollution abatement, etc. Have these defendants managed to win acquittal on "constitutional" grounds or on flaws in the enforcement procedure?

## (F) Regulatory Powers

1. How have the housing and construction regulations been enforced lately? Follow a building inspector around to see if there have been some new problems recently which did not occur several years ago. Is this because of new legislation and tighter regulation, or is it because of substandard practices recently? Do these officials and do the building contractors see present laws as weak, satisfactory, or too tight? Why?

2. What about the weights-and-measures inspections in your area? Have there been any shady business practices occurring with some regularity that consumers should know

about? How often are gasoline pumps, scales, and other measuring devices checked in your area, and by whom?

3. Is health inspection in your local restaurants, schools, and other eating places just a "cozy" affair where no one's license is ever challenged, or have there been any cases recently where inspectors have had to warn or otherwise enforce regulations? What other areas besides restaurants have needed attention from the health inspector? What are some of the problems? How can the public help?

4. Have pesticides been a problem in your area? What about the use of detergents? Are local health authorities concerned about the effects of chemicals upon local crops, streams, parks, trees, etc.? Whatever happened to the tree-spraying program carried out by the city? Is it still being carried on, and, if so, has there been a change in the chemicals used?

5. Do zoning laws in your area keep industry and residential parts of town adequately separated? Do you think the Zoning Board of Appeals has been too lenient in granting variances to businesses who want to expand? Do most zoning decisions "stick," or is there a great volume of "appeal" activity?

6. Does your city have a problem with abandoned junk cars or appliances? Who is supposed to be enforcing the laws about these things, and what are they doing to keep up with the problem? What about junkyards? Do they appear to be properly regulated? Have any recycling plants in your area been the subject of any controversy regarding their adherence to zoning or other regulations?

7. Are there employers in the area who appear to be "skimping" or cutting corners with the wage and hours laws? Whose job is it to see that these laws are enforced? Is there some kind of inspection carried on, or does this official wait for "complaints" to reach his office?

## (G) Opinion

1. What do local residents think should be done about fuel shortages? Are the regulations currently or most recently

put into effect fair and equitable? What changes do they feel should be made in the laws?

2. Have you heard any complaints about the housing short-age or the inability of people to get mortgages? What do they think should be done about it?

3. Some cities have tried to reduce the number of violent crimes by offering to *buy* illegal guns. If this has been started in your area, how has it worked? If it has not been started, is there any sentiment in favor of it, or do local people and government leaders seem opposed? Why?

4. What do local people feel about city employees "moon-lighting"? Do their opinions seem to vary with the type of city employee doing the moonlighting, such as policemen, teachers, others?

5. Have you heard any complaints from a certain neighbor-hood about unfair real estate assessments? Do they feel their taxes are too high compared with those in other parts of town? What do they feel should be done about it?

6. Does the annual report (or the annual budget proposal) touch off a lot of controversy in town? What are some of the most sensitive areas? What are some of the most inter-esting proposals?

7. What do local voters list as their top priorities for political candidates? Honesty? Experience? Youth and vigor? May-be you can set up a checklist of the most-named qualities of a candidate, and see which ones are the favorites.

8. Is the local citizenry satisfied with the closing hours for bars, package stores, and other businesses? Would a survey on reform of Sunday blue laws be worthwhile in your town?

9. How do local citizens see their municipal charter? Have you heard any complaints about "bureaucracy" at City Hall? Can you find any sentiment in favor of an ombudsman?

**(H) Politics**

1. Survey the number of registered voters in town and com-pare it with the number of estimated "eligible" residents

who are not registered. Find out from elections officials what the major reasons are for such apathy. Have any organizations carried on "register" or "get-out-the-vote" campaigns recently? How successful were they? What were some of the problems encountered?

2. How much demand is there for absentee ballots in your town? Who seems to apply in greater numbers: servicemen, students, others? What is done to inform local residents of their rights in regard to absentee ballots? (Or are officials reluctant to "promote" such rights?)

3. What special preparations go on at the local elections board when elections are drawing near? Is there a large expenditure for repair and inspection of voting machines? Does the registrar's office run extra shifts to handle added registration hours, ballot preparation, election night returns, etc., or do the hours remain the same? How many extra people are hired to be in charge of the polls? How much does an election cost in your town? Do presidential elections cost more because of heavy turnout?

4. As an election approaches, can you find local people who have the same last names as some of the leading candidates? Do they get kidded about it? Is there someone whose last name is the same as the governor, a U.S. Senator, the President? How does it feel? Occasionally, you may find someone whose phone number is similar to that of a Congressman or even the White House or the Governor's Mansion. They have interesting stories to tell about some of the phone calls they get when people dial the wrong area code or miss the correct number by one digit.

5. If there is a political convention coming up, chances are you can find some local people who are delegates. Not only can you ask these people for their reactions before and after they attend such a convention, but you might even get one or two of them to be free "stringers" for you just by picking up the collect phone calls from the convention.

6. As major political campaigns get underway, there are normally some books published dealing with issues or

candidates aimed at convincing the "silent majority" of voters that one candidate or the other is an extremist or a conspirator of some sort. Such books hint at scandal in the lives of candidates, or try to erode support through a "guilt-by-association" effort. Check with local bookstores and see what kinds of political books are selling lately—before, during, and after election campaigns. In the 1960's, Kennedy biographies sold well. In the early 70's, books about Watergate were bestsellers. What are some of the new ones? Why?

7. What is the influence of labor on politics in your local area? Do major unions have the power to "make" or "break" a candidate with their endorsement? In between elections, are unions or professional organizations able to get major concessions from City Hall, the school board, or other public agencies and institutions?

**(1) State and Federal**

1. Would you advocate a federal (or state) Department of Consumers at cabinet level? If not, why not? What are some of the major areas you feel need attention from such a department?

2. The 55-mph speed limit on our nation's highways significantly reduced traffic deaths during the energy crisis in the early '70's. What other measures would you recommend?

3. Do you feel that federal antipoverty, urban renewal, and legal aid services programs have caused more legislative and legal problems than they have solved? What are some solutions for this?

4. What is the latest on "privacy" legislation? Are electronic surveillance, credit company ratings, secret dossiers, income tax records, and other invasions of privacy still proving to be sources of irritation to the average citizen?

5. Is the grand jury system outmoded because of all the leaks in recent years? If not, how would you prevent leaks? If so, what would you propose as an alternative?

6. What are some of the new proposals in legislation for aviation, railroad laws, maritime laws? Will government be

called upon to increase its subsidies of these modes of transportation? Where will the money come from?

7. How about new medical, business, and tax laws? What are some of the issues developing in this legislative session?

8. Congressmen and other legislators: What committee are you on? Can you tell us about some of the major pieces of legislation before this committee?

9. What effects do the federal and state payrolls have on your local community? Is there a large military base or other state or federal government institution near your town? What would be the effect of a cutback in personnel or a shutdown of this facility? Get figures on total payroll and compare them with those of local industries and businesses in the private sector.

10. Sometimes the Internal Revenue Service has refund checks coming to people but cannot find them. Check with your nearest IRS office and find out about this and other interesting angles in the process of collecting taxes in your area.

## IN-CLASS AND HOMEWORK ASSIGNMENTS

1. The author mentions a number of problems involved in giving adequate coverage to City Hall, and describes several ways of dealing with them. Assume that you are the News Director of a local station in this area (your teacher may assign a specific station and town), and describe how you would deal with the potential problems discussed in this chapter.

2. In the section "Nobody Here But Us Chickens" there is a list of tactics purportedly used by government officials to control the news by concealing or distorting the truth. Do you feel that such a list is exaggerated? Tell why or why not, and cite specific examples.

3. Describe what steps you would take to be sure that your professional conduct would not be questioned as you begin a new assignment to cover your state legislature.

4. What directories, schedules, and other material are available to help journalists cover units of government in your area? (Specific governmental units such as City Hall, the county building, etc., may be assigned by your teacher.)

5. What are some of the pressures that build up upon a newsroom during an election campaign, and what are some of the ways to deal with them?

6. The author claims that station managers "just turn weird" about Election Night coverage. What are some of the ways in which he says this occurs, and what are some suggestions for handling these situations?

7. Pretend that you are News Director of a station (which may be assigned by your teacher) as Election Night approaches. Based on the needs of the station itself, the community, and the size of the election, draw up a list of the personnel and equipment you will need for the occasion and define the role of each. (Unless your teacher directs otherwise, assume that it is a Presidential election.)

8. What are some of the jobs for Election Night coverage listed by the author that you disagree with? Why do you think these positions are not needed?

# Chapter 9

# The Style of the Newscast

A couple of stations were battling it out a few years ago. They were having a classic "ratings fight" in which each one wanted to be known as "Number One" in town. Posters adorned the studio walls, telling the disc jockeys it was a matter of life or death. There were contests, slogans, jingles, billboards, bumper stickers, . . . the works. The news department was caught up in it, too.

▶ Electronic fanfares would tell each station's audience that they were getting it "first, fast, and furious," or whatever.

▶ Hardly a sparrow could fall anywhere in town without "mobile units" with big call letters on the doors and their lights flashing appearing instantly on the scene.

▶ Politicians ranging from city council members and school board members to mayors and congressmen would be awakened before dawn and asked to make statements to tape recorders which were already rolling as they picked up their phones. Statements? About what? "Anything, baby, we just need the 'actualities.' "

▶ As each newscast drew to a close, an echo-chamber introduction would precede a shortened repeat of the "Big-W Big-Story of the Hour," and the newscaster would

Photo by Chip Hires.

shout his last one-liner almost like a battle cry as the disc jockey started the next record in the background.

The pressure was on and you knew it. If the competition had a story that you did not have, you could expect the News Director to call up and "chew you out" for not being first-first-first. But then, one day, one of the stations leaned a little bit too far.

A bank had been robbed, and both the state and local police radios crackled with cryptic messages about the hunt for the suspects. It began to sound as though one of the patrol cars might have come upon some significant clue. Maybe it was the abandoned getaway car. It was hard to tell. Then, a voice slowly intoned: "Edgar L. Greene, 217 South Orange Street, white male, age 31, five-foot-ten, 182 pounds." (All the information is changed here.) With the speed of lightning, one of the stations interrupted—fanfare and all—and announced that Edgar Greene had been apprehended as the holdup suspect. The station ran the same information in their "top story" for the next newscast a short while later.

The trouble was that Edgar Greene had nothing to do with any bank holdup at all. His name had been called in to headquarters by a patrolman who was working on some other case. It may even have been a complaint filed by Edgar Greene himself. The patrolman's voice might have sounded just like that of one of his colleagues somewhere else in town who was involved in the hunt for the holdup suspect; who can say for sure? What *can* be said for sure is that all the style in the world, all the fanfares, echo chambers, on-the-scene actualities, and all the best efforts of newsmen for years to come would not have prevented Edgar L. Greene from suing that station right out of business if he had been aware of the broadcast and had chosen to take action. Not only could Greene have all but ended the station's broadcast career, but the FCC could have penalized it quite heavily for taking something right off the police monitor and putting it directly on the air. Apparently, in this case, which the writer heard from a friend who worked at one of the stations, nothing more ever came of it. But just imagining what *might* have happened is enough to make you think twice about being first-first-first.

## THIS CHAPTER IS RATED "X"

Why start a chapter on "style" with a story like this? If you have not already guessed, here is why: It is because all the style in the world will never make up for *accuracy.* That is why this chapter is "rated X." You should not be reading it if you have not covered some of the more basic material on how to just get the facts *straight* before you begin to embellish them.

Lack of correct information, as in the example just given, is not the only cause for the erosion of accuracy on many stations. Well-informed newscasters working at a leisurely pace in stations where there is no pressure to be "first" can often distort stories by being too "clever." One New York station had two newscasters who kept slipping in their views on the Vietnam War in the early 1970's. The nation had grown tired of the war, and you may recall that there were many protest demonstrations. One newscaster very subtly managed to stigmatize all peace demonstrators by making them synonymous with hippies and by implying through cleverly worded phrases that they needed haircuts, a bath, or both. The other newscaster held pretty much the opposite view, politically, and would imply that the military establishment took a calloused view of the war by starting his stories with phrases like: "On the Indochina 'killing ground' today, . . ." Although the views of these two newscasters tended to balance each other, both men were supposed to be doing just straight news, not commentary, and enough listeners began to write and phone the station to get the distortions halted.

Style, then, is not only *gathering* the correct facts but also *presenting* them in a way that does not distort or abuse them in any manner. Now that you are aware of these limitations, and of the basic, underlying premises for them, the "mechanics" of it all can be discussed.

## "SHOW AND TELL": A CONVERSATIONAL APPROACH

Even as an elementary school pupil, you could always tell when someone was reading to you from a book and when someone was just telling you something in his own words. It you were to pick up a newspaper even today and begin reading it aloud to someone else, that person would probably be able to tell pretty quickly that you were reading—not telling—the story. What your listeners would like you to do on radio and TV is to "tell" the story rather than just "read" it. The news you hear when you turn the radio on is usually more like a normal conversation than the news you find printed in a newspaper. It is written for the ear, even on television. Although TV can reinforce what is being "told" with pictures, maps, and charts, it does not attempt to be a newspaper. Little or no actual "reading" is involved when you are watching TV, and none at all is involved with radio. If you do not want to confuse, mislead, or bore your audience, you have to be pretty good at the old game of "Show and Tell."

Since people generally speak more informally than they write, newscasts usually sound more informal than stories carried in the newspapers. It is, however, possible to carry the informality too far. A newscaster who does not sound knowledgeable, authoritative, clear, and accurate can lose the confidence of his audience pretty quickly. You can throw in slang, clichés, colloquialisms, and all kinds of gimmicks in an attempt to be informal, but you just may wind up being *too* informal. You have to know where to stop.

What is it about a newspaper that makes it sound more formal? Why cannot newspapers "tell" their stories, too, just like the broadcasters? Well, just start with things like abbreviations, headlines, statistics, and information in the form of long "lists." These are much harder to get across to people who are listening rather than reading. Things like connecting a speaker with his quotation can just be done with quotation marks in a newspaper, but how do you put quotation marks on the radio? It is tricky at first, but there are ways to do it. In fact, there are some things that broadcasters can do that the newspapers cannot do. For one thing, because you are talking to your listener in a conversational tone of voice, you have a chance to get much closer to him than does the writer of a newspaper story. With the right choice of words and the right tone of voice, you can make him "feel" it when a story is funny, tragic, urgent, exciting, or whatever. He can identify more closely with the people in your stories, feeling sorry for them, disagreeing with them, and so on, frequently to a greater degree than he can with the print media. This is especially true when he hears their voices on tape, and even more so when he can see their facial expressions on film.

Since you are dealing heavily with feelings and speaking more informally, you can use these factors to be more *interesting.* This is important in the news business. The newspaper people may look down their journalistic noses at you when you start talking about being "interesting," but they forget that your listeners or viewers cannot turn the page. What they *can* turn is that dial! If you are bored with an article in one newspaper, you do not go out and buy another newspaper. Your eyes just shift to something else on that page or over on the next page. If you get bored with what is coming out of your radio, what do you do? You just reach out a little finger and push a button. People can read newspapers at different speeds—browsing, skimming, turning back, etc., but they just cannot do that with radio or television. Broadcasters not only have to keep them all together; broadcasters have to keep them *interested.* You could have all the facts right there, just like your colleague on the newspaper, but from a dollars-and-cents standpoint, turning to another page and turning to another station are not the same thing. Just the way you are telling the story is also your way of holding your audience or causing them to turn to another station. Learning to be a good broadcast writer is somewhat like learning to be a good wrestler—you have to know all the basic "holds."

## SEPARATING THE JOURNALISTS FROM THE "RIP-AND-READERS"

One of the most fascinating things in the newsroom when a Cub Scout Den or Brownie Troop comes in for a tour of the facilities is that wire service machine over in the corner. The children just cannot take their eyes off it. They all go home clutching their little pieces of wire service copy salvaged from your newsroom trash barrel. That AP or UPI wire has a mesmerizing effect.

Unfortunately, it has a mesmerizing effect on some of the people who work there, too. The machine just keeps grinding out stories day and night, and the rhythm of the keys clickety-clacking on the endless paper provides an atmosphere in which many individuals come to believe they are really top newscasters just because they can read it. Some of them will go on believing it for decades, at stations large and small. Oh yes, they have called up the state troopers and the local desk sergeants, and they have been writing up their own local stories from these calls for years. Some of them can even weed out the police jargon in the way which was shown in the chapter on police coverage, but this is not the kind of stuff that is going to win the Pulitzer Prize.

So far, the discussion has been about gathering and presenting facts correctly—without distortion—and about making it interesting and saying it all in a conversational manner, and, noting that, you must be knowledgeable, authoritative, and accurate. "But how," you may ask, "do you get all of these things together? Where do you start? Where do the words come from?" The start has something to do with your personal life style. Obviously, the thoughts that go onto paper from the typewriters of the world's greatest newscasters do not come from a vacuum. These people have adopted an appropriate life style which allows them to choose many of the seemingly clever words and phrases and much of the background information they need from their own living experiences. Although you may agree or disagree as to whether English courses are the best prerequisites for unemployment, a certain ability to work with the fundamentals would help. You need a fairly good vocabulary and a fair share of grammatical skills with which to throw that vocabulary around. This does not mean that you need a Ph.D. in journalism to get started in a broadcast newsroom (many Ph.D.'s, the writer suspects, would not have the foggiest idea what to do if a local station hired them tomorrow and left them alone in the newsroom) but a good education would not hurt your competence.

Besides a formal education, there is just the plain business of "keeping in touch." If you are not subscribing to *Time, Newsweek, U.S. News and World Report,* or some other leading magazine that will keep you abreast of the latest ideas in the arts, sciences, and current events, then that would be a good place to start. Then, you will want to broaden that basic understanding by keeping up with at least occasional issues of *Sports Illustrated* or of one of the "intellectual" magazines like *Harper's* or *Atlantic Monthly.* This need not cost you a fortune in subscriptions; public libraries have been around for years.

Of course you will want to keep up with the latest developments in your own industry if you are serious about broadcast journalism at all. Listen to various kinds of newscasts on the radio, not just on a favorite station but on the networks and on small and large local stations as well. Watch newscasters on TV. Compare the networks. Analyze the techniques. Ask yourself, "How do they take a story that's going to be at least a thousand words long in the newspaper and get it down to one- or two-hundred words on the air?" Start reading the sports page in the newspaper if you have not been doing it lately, and listen to the sportscasters so you will not be "out of touch" when you are called upon to do a sports story or two. Keep up with those articles on theatre, art, and music in the news magazines, so the names of the people, the works, and the trends will not escape you when you need them. Make it a point to read the editorials and the critics and columnists in the newspapers. Do not delude yourself into thinking that a steady diet of AP or UPI radio wire stories is going to broaden your mind. Even the wire services themselves would never claim that.

Getting *out* of touch is not that hard to do. The writer found some newsmen at one station in the New York City market who had been sitting at typewriters rewriting and embellishing stories for years. They honestly thought their job was simply to paraphrase all stories that came in on the wire so that listeners would not be able to recognize the similarity in the wire service stories between their station and others nearby. They never picked up a phone to check anything out. They never added any background knowledge from what they should have been hearing and reading elsewhere. It seemed at times to be almost to the point where the President of the United States could have staggered into the newsroom and collapsed over the desk and these fellows would wait until the story came on the AP or UPI wire before they ran it. If Congress votes to cut off funds for something, you should have some idea of what the issues were behind the vote before the wire service spells it out for you. If the U.N. Security Council is called into emergency session, you should have in your mind a background of names, places, and events that can help you tell your listeners why. Paraphrasing wire service copy does not make you a journalist; it makes you a glorified parrot.

One more point about life styles: discipline yourself to be suspicious. Double-check your sources, question them, and, above all, do not "fake" it if you do not understand. If the words or phrases in a news release or statement are unclear, check with someone who might be able to clear it up for you. If your own understanding of the material is fuzzy, imagine what condition it will be in by the time it reaches your listeners. It might even be downright *wrong* by the time you get through rewriting it! You should know enough about your subject to be able to answer questions if someone calls up after the newscast, including questions about what the story means in general aside from the latest development. Just telling people that you "got it from the wire service" and you do not know any more about it is usually a "cop-out" on your part, unless the story is legitimately about something you could not possibly anticipate or prepare for, such as an earthquake or plane crash in some remote part of the world. If your idea of good journalism is to just rewind the mayor's latest statement and play the whole tape verbatim—hiccups and all—then this is another form of "copping out" on your part if you have not taken the time to study his topic or to ask him any questions.

## TALKING TO YOUR TYPEWRITER

It has already been mentioned that broadcast news is "conversational," but it normally takes two people to have a conversation. In this case, you will have to imagine that the two people are yourself and the listener. There are several ways to "test" your story to see if it is conversational. One way is reading it back to yourself aloud. The places where you pause or stumble *off* the air are the places where you would have paused or stumbled *on* the air. Try to weed out those mispronounciations (or hesitations when you are not really sure how to pronounce something), those awkward pauses, and so on. That is *half* the job: At least you will be able to read it, but this does not guarantee that others will be able to understand it. Unfortunately, this is as far as many newscasters go in their careers. Others at the station can sense that their newsman is not exactly another Walter Cronkite, but they do not really know what to tell him so they just let it go.

This may be your case. It you have been writing your own stories and reading them on the air for awhile, you may have built up a sort of immunity to the rough spots. You will not stumble over it because *you* wrote it! Hand it to someone else and have that person read it to you. Listen for where he or she stumbles. Those are clues. The acid test, though, is to hand your own version of a late-breaking story to a newsman whose newscast is already on the air. He has to read it "cold," and with his microphone already on. If he has trouble with it on the air, he may be diplomatic enough not to complain later on but that does not mean the story was perfect. Take the hint and see what you can do to improve the situation. In fact, get in the habit of writing all your stories as though someone else might suddenly have to read them at any moment.

The fact that you and other newscasters can read such stories without stumbling is not the only test, though. *Listener comprehension* is a big item. They are all out there waiting for your newscast: the ones who cannot hear well, the ones who are driving in heavy traffic or fighting with their wives, the ones whose extremist views will distort anything they hear, . . ., and the ones who just do not get it. (Sometimes these latter types will seem to be in the majority.)

In all fairness to the listener, though, you must remember that he cannot get an "instant replay" of your newscast the

Photo by Chip Hires.

way he can watch those spectacular plays over again during a ballgame on TV. If he misses part of a sentence, or if he does not understand something the first time you say it, quite often it is just gone. He cannot start reading a line over again as he can in a newspaper. This is why the style is not just conversational, but it is also arranged in a special *sequence* that is easily picked up by the ear. Another ingredient is a subtle form of *repetition*. Any politician can tell you that the best way to get a point across is to repeat it in several different ways.

Of course, before devices like sequence and repetition will work you have to get your listener's attention in the first place. Newspapers do this with headlines designed to catch your eye so that you will want to read the article which follows. In broadcasting, it is done with a strong "lead" sentence or phrase which serves to catch the ear rather than the eye. Unlike the first sentence in a newspaper story, the lead sentence in a broadcast story does *not* spell out the entire "who-what-when-where-why" in condensed form. Instead, like a colorful headline in a newspaper, it simply alerts the listener to the topic and directs his attention to the story before you hit him with the details.

Here are some examples. Where a newspaper would say:

"Special Prosecutor Leon Jaworski today suggested to U.S. District Judge John J. Sirica that he conduct his own inquiry into whether former President Richard M. Nixon is healthy enough to testify at the Watergate cover-up trial."

a broadcast station might put it:

"Judge John Sirica has been asked to see for himself whether former President Nixon can testify at the Watergate cover-up trial, or whether he's too sick. Prosecutor Leon Jaworski filed a motion today . . ."

The main ideas remain intact, but things like middle initials and parts of lengthy titles have been dropped. The sentences in the broadcast version are shorter. If you try to read that newspaper version out loud, chances are that you will run out of breath.

Radio Station WNEW, which came out with a broadcast stylebook back in the early 1960's, used this as an example of coverage when a water main broke on a major subway line during rush hour. Their competitor had reported:

"A water main break at 6th Avenue and 46th Street has caused a disruption of service on the I.N.D. Sixth Avenue line."

while WNEW put it this way:

"For midtown subway riders, it's a case of water, water everywhere, but not a train in sight."

And then they went on to fill in the details.

What they were trying to do, of course, was get the listener's attention first by using a sentence that not only caught his interest but which was almost so simple that most listeners could repeat it back to them, word for word, had they been asked to do so. It is doubtful that anyone could have repeated the competitor's lead sentence.

One other example from their style book concerned a Supreme Court decision. Competitor's version:

"The United States Supreme Court today reversed an appellate court verdict and set aside the conviction of seven Alabama civil rights demonstrators."

WNEW version:

"The U.S. Supreme Court has knocked down police barricades in Alabama."

. . . and then, of course, they fill in the rest of the story.

The trouble is, you can go too far with the leads, too, just as easily as a newspaper can sometimes overdo it with a screaming headline that does not quite match the story. Just because the lead is strong does not mean it is going to be a great story after that. Trying just a bit too hard to be clever, one of WNEW's writers reportedly said there was "grave trouble" on the labor scene and then went on into a story about a cemetery workers' strike. The writer was in grave trouble, too, according to WNEW, concluding that, "the leads can't come from left field."

United Press International has been putting out a broadcast stylebook for many years, and agrees with the practice of using good, attention-getting (but not weird) leads. UPI adds a few qualifications of its own:

► Do not make the first sentence a question, because it sounds too much like a commercial.

► Do not lead off with a quote, because it is too easy to confuse just whose quote it is.

► Never start a lead sentence with just a name. Always precede the name with a title or an identifying phrase. If your listener misses this identification, he may miss the point of the entire story.

On this last point, even newspapers have begun to use the "broadcast" style for reporting names with titles. Years ago, they would put the name of the individual first, then follow it with his title. Many of the combinations were very awkward, like this:

*Old way* (wrong):

"Henry Kissinger, Secretary of State, said today . . ."

*New way* (right):

"Secretary of State Henry Kissinger said today . . ."

Longer titles may be broken up and put before and after a person's name, such as in:

*Awkward:*

"Arthur Burns, Chairman of the Federal Reserve Board, . . ."

*Smoother:*

"Chairman Arthur Burns of the Federal Reserve Board . . ."

One might expect that with all these style books around, stations all over the country would be trying to imitate these approaches. Not so. Unfortunately, there are still major stations, even "all-news" stations, where the way to prepare a newscast is to take stories right off the wire, hold them under a photocopying machine, and read the copies word for word over the air. It is not unusual to hear the same story repeated in exactly the same words every hour or two for several hours on at least one major all-news operation that the writer knows.

Generally, though, the larger stations and the networks have their own stylebooks by now, and their people are certainly not beginners, so examples of poor presentation on such outlets are the exception rather than the rule. The problems are usually with smaller stations who can barely afford to hire, much less properly train, newscasters.

The writer was driving along an interstate highway not too long ago, near a small town where he had worked for a local radio station under at least two different sets of call letters. As he turned on the car radio and tuned to that particular spot on the dial to see if they were still in business, the "news" came on. They had a lead story that went somewhat like this:

County Sheriff's deputies really earned their pay last night, taking care of disturbances in Branston, Coleville, and Mopohack. Several persons reportedly taking a hayride outside of Branston were halted after neighbors called to complain of the noise, and before the officers could find out who was in charge, a fight broke out, resulting in several arrests and a stabbing. Several persons were taken to the hospital. Brothers Eugene and Gary Carson, ages 18 and 17, were charged with intoxication and resisting arrest. Officers thought they had successfully brought the group in for booking when Eugene allegedly grabbed a chair at the Sheriff's office and brought it down on the head of Deputy John Farringer, sending him to the hospital for stitches and picking up an additional charge of assaulting an officer. Eugene's brother, Gary, joined in the meelee during the booking and was subdued by Deputies Laars Heydahl and Leonard Santibucci. Back at the hayride scene, a Miss Dorothy Fenstermacher, 20, was arrested for disorderly conduct and resisting arrest. Miss Fenstermacher's boyfriend, 21-year-old Angelo Annunziato, was charged with stabbing a 23-year-old Emil Rabinowitz, reportedly after attempts that Rabinowitz was allegedly trying to make at gaining Miss Fenstermacher's attention during the hayride. Annunziato was released on his own recognizance pending a court appearance before Justice Theodore Shields on September 19th.

(That was the Branston incident. There was more:)

Meanwhile, in MoPohack, a car went out of control on Route Six near Shenrock Place, and seven young persons suffered minor injuries. 21-year-old Ray Stoezl was charged with driving while intoxicated and with driving while his license was suspended. A passenger in Stoezl's car, Alberto Rodriguez, was treated at Bucknam Community Hospital for lacerations and contusions, and released. The Coleville incident involved a complaint by Mrs. Jack Starke of 1013 Kent Road who said she heard a prowler at about 1 A.M. Upon investigation, deputies discovered a 48-year-old Sean O'Rourke of no certain address, sleeping in the garage of Mrs. Starke's nextdoor neighbor, Scott F. Williamson. O'Rourke, who said he was unemployed and just passing through, was charged with breaking and entering and vagrancy. He was remanded to the County Jail in lieu of bond for a court appearance on September 20th.

Beautiful, simply beautiful! About 13 or 14 names, including deputies, judges, vagrants, and what-have-you, many of them defying pronounciation. In addition, their ages and various charges ranging from drunk driving and disorderly conduct to stabbing and assaulting an officer were given. Reading time was about 2½ minutes for this masterpiece, which was little more than a glorified police blotter. That is more than half of the normal "five-minute" newscast when you allow for things like weather and a commercial. The people at this little radio station would probably be very hurt if you dared to suggest that they were not serving their local community, but who can keep track of—much less care about—all those details?

As was said, this is not an exact copy of the story the writer heard but, for purposes of discussion here, close enough to give you an idea. Assuming that this were to be the kind of journalism being turned out at a station where you were just joining the news staff, where would you start hacking away?

*Ages*—You do not really need them, unless they have some special significance in themselves. Unless a group of kids ranging in age from 9 to 13 all get arrested for smoking pot, or unless the people from the hayride who assaulted the deputy sheriff were in their 90's, all this "21-year-old" and "23-year-old" business does nothing for your story. If someone dies who is very famous, his age may be worth reporting. If somebody's grandmother is a football star, we report her age (if she will give it to us!). If ages do not really add anything to your story, leave them out. If you do use an age, it is "21-year-old Mary Smith," not "Mary Smith, 21, . . ."

*House Numbers*—Strictly *out*. Unless there is a fire in which several persons are killed, or unless a major gambling or narcotics raid is made on a specific apartment (and that means major) the number is irrelevant. You might identify a murder victim as being from a particular street if he is local, but you would only identify less significant people such as those nabbed in a gambling raid by what town they come from. (Thus the murder victim might be from "East Washington Avenue," and the gambling suspect "from New Haven.")

*Policemen's Names*—Use them only if they are doing something heroic, controversial, or getting hurt. If they are just doing their routine job, it is not news. Much as you would like to give police all the credit they are due, in a broadcast news story a policeman's name becomes just one more name to remember. The policeman who makes news is the one who disarms a gunman, talks someone out of jumping off a bridge, saves someone's life, etc.

*Police Jargon*—Phrases like "remanded to jail," "in lieu of bond" and "released on his own recognizance," just do not belong to radio and television. If you have not seen the explanation of police jargon and how to translate it in the "Police Beat" chapter, please read it over. Try not to make your station sound like an electronic police blotter.

*Large Numbers*—The numbers from 1 to 999 are easy to see and read aloud. Very few people stumble over them. As soon as you get any larger than that, words must be substituted for numbers in the "thousands" column and sometimes for the "hundreds" column. Thus 1,102 becomes "11-hundred-2." The number 1134 should be typed out as 1-thousand-134. If a local board passes a budget of $1,937,268.25, it should occur in your story as "just over 1.9 million dollars." The word "dollars" is spelled out at the end of the number, rather than using the dollar ($) sign. If an area firm receives a contract for $5,987,622, your broadcast copy should read, "close to six million dollars." To attempt to spell these figures out will bore some listeners and confuse others.

*Abbreviations*—Abbreviations are almost never used in broadcast copy unless they are the kind that are intended to be read aloud as abbreviations. Things like the Y-M-C-A and the U-N are all right, and of course you would leave out the dashes between the letters if they form words, like NATO. Government agencies like the F-B-I and the F-C-C are familiar. You might get away with "St. Louis," but it would be safer to make it "Mount Washington" or "Mount Vernon" instead of "Mt." Names like Mr. Jones and Mrs. Smith are all right, but do *not* abbreviate:

▶ names of cities, states, or countries
▶ days of the week or names of months
▶ titles of corporate or government officials
▶ words like "street," "avenue," "boulevard," in addresses.

You might get away with saying "G-O-P" for a Republican if you do not overuse it, but watch out for "newspaper style" identification of Congressmen and Senators:

*Wrong:* Sen. Lowel R. Weicker (R.-Ct.)

*Right:* Republican Senator Lowell P. Weicker of Connecticut.

Except for the G-O-P example, political parties are never abbreviated. Things like the S.L.A. may look familiar in print, but you would be better off saying "Simbionese Liberation Army" on the air. The same goes for the N.L.F. in Vietnam. Memories fade quickly, and few listeners will recall that those initials stand for the National Liberation Front. *Rule:* "If in doubt, spell it out."

*Quotations*—Identify the speaker *before* you quote him, not after.

*Right:* "Democratic Council candidate George Brown says Republican Councilman Lawrence Findler is not telling the truth about his finances. According to Brown . . ." (Go ahead and quote him, now that it is clear who is making the accusation.)

*Wrong:* "Republican Councilman Lawrence Findler is not telling the truth about his finances. That is the charge made today . . ." (Your Republican listeners who sympathize with Findler are so upset they may miss who is making the charges. Some of them might even think *you are* making the accusation.)

*Names and Titles*—First names may be left out if the person is well-known and constantly in the news. If the Mayor's name is John Brown, he can just be "Mayor Brown" in your newscasts, or "Riverdale's Mayor Brown" if you are serving that many towns. When he comes up for the second or third time in a story, he may just be "Mr. Brown." Occasionally, you will see the wire service leave out the "Mr." for the President, a Cabinet member, or some other high-ranging government official, but there are stations where newsrooms are ordered to put it back in. The writer recommends leaving it *in* as much as possible. For titles, see the previous discussion of "leads," where Henry Kissinger and Arthur Burns were mentioned.

## NEWS JUDGMENT AND GOOD TASTE

Every station has an "image." Some stations work very hard to project a certain kind of image, while others get their image just from *not* working very hard on it. Whether you are working for an outfit that sees itself as a vigorous, youthful, "hustling" station where everybody is really "with it," or whether they pride themselves on things like soft, easy-listening music or informative and educational "adult" programming, a news department that is not too fussy about what stories do (or do not) go on the air, can easily become the "lowest common denominator" that drags the rest of the station's image down.

Here are some suggestions that will help to keep that image sparkling:

(1) Avoid libelous terms: Carelessly referring to someone in a story as "corrupt," or involved in "swindling" or "flimflam" or some other shady practice, can get you a lawsuit. Just as easily, you can be sued for declaring somebody "bankrupt" before the court does, or by labelling him as an "addict" or "drunk" or even "hot-tempered." To call an incident an "attempted suicide" without quoting an official source might result in libel action against you from the person who was despondent but who now sees a good way to gain attention by suing you. "Unmarried mother," "illicit relations," or even "illegitimate" are terms that can get you more than just a complaint. Atheists and Klan members can even sue you for calling them by the names of the organization to which they belong.

(2) Gory stories are *out.* The station that has nothing better to talk about than the list of ambulance calls overnight or all the muggings and break-ins from the police blotter should not be on the air. If these things are of a *major* nature, then perhaps an occasional one can be allowed but detailed descriptions of injuries and damage day in and day out are enough to turn people off, or to have them turn you off.

(3) Bomb scare and evacuation stories: *verboten.* When you run stories like these, you are playing into the hands of the kooks who want to see their anonymous phone calls make people scramble. This is in the same category as the anonymous caller in the "Civil Disorders" chapter who tells you there is a "riot" somewhere. Do not give him the satisfaction. If a bomb actually goes off, then it is a story. Bombing incidents in New

York City used to touch off a rash of bomb-scare calls to all the radio and TV stations in the area for the next few days. After a while most stations learned not to give the calls any play.

(4) Do not run stories to death. If you have newscasts every hour or even every half-hour, you risk sounding like a broken record. If a major world figure dies (like France's DeGaulle or Egypt's Nasser some years ago) word of his death can be a major story for about the first two or three hours. After that, do not "bury him every hour." The wire services may go overboard with all the statements from other world leaders, the thousands weeping in the streets, etc. This is a time when your policy toward the wire service should be "select, don't settle." Try leaving out a story like this on every other newscast, or somehow rotating it or putting it at the bottom with fewer details so that listeners who have been with you for several hours are not tempted to pound on their radios.

(5) Leave out "routine" developments in long-running stories. For example, when a war has been going on for quite some time in the Middle East, Southeast Asia, or elsewhere, the public "tires" easily of hearing small details. One jet strafing a couple of trucks, one patrol running into an ambush, etc., are not really news anymore. To recite all this stuff hourly is a waste of time.

## THE USE OF TAPE RECORDINGS

Along with the growing number of very portable and very versatile recording devices over the past few years, there has also been a growing number of very good—and very *bad*—tape recordings heard on newscasts. Somehow, there are those among us who think that the higher the stack of cartridges is, the better the newscast will be. It just does not work that way.

The possibilities for doing a really good job with tape, of making that "picture with sound" that is worth a thousand words, are just as endless as the possibilities for doing a *poor* job. On one hand, a reporter can prepare for on-the-scene coverage as discussed in the chapter on that topic, and go out and get:

▶ a candidate responding to cheers (or jeers),

▶ a protest leader with a lot of charisma "socking it" to his followers or to his opponents,

▶ the sounds of a community at work or play—from traffic noises, industrial sounds, and jackhammers to picnics and parades,

. . . while on the other hand, a tired newscaster can dial the "umpteenth" phone number on the wall, roll his tape recorder, and then back the thing up and play it word-for-word on the air, no matter how "tinny" or "canned" it sounds. Tapes like this last one just mentioned—aired just for the sake of having tape—can do far more harm than good.

Not only the *technical* quality of the tape (tinny, fuzzy, etc.) should determine whether or not it gets used on the air, but often the *content* of the material is a deciding factor regardless of how good the technical quality may be. WNEW, in that stylebook mentioned earlier, had this example:

*(Written intro:)* "If they hadn't gotten greedy, two Queens gunmen might have escaped tonight, after robbing two Ozone Park drugstores but the bandits apparently tried for number three and it proved to be their undoing. The holdup men walked into the Leffert's Pharmacy on Leffert's Boulevard and owner Jack Nodiff told what happened:

*(Tape:)* "These men had come in first—in other words when they came in, there were no police officers in the store. The police officers came in approximately 30 seconds after these men had come in, so either these men had come in to throw the police off the track or they came in merely waiting for my customers to leave. However, the police were alerted to these other holdups in the area. Incidentally the other two drugstores which were held up were within proximity of three blocks of my store."

*(Written story:)* "In the ensuing gun battle, one of the bandits was killed, the other seriously wounded. A woman accomplice escaped. She's being hunted now. The police had a casualty too. One officer was wounded, but not badly."

In this example, the tape did more harm than good. The part about the shoot-out between the gunmen and the police was added almost as an afterthought, along with the fact that one of the bandits was killed! The store owner was so wrapped up in an insignificant set of details that his description served only to "blur" the whole story. This is where it takes courage as a journalist to leave something out. If you were the stringer who went out to the scene to record something like this, it was probably all very exciting with the police cars, ambulances, bodies on the floor, and the whole business right there in front of you. You may have gone to a lot of trouble to get there, such as leaving home when you thought you had the night off, or going through rain, heavy traffic, or whatever. Under these circumstances, it is very hard to tell yourself that what you brought back on that tape really is not good enough. It may even be harder, if you are a newscaster receiving this material from a stringer, to tell him you really cannot use it. After all, he is out there trying to make a living just like you, and for you to reject his stuff makes you the "bad guy."

This whole matter of whether to use, or not use, tape will take discipline, teamwork, and understanding all around. If you have stringers out gathering sounds on tape for you, one of the first things they will have to learn is *not* to be hurt if you do not run their tapes and *not* to expect their tapes to be run just because they went out and got them for you. Talk this over calmly with your colleagues *before* a situation like this comes up. The writer has seen the morale in a number of newsrooms suffer on just this very point.

If you do not have stringers out, that still does not give you license to run everything you gather on that tape recorder of yours. All too familiar is the small-town reporter who interviews the Fire Chief at the scene of the blaze. The Chief tells him which engines responded until the reporter gets lost in numbers and names of hose, ladder, and truck companies. Then the Chief goes into a big explanation of how many feet of 2½-inch hose they used and what time the various alarms came in. All this is great stuff for a weekly newspaper to run in the eighteenth paragraph, but it certainly does not belong on a radio station. You have to stop and ask yourself, "Does this *help* the story?" If it looks like you can do a better job with your typewriter, then by all means do it. You do not have to prove to your audience on every newscast that your station owns a portable tape recorder.

Concerning the subject of tape recordings, there is a "sore point" that comes up sooner or later in any station where someone *other* than the newscaster is going to play the tapes, and it will be brought to your attention now to save you a lot of trouble later on. There is probably nothing that can make you more furious as a newscaster than to call for the voice of an important person in the news and to have the "dingaling" who is running the control room play the voice of Smokey the Bear instead. Not only does it blow the whole show, but since the audience heard *you* introduce it, most of them think it is *your* mistake. Your bungling friend sits there on the other side of the glass in all of his anonymity while you sit there with "egg on your face" trying to salvage what is left of a newscast which has just been all but destroyed. In the writer's own experience, he has had tapes rewound on the air, played at the wrong speed, cut off at the wrong cues, the wrong speaker or a commercial played instead of what he called for, and even empty control rooms where the guy who is supposed to play the tape has left to go to the bathroom while you sit there marooned with a "live" mike! There are some ways to try to deal with this kind of thing (some more effective than others) but basically you will have to try to figure out that person on the other side of the glass. Here are a few suggestions on how to get started, but you will have to take it from there.

First of all, that other fellow is probably an engineer or a disc jockey. Either way, he has his own things to think about. The engineer may be all wrapped up in a mathematical formula or thinking about the transmitter or some other technical matter. The disc jockey is probably mumbling some really neat record introductions to himself or talking to one of his many fans on the phone. Either one of them may be filling out a log, taking readings, cueing up various records and tapes other than the ones you will want played, etc. In other words, they are usually in another world. You may walk into that control room and say something in perfectly clear English, and it will go in one ear and out the other. You may have written something out very carefully and shown him the cartridge or tape you want played, and all you get is a glassy-eyed stare. This really happens.

The reasons for such an arrangement are usually either of two things:

► One, the station cannot afford the extra tape or cartridge machines for the newsroom, or . . .

►Two, the engineers are under a union contract which says they push all the buttons and you just read.

If there is a union contract with engineers, chances are that they not only must be the ones to *play back* the tape but that they must be the ones to *record* it in the first place. In a case like this if you plan to make any phone calls in pursuit of taped interviews, be sure you go personally to these engineers first and be sure that a newly erased reel of tape is properly mounted on the appropriate tape recorder before you start. If you get the person you are going to interview on the phone first and then expect someone to start a tape recorder for you right away, you will find out that is just not the way.

If you do manage to get something on the tape, you still have a long way to go before you get it played back properly. Assume for the moment that you are still working with raw, reel-to-reel material and such things as editing or putting the material on cartridges are out of the question. In such a case, you will have to select an excerpt from that interview that needs no editing. Type a carbon copy of your story which contains:

► the words *just before* that which you want on the air, indicating clearly that the engineer is to cue up the tape *just after* these words,

► the first words you should hear on the air,

► the last words you should hear on the air,

► the exact timing of the excerpt in number of seconds.

Give the carbon copy of your story to the engineer, and stay there to supervise him while he cues up the tape to the appropriate spot. Otherwise, you will be surprised during your newscast to discover that he just has not remembered to do so, and the tape will not be ready. If there is more than one tape machine in the control room, note which machine this tape is mounted on, and mark it with a crayon in the margin of your script, so that he will not "roll" the wrong machine. Then pray. It might help.

Much more common, perhaps, is the situation where you hand a stack of cartridges to a disc jockey. Here again, carbon copies of the stories involved would help. Put a title at the top of your story which matches *exactly* the information on the label of your cartridge. The text should have your last words as you introduce the cartridge, and the speaker's last words on the cartridge itself, plus the timing. Number his cue sheets and yours in exactly the same order, and stack the cartridges in that order. Scribbled labels, or labels that have the speaker's name while the matching cue sheet has something else for a title, can all lead to confusion. Just as you stood around and supervised the engineer in the previous example, do something that will force the disc jockey physically to acknowledge the presence of the cartridges and cue sheets. Place them in his hand, read over the cues with him, watch as he puts the first one in the cartridge machine, or something. If you just tiptoe into the control room and meekly slip them onto the counter while he is busy rapping with his vast audience, you may find, as the writer did, that he is out to the bathroom when it comes time for that first cartridge.

In any case, if someone other than yourself is playing any of the tapes for your newscast, it is wise to type in a line or two in parentheses, or lower case, or some way in which you can distinguish it from the regular script, which you may read in the event the tape breaks, the cartridge misfires, or whatever.

How long should tapes be? Well, on radio, usually no more than 40 seconds at the very most. Cuts as short as 10 seconds have been very effective, especially with formats like ABC's "Contemporary" Network. If a correspondent is filing a detailed report—say for an example a stringer who covered last night's school board meeting—he might run up to between 50 and 60 seconds if he has done a "wraparound," which includes his own voiced report plus an inserted actuality. The meeting he is covering would have to be the biggest thing that has happened locally for quite a while, though, because even on the networks you rarely hear a newscast audio cut of more than 30 seconds. Anything longer than that is often a sign of poor editing.

Of course, with radio, you should be geared for a lot of repetition. Newscasts on most stations come every hour, and on a great many stations every half-hour. If a politician or someone else gives you a lengthy statement, take out several excerpts which qualify as newsworthy and rotate them. For example, having taken excerpts *A*, *B*, and *C*, run excerpt *A* on tape in the first newscast and mention *B* and *C* in your written copy. On a later newscast, run *B* on tape and use brief mentions of *A* and *C* in your written copy, etc. This way, you get more mileage out of your tape and your listeners will not hear exactly the same audio cut repeated over and over again.

## FILMS AND VIDEOTAPE: THE STYLE OF TV

The basic principles of journalism in this book apply to both radio and TV, and the writing of newscasts in "conversational" style has also applied. Where the two media differ significantly for newscasters is in television's need for a good visual product versus radio's sole concentration on sound. In the preceding section on tape recordings, you were geared to the needs of radio. You were warned against the use of tape "just for the sake of having tape." On TV, it is not that simple. You cannot just decide not to use the picture. It is going to be there anyway, so your decision is *how* to use it, and use it well.

Of course, TV is the medium that takes you there—live—to the moon, or covers the activities of Presidents, Popes, and Prime Ministers with everything from satellite relays to multi-camera coverage of nominating conventions, which runs into the millions of dollars. However, this is what the *networks* are doing, and no local station could ever afford to do that kind of thing on its own. Other than sports and certain local emergencies, TV stations do very little live remote broadcasting. Most TV newscasts rely heavily on film and videotape, backed by slides and wire service Photofax machines. Many have their own resident artists just as department stores have people who do their windows and displays, and here and there you see some imaginative graphic work in the form of maps, charts, and other visual aids. Beyond these facilities, the work is very similar to that in radio news. Those who walk into a TV newsroom expecting to spend most of their time smiling at a camera face a rude awakening when they find they still have to make those phone calls, type stories at a typewriter, and go out and gather stories.

What this means for TV here in the chapter on style, then, is not all that different from what has been said about radio. Many TV news producers are just as guilty of the "tape-for-the-sake-of-tape" syndrome as their radio counterparts, only now it is film for the sake of film. Not only that, but they are subject to the same temptations to use something because of its technical quality rather than its journalistic value. On top of this, though, TV news directors are accused of "motion sickness," or a belief that if it does not move, it is not news. They will tell you that they want to get away from just a head-on shot of the anchor-man looking up and down at the camera from his script. Okay, fine, but very often there are ways in which still photographs and drawings are effective ways of communicating. Not only are they cheaper to produce, but they can often help TV cover abstract topics such as fine arts, advanced medical science, technological invasion of the environment, etc.

Assuming, then, that you are writing a few stories to get ready for a TV newscast, you will simply want to take into account what your audience is going to be *looking at* throughout the entire process rather than just listening. This is accomplished by dividing your paper into two columns: video and audio. The video column, at the left, takes up about one-fourth to one-third of the paper. The other two-thirds to three-fourths of your paper contain just what it did for your radio newscasts: the words that either you are going to say or which are going to come from the sound track of a videotape or film. So far, it is simple.

What is not quite as simple is the fact that your microphone does not go off when a tape goes on, as it did for radio. You may find yourself "narrating" for part of a film and then letting the sound track take over for another part. Several different pictures will come and go while you are reading through a paragraph. The variations are endless, and the techniques for presenting pictures effectively are improving all the time. Instead of grabbing an extra batch of rip-and-read wire copy to "pad" the closing seconds of your newscast as you glance at the clock the way you did in radio, you will find yourself wearing a stopwatch around your neck in the newsroom and including in your script just exactly how much time everything takes and on just exactly which syllable to start and stop using various still or moving pictures and when to switch to another source.

Another important factor for television is that you most likely are not doing your newscasts alone, as you would be able to do in many cases for radio. TV divides its news into several areas:

(1) Writers: Those who gather, compile, edit, etc.

(2) Talent: On-camera correspondents, anchormen, special reporters such as weather and sports people.

(3) Producers: The people who "orchestrate" a given show by coordinating the efforts of writers, talent, film people, cameramen, control room personnel, etc.

(4) Executives: News Directors or News Vice Presidents who hire and fire, set overall policies, scheduling, crews, budgets, etc.

In addition, many stations have intermediary positions such as "assignment editors" and "unit directors." Other stations have overlapping functions for their personnel, such as News Directors who also function as producers or assignment editors, or anchormen who go out and shoot some film every day just so they keep "in touch" with the real world and do not become isolated behind their big desks that you see on camera.

Beside these factors, formats differ more widely on TV now. Some stations still use the "superstar" format with a dominating personality who gives the news, while other have begun to use a "team" approach. In the space of this volume, then, it is not possible to give you all the production techniques necessary to accommodate all of these needs and more. Obviously, that can better be done in a book on television techniques. It should be pointed out, however, that when most books on television news get down to the chapter on writing, they give you pretty much the same tips as presented in this chapter. The major difference occurs when they begin to discuss how to "let the picture do the talking."

Maury Green, in his book, *Television News: Anatomy and Process,*\* has a couple of excellent examples of this point:

At the 1960 Democratic National Convention, the (then) governor of New Jersey, Robert Meyner, was asked a politically embarrassing question during a news conference. . . . He did not answer immediately. He looked down at the table, he picked up a fork and played with it, he studied the ceiling. The camera kept on rolling while he searched for an answer. Finally, after 20 seconds of hesitation, he found it.

As Green points out, a radio listener would probably wonder if the station had gone off the air. A newspaper reader would have chuckled just slightly. But on film, says Green, "It was excruciatingly funny." He says he watched the film several times with different audiences, and that in each case they would start chuckling at about 7 seconds, they would all be laughing at 15 seconds, and by the time Meyner spoke at 20 seconds he was drowned out by the laughter. This episode, says Green, could only have been possible on film.

The other situation was one in which Edward R. Murrow asked Dr. J. Robert Oppenheimer about the chance that humanity might destroy itself by accident with nuclear weapons:

For something like 45 seconds the brilliant nuclear scientist pondered the question, and for the full time the camera held on Dr. Oppenheimer. Murrow did not interrupt; there was only silence. Finally, the physicist replied. "Not quite." In a medium addicted to sound and fury even 5 seconds of motionlessness and silence is an eternity, and nine times that is unthinkable. Yet that 45 seconds was one of television's finest moments. The suspense of watching one of the world's great scientists think through the intricate ponderables of the proposition was almost unbearable, and his answer, when it finally came, left the viewer with the certainty that his world had been given no more than a momentary reprieve.

\*Excerpts reprinted by permission of Wadsworth Publishing Co., Inc.

It took not only teamwork among all the people producing that show, but a tremendous understanding of context to elevate it to greatness. Green credits "the wisdom of the director in holding the static shot of Dr. Oppenheimer, and Murrow's wisdom in holding his tongue, . . ." for creating this particular moment in a way which could never be duplicated on the radio or in print.

If you are headed for television news, you will want to go much further into a study of the techniques behind these examples.

## BARNUM AND BAILEY WOULD BE PROUD . . .

As was mentioned back in the chapter "The Basics," there is nothing more out of style these days than interrupting programs with sensational-sounding electronic hodgepodge just to promote the claim that you have the story first. This disease, known as "bulletinitis," went out in the late 50's and early 60's in most major cities. Here and there, you may find a station that still uses news bulletins as a form of promotion.

Self-promotion still has not disappeared altogether, though. Somehow, our industry clings to that "show biz" mentality. The flavor of this "beating your own drum" as practiced by the all-news stations which came into vogue in the 1970's was captured in this tongue-in-cheek piece by Harry Waters in the *New York Times*. He calls it, "Hickory Dickory Dock, News Around the Clock":

7:00 a.m. Morning there all, Rip Read here . . . your WPOW all-news anchorman, bringing you round-the-clock, up-to-the-second news, news and more news . . . TOTAL news . . . (beeping sounds in background, sirens, an echo chamber chorus wailing "Neeeeeeeews . . . dum da dum . . . on Doubleyew . . . Pee . . . Oh . . . Doubleyew"). Okaaaay, . . . coming up in five minutes we'll have a WPOW report on that big Mafia trial in Bayonne, coming up in seven minutes the latest word on the weather from WPOW's own meteorological-satellite center, coming up in the next half hour special features from WPOW experts on theatre, science, sports, traffic, restaurants, consumer affairs, and family counseling. But first, this message . . .

7:02 Commercial
7:03 Commercial

7:03½ WPOW promotional message ("Newscaster Rip Read came to WPOW in 1967 after a distinguished journalistic career with the Grand Forks Gazette . . .").

7:04 Commercial

7:05 Hi, Rip Read back, bringing you round-the-clock, up-to-the second news, news and more news. Here are the top stories of the hour. The Red Chinese thrust into the Middle East has reached the Gaza Strip . . . the President has just concluded his press conference from the War Room at the Pentagon . . . an unidentified submarine has just surfaced off Miami Beach . . . Richard Burton reportedly has been seen alone and disheveled in a Havana bar . . . More details later, but first let's go to Superior Court in Bayonne for WPOW newscaster Bill Fern's report on that Mafia trial. Come in, Bill.

Hi, Rip. Well, all of us here are still waiting for that sensational mystery witness, known only as the Lady from Seacaucus. District Attorney Doyle has promised that she'll clinch the state's case against Tony The Toad. Of course, we've been waiting for this mysterious femme fatale for three days now, . . .

Yeah, we know Bill.

Uh, . . . well . . . uh, suppose I call you later. Okay, Rip?

7:08 Thanks, Bill Fern, for that late-breaking word from Superior Court in Bayonne. Now here's a message . . .

7:09 Commercial

7:10 WPOW Promo

7:10½ Commercial

7:11 Okaaaay, . . . Rip Read back to update those big breaking stories. The Sixth Fleet is racing toward the Suez Canal in response to that Red Chinese invasion . . . That unidentified Miami Beach Submarine has now anchored off the Fountainbleau . . . No word yet on Richard Burton, but now here's some personal advice to a listener from WPOW's family counselor, Doctor Essie Esalen.

(Male voice): Doctor Esalen, here's a letter from a troubled housewife in Haverstraw. "Doctor Esalen," she writes, "I have just learned that my husband has been involved in an affair with our babysitter for the past four years and my son recently asked to have a transsexual operation. What do I do?" Doctor Esalen?

Well, Tom, it seems perfectly clear to me that this woman is subconsciously punishing herself by overreacting to the actions of her husband and son. In short, she's what we call a latent masochist. My advice to her is to seek professional psychiatric counseling before this disorder gets completely out of hand and destroys her family life.

7:13 Commercial

7:14 Commercial

7:14½ Commercial

7:15 Rip Read back. We're still awaiting word from WPOW's Bill Fern on that sensational mystery witness at the Mafia trial in Bayonne. Coming up in five minutes, a traffic report from WPOW helicopter pilot Ray Rotor somewhere over the Gowannus Expressway. But now let's hear from WPOW's citizen troubleshooter Dyer Plight, . . . *the* man to call when you're not getting a square deal. Dyer?

Well, Rip, today your WPOW citizen troubleshooter responded to a plea from a Mrs. M.G. of 1236-B Avenue R in Jamaica. Mrs. G. wrote us to complain about a giant pothole that had gone unrepaired in front of her house for almost two years. Well, your WPOW troubleshooter immediately called the Department of Sanitation. I got nowhere with them, so then I called the Department of Public Health. Nowhere with that crowd either. Finally I called the Department of Public Works and *they* tried to tell me that I should have contacted them in the first place.

Typical bureaucratic cop-out, huh, Dyer?

You guessed it, Rip. Anyway, I tore into the department manager so heatedly he finally agreed to send a special truck to fill Mrs. G's pothole.

I bet Mrs. G. was plenty grateful to WPOW, huh, Dyer?

Well, not exactly, Rip. It seems that the truck backed over her favorite rhododendron bush and now she's complaining that . . .

Excuse me, Dyer, but I've just been handed a WPOW Insta-Flash. This is a WPOW Insta-Flash! WPOW has just learned that Richard Burton has *not* been seen in Havana as earlier reported. This has been an Insta-Flash from WPOW, your round-the-clock, up-to-the second all-news radio station . . . (beep, beep, dum da dum . . . Neeeeeeeewws . . . on Doubleyew . . . Pee . . . Oh . . . Doubleyew)

Okaaay, . . . coming up in the next hour, the latest word on that mystery witness in Bayonne, . . .

Click.

You may chuckle, but that format is not too far from what still passes for "all news" even today. Self-promotion is not the only evil, though. There are the practices of "Afghanistanism" and "padding."

"Afghanistanism" is accomplished simply by ignoring the local scene entirely. Many small rip-and-read stations have an announcer or two who may sound very authoritative and who can read what comes off that wire in pear-shaped tones with the greatest of articulation. Even some larger stations do this on Sunday mornings when they think nobody is really listening. There could have been six shootings and a hotel fire over night in your own town, but since you have no newsman on duty there is no word of it on your station. Instead, your Sunday morning disc jockey reads wire service stories about grocery store holdups which took place overnight in the city where the wire service has its office. This is often because the one writer on duty in the wire service bureau is rewriting from that town's local newspaper. The practice of "Afghanistanism" is not limited to small towns and small stations. If the writer recalls correctly, there was a day in which the subway fares had gone up in New York City and people were jumping over turnstiles and protesting in subway stations. On the same day, there were antiwar protests going on at Grand Central Terminal, a militant group known as the "Young Lords" had taken over a church in Harlem, and the mayor of nearby Newark, New Jersey, had been indicted for alleged mafia connections. If not exactly all of these stories occurred on that day, suffice it to say that it was a day *like* that, one way or another, and yet on one major station the newsman on duty ignored all of these stories and led off a "drive-time" newscast with a story about the arrival of Vice President Spiro Agnew in, yes, Afghanistan, on some kind of world tour. The "style" of such a newscast is just great. It is a very safe way to fill up air time without any controversy. No one will challenge any of your stories. In fact, no one will care.

A limited form of "Afghanistanism" is "padding." This is the practice of covering only one or two local stories—maybe just phoning the desk sergeant at police headquarters and calling that your local news—and filling in the rest of your newscast with world-and-national copy from the wire. Russell Baker caught the essence of this practice in an article in the New York *Times* which he did in 1971, entitled, "The Pickled News."

WASHINGTON, FEB. 17—**The 1971 all-purpose, any-day, any-week news roundup:**

Gunfire erupted today along the troubled Middle East as riots broke out in major cities on four continents, leaving a wake of death and destruction. The cost of living, meanwhile, rose to new zeniths, matching the tonnage of all the bombs dropped on the Ho Chi Minh Trail since World War II. Government officials hinted.

Winds of hurricane force slashed across, leaving thousands stalled in record traffic jams leading to all beaches and mountain resorts for the first time since the Paris peace talks get nowhere again today in response to the President's call to the young people of America.

At a prayer breakfast the Rev. Billy Graham.

Interdiction, meanwhile, continued throughout the coming rainy season, as ominous signs of an enemy buildup continued to continue. Saigon said, Whitehall wondered tonight, Paris decreed, Cairo threatened again and Moscow continued to show signs.

Meanwhile, in Washington, the powerful and influential Wilbur Mills indicated along the Potomac.

Raging out of control for more than ten years, a lethal blanket of oily black secret intelligence estimates coming across the President's desk has been met by Government economists with optimism about the prospects for the second quarter.

Latin-American revolutionaries bombed.

The bodies were found trussed with ropes, a pool of blood lying in a nickel-plated revolver. Interviewed today on his one-hundredth birthday, the centenarian reminisced, despite a cost overrun of nearly $2.5 billion on the Air Force's long-awaited new visor cap.

Casualties were the lightest, for which most veteran observers credit President Nixon's policy of casualtization.

Premier Kosygin met for nearly three hours.

In response to questions, Ronald Ziegler declined.

Cries of "Off the pigs!" swept through the fierce Meo tribesmen as firebase Mayor Lindsay, looking self-conscious in a hard hat, walked 86 floors to his office after the latest power failure had left traffic paralyzed for more than all the machine-gun bullets fired in France during the First and Second World Wars, regardless whether the industry agreed to meet union demands before the midnight deadline in defiance of President Nixon's call to the young people of America.

Angry, fist-shaking black militants declared.

A new study suggests that enjoying yourself is a leading cause of cancer.

Rocks brought back from the moon evoked scientific debate today. Hanoi charged as the State Department dismissed without comment. The judge said the severity of the sentence was justified by the youth's repeated refusals to have his hair cut. Additional soldiers were found not guilty of massacre at My Lai.

Senator Edward Kennedy.

The sluggishness of the stock market is attributed by some analysts to emergent nations, underdeveloped peoples, disadvantaged elements, the inner city, senior citizens, culturally disadvantaged children, the slow growth rate of Latin-American economies, Tupamaro kidnappers, Timothy Leary, the boycott of lettuce and Congressional concern with excessive violence on television.

Vacationing at San Clemente. Alarming rise in heroin addiction. Berlin. Geneva conference. Mission control at Houston reports nominal gunfire along the Suez Canal and rising interest on college campuses.

That Japanese rail disaster's death toll is still rising tonight. Governor Rockefeller flew to Washington, President Nixon to Key Biscayne and two hijacked airliners to Havana. Highly placed government sources revealed, suggested, indicated, said they believed, expected, denied, were reluctant to comment for publication, awaited and were pleased, despite reports.

Physicians now believe that happiness may be a leading cause of heart attacks, in spite of the President's plea for the silent majority to back his program for revenue sharing which captured documents indicate may be the objective of the anticipated Red offensive.

Rain, sleet and intolerable heat battered thousands of square miles today.

Meanwhile, record-breaking pornography.

Mr. Baker's "all-purpose, any-day" newscast can still be heard in its radio form on some stations. Just ask some disc jockey about how he has been busy chatting with friends on the phone or in the studio until the record runs out and the precise moment for the newscast has arrived. He "punches up" the news theme on the cartridge machine and reaches into the wastebasket for the newscast he gave an hour ago. If he is lucky enough to find it, he "ad libs" his way around it, trying to make it sound a little different this time. If he cannot find it, he recalls a great many of the magic phrases just shown you in the Russell Baker article. He puts on a great show. Yes, Barnum and Bailey would be proud.

## "WINGING IT"

Suppose you are driving home in rush-hour traffic after a hard day's work. The music on the radio is keeping you company. Then the station's announcer comes on with one of those traffic news reports:

Traffic on the Long Island Expressway is bumper-to-bumper, . . . Likewise on the B-Q-E and the Belt Parkway. Traffic is stop-and-go on the West Side Highway and the Henry Hudson Parkway with delays in the one-hundred-eighties. The Deegan is moving along smoothly, and the East River Drive is heavy with some delays. Traffic is heavy but moving on Routes 1 and 9 in New Jersey, with delays along Route 3 in the construction zone. Mass transit is reported on or near schedule.

He sounds very knowledgeable, does he not? Would you believe he is *staring at the ceiling,* making all that up? Of course, he is one of the "regular" people on the staff. No substitute could "wing it" like that. The substitutes have to call up all those numbers on that brown, fly-specked list on the wall, asking about the latest traffic conditions from the various agencies which have jurisdiction about such matters. Anyone who substitutes very often may find that he can save all those phone calls just by tuning-in another station nearby and copying down what their helicopter pilot is saying. It is all so easy —and it is also unethical.

"Winging it" is a phrase used to describe the kind of throwing motion you make when you are playing a game of Frisbee. Whether you are doing it with a toy plastic disc or with a news story, there is always the risk of missing your intended target completely. Missing the target with a news story in this manner can have disastrous results!

Even the wire services have been known to "wing it." Back when Lt. William Calley was on trial at Fort Benning, Georgia, one of the wire services had two versions of the story on the outcome of the sentencing already written and punched-out on tape. Calley had been convicted the day before of participating in the murders of civilians in the South Vietnamese village of My Lai. Now, the sentence everyone was waiting for would most likely be the death sentence or it would be life imprisonment. The punch-tape was all set up to roll at the flick of a switch and type out the sentence for thousands of radio stations across the country. The word was flashed from the Calley trial to the wire service: life in prison. Someone at the wire service threw a switch and rolled—you guessed it—the wrong tape. Within a sentence or two, the wire service people noticed their error and broke in with a warning to subscribers not to use the story.

What is indicated here is that there is a fine line between carelessness ("winging it") and outright deception. Probably

Photo by United Press International.

neither the man giving the traffic report nor the wire service giving the incorrect death sentence had any intention of lying or of deceiving the public. If you were to ask any of the people involved, they would be likely to tell you that their motive was to cut corners—to save work—to help speed things up a bit. The Chicago *Daily Tribune* wanted to speed things up a bit in 1948, and based on some early returns they rolled the presses with an enormous headline declaring that Thomas E. Dewey had won the Presidential election. The real winner, Harry S. Truman, took great delight in holding up a copy of the paper for photographers the next day. (See photograph above.) Back at the newspaper, someone had apparently been so anxious to be first that they were "winging it." The moral of this goes right back to the very first premise made in this book: "Being First Is Not as Important as Being Right." And "winging it" will not help you to be right.

# PRONUNCIATION, VOCABULARY, AND JOURNALESE

Every now and then, you come upon a fellow who gives the "first impression" that he is a good newsman. He will submit an audition tape that makes you wonder why he is not one of the leading network newscasters. He will take that portable tape recorder out to the scene and come back with some of the greatest interviews and actualities you ever heard. Your every wish as a News Director is his command. His loyalty is unsurpassed, his work is diligent. Just one thing is wrong: Some of the words are "over his head," and when he mispronounces them on the air he makes you the laughing stock all over town.

Sometimes there is nothing that can make listeners laugh at a station more, and make them turn to another station more quickly, than to hear the names of foreign countries, political leaders, and other familiar names and terms in the news mispronounced. It might be more than just a weak vocabulary. It might also mean that your newscaster's awareness of current events is much too "shallow." A combination of *both* weaknesses—vocabulary and current events—can really shatter whatever else your station may be trying to build up as an image.

Here are some examples the writer actually heard on the air:

▶ a "librarian" freighter sinking.
▶ a candidate running in the Sixth "Congregational" district.
▶ "Calvary" troops advancing in war maneuvers.
▶ Racial *imbalance* pronounced like the word "ambulance."
▶ The initials of the Department of Health, Education and Welfare (HEW) pronounced as a word, "hue."
▶ a moment of silent "mediation" in public schools.
▶ Dr. Timothy Leary and his "hallucinary" drugs.
▶ The Navy firing its "Po-*SID*-ee-on" missles.
▶ Gen. MacArthur's body lying in the Capitol "rotundrum."
▶ Sen. Vince Hardtack winning an Indiana election.
▶ a candidate making serious "allocations" against his opponent.

There are hundreds and hundreds of examples like these. Anyone who has been in the business a while can tell you a few. There are even some cases where the words are pronounced correctly, but where the newscaster is not sure whether Senator McGovern is from New York or New Jersey. If you do not see what is wrong with each of the examples, that is the first problem: Start right there. Problems like these will come back to haunt you later on if you do not start working on them right now. Remember those news magazines mentioned earlier? Keeping up with them will make a difference.

As explained in the "police" chapter, people who work in certain fields sooner or later begin to talk to each other in a sort of coded language all their own. Just as the desk sergeant may tell you there was a "B-and-E" for "Breaking and Entering," so the waitress at the sandwich shop will order a "B-L-T" from the kitchen when she wants a Bacon, Lettuce, and Tomato sandwich. The temptation in our own field is to use the same words over and over again because they sounded good the first time. It is like telling a joke over and over again: It was only funny the first time. Many stations have begun keeping a list of "no-no" words posted on the newsroom wall for their writers to avoid. The words have either been so overused they have become stale, or they are used only by journalists and you never hear them in daily conversational usage.

Here is a typical "no-no" list:

| | |
|---|---|
| averted | indeed |
| curbed (for spending) | Sino-Soviet, Anglo-American, |
| feared (as in "feared dead") |    Afro-Asian, etc. |
| post (for "job") | triggered |
| on-the-heels of | rash of |
| weatherwise | blaze (for fire) |
| stave off | stepped-up |
| bevy of . . . (fires, storms, | impending |
|    etc.) | surge (of cold, arctic air) |
| on tap | cited (for named or charged) |
| voiced | ventured |
| bloodless coup | seek, sought, seeking |
| pave the way | upcoming, outgoing, |

incoming, downgrading
forward-looking
oust, ouster, ousted
hike (for pay increase)
perpetrator
youths
crackdown
spokesman, spokesmen
observers, sources say
grinding (crash)
proposal, proposed
dispatches
purported
probe (for investigate)
proliferating
upsurge (in crime, economy,)
withering (criticism, enemy
    fire)
slated
rapped (for criticized)

elsewhere, meanwhile
bearing fruit
terror stricken
strong measures
hopeless deadlock
meaningful, useful
blast (for explosion)
mad-dog killer
savage attack
brutal murder
wild-eyed assailant;
    assailant
terrorized
early settlement
impasse
bridge the gap
persons
the weatherman
white stuff (for snow)

## IN-CLASS AND HOMEWORK ASSIGNMENTS

1. Get hold of a newspaper and pick out at least three sentences which cannot be read out loud easily. Rewrite them in broadcast style and explain the changes you have made.

2. The author discusses your life style and how it should be applied to your style as a broadcast reporter. Describe your own life style in a few paragraphs, and then evaluate it in terms of your potential for success in broadcast news. Start with your strong points first in this evaluation, then mention some areas which you think need improvement and how you propose to bring about such improvements.

3. Explain what is wrong with each item in the list of examples which the author says he has actually heard mispronounced on the air. Add some of your own, if you have heard any.

4. Copy the list of words and phrases listed as "no-no's" and make your own list of suitable alternatives.

5. Select a story from today's local newspaper and rewrite it so that you can read it aloud in 30 seconds or less.

6. Tape record some local newscasts from an area radio station (or use a tape recording provided by your teacher) and rewrite stories which you think can be "tightened" or made a little clearer. Explain your changes.

7. Rewrite the crime story about the Sheriff's deputies and the hayride, etc. You may break it up into as many separate stories as you feel necessary.

8. Rewrite the "WNEW" example of the abuse of tape. Make up an imaginary "taped" excerpt to replace the one they have used.

9. Pretend that union rules will not allow you to touch any recorders. Rewrite the story for the previous question (8) in a "cue sheet" form with a carbon copy for your engineer. Put all of the things on it that are called for in the part of this chapter which covers this situation.

Photo by Chip Hires.

# Chapter 10

# The Industry and the Profession

Admittedly, broadcasting is not the most "stable" industry you can find in this country. Very often, a slight change in the winds of office politics or a slight dip in the ratings can bring about sudden unemployment. So can a new manager. There are many factors that cause broadcast stations themselves to have a lot of "turnover," but there are also many personal hangups among individuals themselves.

## WHY SOME GUYS JUST CANNOT HOLD JOBS

Not very long ago, the writer had the opportunity to screen a number of applicants for news jobs at a radio station in a major market. The economy was in one of its downward trends and some newsrooms at networks and major stations nearby were trimming their staffs. Some of the applicants worked briefly as substitutes so that the station could get a good look at them. Others just submitted tapes and resumes. In many cases, they had voices that would make Walter Cronkite sound like a choirboy and could type stories that would do credit to any network. At first glance, most of these people appeared to be the best that broadcast journalism had to offer, but a few of them would never be offered a full-time job if there was one and perhaps not even invited back as substitutes. Why? It is only fair to let you know:

### Nelson Know-It-All

First, there is *Nelson Know-It-All.* He cannot resist telling us all about how they do it at that 50-kilowatt station he worked for (or that network or some competitor who is somehow "bigger" than we are in power, staff, coverage area, or ratings—you name it). He clearly implies that he is doing us the favor by coming and gracing our newsroom with his presence, and that we all ought to be grateful that he is here. (A variation of this is the "Know-It-All" who comes from a college station or a broadcast or journalism school where they *always* do it right.)

### Irving Image Changer

Then there is *Irving Image Changer.* Despite all the directions we gave him, memos on the wall, hints, etc., about our own style and format, our own procedures, our own image on the air, etc., he wants the station to sound like *his* favorite station or network while he is on duty with us, and he proceeds to do a complete overhaul right on the air. If the station is known for soft music and a "gentle" news style, he will come out with all tape machines blazing in a big audio duel with the competition, putting three or four actualities in a little one- or two-minute "headline" edition of news, driving the control room people right up the wall.

### Sam Supermilitant

There is also *Sam Supermilitant,* who wears a big chip on his shoulder, waiting for the front office to knock it off. If there is the slightest irregularity in his paycheck, work assignment, or, worse yet, a critical word from the boss about his spellbinding newscasts, he moves with trigger-finger speed to dial that phone and "chew out" the accounting department, the News Director, the Program Director—you name it. They are all "against him."

## Eugene Unionist

A variation of the Supermilitant is the *Eugene Unionist.* If there is a union involved, he calls up the union office and expects a bolt of lightning to strike down those who may have offended him back at the station. (If you are in a union situation and you have something like this in mind, the writer suggests that you see your *Shop Steward* first. Normally, he is one of the guys who has worked there for quite a while and has not only encountered your kind of problem before but may have a solution that did not occur to you right at his fingertips.)

## Freddy The Fumbler

There are also *Freddy the Fumbler* types. These are really nice guys who would give you the shirt off their backs. Trouble is, they are always just a little bit disorganized in their personal lives and it "spills over" into their work. They get to the station a little late because they missed the bus, had a flat tire, ran out of gas, or they cannot guarantee they will be on time when you ask them to come and substitute because they are working somewhere else where the shift overlaps ours. When they finally arrive at the station, they have to call their wives, relatives, friends, other employers, etc., to let them know they will be late when they get through with *us.* Somehow, their stories keep getting mixed up, the wrong tapes get on the air, and a whole rash of mistakes just seems to break out whenever they are around. Nice guys, if they could only get organized.

## Sidney Story Teller

And then there is *Sidney Story Teller.* He is the greatest one for bull sessions. He always has one more joke or story for the disc jockeys, salesmen, engineers, secretaries, etc., before he gets back to the newsroom and gets down to work. Sometimes he is the chronic complainer variety, with a whole list of things you would not believe were wrong with the station, the management, the people in other departments, etc. At other times, he is just a good breeder of gossip or he sees himself as the world's greatest comedian. (A variation of this is *Charlie Comedian,* who spends a great deal of effort on company time trying to crack someone else up who is on the air by dropping his pants, holding up signs, wearing wastebaskets on his head, etc.)

## Vinnie Vindictive

*Vinnie Vindictive* is another one. He feels he has to defend to the death everything he just did on that last newscast when the boss either calls up or wanders into the studio to suggest the slightest modification. He does not have the insight to say, "Oh, you didn't like that, sir? Okay, we can change it," without having to admit being wrong. Instead, he bombards you with reasons for having done whatever it was. If you are the one who called him, you sort of "cringe" by your radio for his next newscast, because he has that slight snarl in his voice as though to tell the whole world he is only doing it this way under protest. (In fact, there was a guy who went one step further in this league back in the 1950's and resigned right over the air on the old Herald Tribune Network. It seemed as though every few months for the next few years, he would resign over the air on another unsuspecting station out in the suburbs. He proudly showed the writer a scrapbook of newspaper clippings resulting from this strange activity. He had one of the best voices in the business when the writer last saw him some years ago, but any station where his reputation had preceded him probably would not touch him with a ten-foot pole!)

## El Exigente

Of course, you will not forget *El Exigente.* Like his counterpart in the well-known TV commercials, he keeps you on the defensive. (News Directors are often prone to this type of behavior.) His brand of journalism is always a little better than the next guy's. He looks down his nose at most other people's efforts, and lets you know one way or the other that no one can hope to match his flawless work. He constantly finds fault with others, usually gossiping about someone who is not present at the moment, but sometimes even putting you down right to your face. He tries to give the impression that he is highly dedicated. Maybe *he* feels dedicated, but the others feel he is "something else."

### Peter Pear-Shape

*Peter Pear-Shape* is another familiar newsroom character. This fellow can charm you with his melodious voice, and judging from his audition tape you wonder why he is not at a bigger station. That is, until you sit him down to a typewriter or send him out with a portable tape recorder. At one, he can hardly spell "cat," while at the other he either comes back empty-handed or brings you something that is too poor to put on the air. An interview with him does not uncover these things when he applies for a job. This is because he can talk endlessly about radio and TV stations, use all the appropriate jargon and drop names as though he is an old hand. He *is* an old hand—at occupying a chair and holding a coffee cup in both hands.

### Ronald Resonant

*Ronald Resonant* is usually a well-meaning and dedicated young man. He takes himself very seriously. He may be all of 20 or 21 years old, standing there in the newsroom, but he tries very hard to sound like he is in his 50's on the air. If he would only relax and be himself, at least there would not be any credibility gap. He overpronounces his words to impress you with his reading skill. He tries to sound *very* authoritative and serious, perhaps to compensate for the fact that there is not very much education, experience, or just plain maturity behind that voice. To borrow a phrase which the ABC Network-owned stations once used in their ads, he tries to make "an Easter egg-roll on the White House lawn sound like the invasion of Normandy." He never gets past the audition at larger stations but you hear him quite often on the smaller stations because the price is right, especially on weekends. This poor fellow tries hard and his loyalty is usually beyond reproach, but unless he has something else going for him, he probably will not last very long and he certainly will not advance in the profession.

## AUDITION TAPES, RESUMES, AND INTERVIEWS

Word got around one year that a station might have a full-time opening just at the time when other major stations nearby were laying off newsmen in droves. As mentioned earlier in this chapter, the economy was in a slump and a lot of good talent was being turned loose. Immediately, the resumes and phone calls started pouring in. The writer had seen this process taking place before at smaller stations whenever summer came and college students were out on vacation. They would approach the Program Director for summer jobs as disc jockeys, and when they did not succeed they would try the newsroom.

In the New York City market, though, the station was not dealing with college students; it expected some real "heavies" to be applying. Some of the applications were good, there is no denying it, but in a majority of cases the writer had not seen *worse* presentations than those crossing his desk at that point. Many were so sloppily done, they did not even merit an answer. Some of the applicants he interviewed in person came on with all the finesse of a big dog climbing into someone's lap, and he would let go a sigh of relief when they finally left. If, as you read this, you are planning to go out looking for a broadcast news job sometime soon, here are a few pointers.

The practice of sending out a whole "flock" of tapes and resumes, and then of waiting for the News Directors of the world to beat a path to your door, is *not* going to accomplish very much. Most stations receiving this kind of application will know you are just on a "fishing trip" and they will not waste their time with you. Among some of the worst resumes are those produced by a few commercial broadcasting schools (fortunately, not *all* broadcasting schools) who run them off on an old beat-up ditto machine. They give each of their graduates a stack of these resumes with his vital statistics fuzzily reproduced thereon, along with an equally fuzzy form letter that tells that he has just graduated from their school and that he is looking for a job. The letters are simply addressed to "News Director" with the call letters and city. Inside, they begin, "Dear Sir,"—no names, no street addresses, no effort at *personal* contact. These go right into the waste basket.

Before you approach any station for a position, do your homework. Take the trouble to find out the *names* of the General Manager, Program Director, and News Director. These are readily available in any *Broadcasting Yearbook*, along with the correct street address and phone number for the station. If you are writing from out of town, address it to the News Director by name, not just "News Director" and "Dear Sir." Even if News Directors have been changed since the yearly index was published, the person who answers your inquiry will still be more impressed by your having used a name at all. Too many applicants fail to exercise even this simple courtesy. Your resume may be photocopied, dittoed, mimeographed, etc., but your letter of application should be individually typed.

If you are dropping by a station personally, try to confirm with the receptionist (if they have one) the name of the News Director just in case there has been a change. Even if the first person you come to happens to be the News Director himself and you use a name, there is a good chance it is the right one if you took the trouble to look it up. These may seem like very small points, but face it: If you have not bothered to find out his name and remember it, why should this News Director to whom you are applying bother to find out or remember yours? As Dale Carnegie put it in his book *How to Win Friends and Influence People,* the nicest thing to say to any person is his own name.

Aiming too high for your experience is a waste of your time and that of the News Director you are trying to convince. If you are just getting into the business with no special qualifications and less than a college degree for education, stick to stations of 1000 watts or less in towns of fewer than 100,000 population for your first job, or stay as close to those figures as you can. (The term 1000 watts refers to a common designation for AM radio stations. FM and TV stations differ from this, using generally higher figures.) If you have had a year or two behind the microphone (and behind the typewriter and tape recorder) then you might try stations of 5000 watts (AM) and up in towns of more than 100,000. After a few more years, you can set your sights even higher, but do not expect to walk into a 50,000-watt (AM) station in one of the nation's ten largest cities and get an interview—much less a job—if you have never had any experience before. You would be competing with seasoned veterans who have many years of on-the-air experience behind them.

There must be a job *opening* before they can hire you. Stations can sometimes add on stringers, substitutes, and other part-time people for vacations, sick days, or expanded coverage of major stories, but generally if they are not already looking for someone, you are not likely to find a job, regardless of your qualifications. How can you find the stations that are looking for full-time news people? Here are a few hints:

1. Follow the ads in *Broadcasting* magazine and other trade journals. At least in these publications, you will know which stations have openings, because they are advertising them. For *Broadcasting,* the address is: 1735 DeSales Street, N.W., Washington, D.C., 20036. Use the same address if you want to get a copy of their "Yearbook" directory. You may prefer to write for rates first, because in recent years price increases have put subscriptions a bit out of reach for beginners and students. At some stations, a few people on the staff can "split" the cost of a subscription, and you may find someone with similar interests who would be willing to "buddy up" with you.

2. Stake out the geographical area in which you would like to work. Phone ahead to a few stations in that area, and say you would like to just drop by for a moment. Try to avoid the word "interview." Just say you will be on the way through the area and that you are looking for possible job openings, but that you know they are busy and you just want to introduce yourself and see if they know of anything in the area. This way, they are not so much on the defensive. They have not committed themselves, and, as far as they are concerned, you are just "visiting." This is not cheating—nobody is going to admit to some stranger over the phone that there is a job waiting. They will want to get a look at you first, and then, if they have something, they will let you know. If not, at least you have made a contact

and you have filed an application with them. When you call up in the future they will at least have had a chance to meet you before and your opportunity will be greatly enhanced.

3.  Do not demand an audition. If they are in the mood to give you one, fine, but it is better to have a tape ready. If you do not have a tape recording of yourself delivering a newscast, that will be your first project before you can undertake any effective job-hunting. For this, you will have to look up a a recording studio or a small radio station in your area and make arrangements for a recording session and some material to read. Have a few copies made of the tape, because many stations to whom you apply will give you back a different reel of tape instead of the one you originally submited. Others will give you nothing back at all.

4.  If you are a beginner, a free-lance relationship with a small local station might be better. This way they do not have to hire you. You can get to know the people in the newsroom, you can try sending them some stories, and see what they accept for broadcast. If you have a portable tape recorder and you are able to send them "actualities" or on-the-scene interviews over the phone from the scene of a story, you might develop the "knack" of doing this and start charging a dollar or two for the stories they accept for broadcast. They are not paying you for your time as they would a regular employee; they are just buying the story on a piece-work basis. The writer has seen college students at a campus near the state capitol do this with half a dozen small stations around the state. From this kind of relationship, you can build toward part-time work as a substitute and from there to a full-time position, depending on where the openings are and how they like your work.

## UNIONS: THEIR ASSETS AND LIABILITIES

Just the word "union" evokes an emotional response from most people. It depends largely on who you are and your present role and past experience. To a Shop Steward who has just led his co-workers through successful negotiations and a good contract settlement, it is one thing. To a station manager who has just beaten back an attempt to organize his employees, it is another. This book will try to examine both sides of this often-sensitive part of our industry here, because to avoid it would be like playing "ostrich."

Some of the major unions involved with the broadcast industry are:

▶ AFTRA, The American Federation of Radio & Television Artists,

▶ I.B.E.W., The International Brotherhood of Electrical Workers,

▶ NABET, The National Association of Broadcast Employees and Technicians,

▶ SAG, The Screen Actors' Guild, and

▶ W.G.A., The Writers' Guild of America.

The ones whose initials are separated with periods above are referred to by their individual initials. The others are usually pronounced as words ("AF-tra," "NAY-bet," and "SAG").

Newsmen are not usually included in I.B.E.W., which covers engineers almost exclusively, nor are they likely to be in "SAG," which concentrates its efforts on actors for movies, filmed commercials, and television. W.G.A. organizes writers for the networks and larger stations, as well as for newspapers and other print media, but does not concentrate on the "on-the-air" personnel. This leaves AFTRA and NABET.

AFTRA is the union where you will find most of your well-known network radio and TV newscasters, like Walter Cronkite, David Brinkley, Howard K. Smith, and others. It also includes the big-name performers like Johnny Carson, Bob Hope, and a long list of others ranging back through the years to charter members like Eddie Cantor, Edgar Bergen, and Jascha Heifetz. It is the dominant union in this field, and it concentrates on the larger stations and the larger cities as well as the networks, but it is often found in smaller towns and stations.

AFTRA'S major activities are on the economic front, negotiating and then enforcing contracts, seeking better wages and working conditions, and taking care of the special needs of different types of performers and the requirements demanded of them.

AFTRA has some 30 "locals" throughout the country, based mainly in the major cities. Local boards of directors are selected by the members in each local, and you are likely to recognize most of the names on a given board because they are mostly well-known air personalities from that particular area. Salaried executives and a paid local staff are retained by the local to carry on the day-to-day business.

The contracts negotiated at a national level for networks and network-owned stations are first hammered out in various committees who draw up basic demands on wages, fees, working conditions, and other categories. AFTRA's national convention approves these demands by delegate vote, and then the bargaining team goes to work. At individual stations on the local level, the members are the "convention," and the negotiators follow their lists of demands in bargaining with employ-

Photo by United Press International.

ers. The salaries and fees set forth in all AFTRA contracts are considered the minimum. They are what you start with. You are always free to do better, but wherever there is a contract in effect you are not allowed to accept less.

Each local sets an initiation fee and a scale for dues. The dues are usually based on your earnings bracket for the previous year. AFTRA has a pension and welfare plan, accidental death insurance, Blue Cross and major medical insurance, and other benefits included for the cost of the dues.

NABET, the National Association of Broadcast Employees and Technicians, has a similar operation but as its name implies does not limit itself to on-the-air personnel. You are more likely to find NABET in stations where all employees ranging from secretary and engineer to copy writer and disc jockey want to be represented by the same bargaining unit.

If the station to which you are applying has no union to represent its employees, this means you are on your own. In many small stations there is little or no danger involved in this kind of arrangement. Relations between management and employees range from the almost paternal to the barely tolerable, depending on the market and the availability of qualified talent. Some owners treat employees like members of their families and the station's operation is very stable over the years. Others get all the mileage they can on a strictly businesslike basis, and employees either advance to larger stations or drop out if they are dissatisfied, but rarely does anyone "stand and fight," challenging management on its own ground.

In networks and in larger stations, management has usually been able to accept unions as a way of life and to bargain with them in a businesslike manner. The manager doing the bargaining may own a few shares in the company, but he does not own the whole firm. Negotiating with employee unions is part of his job. At many smaller stations if the manager is not the owner he at least knows the owners personally and can probably count them on one hand. In the smaller stations where there is no union, you are likely to find an intense fear of unions and any effort to organize will be met with a tooth-and-nail fight.

Unless there is a definite consensus among your fellow employees that conditions warrant having a union in a station where there presently is none, you would be safer not acting as a one-man organizing team. Union literature is correct in saying that your right to file for an NLRB* election is protected by state and federal law, but *only* after your intentions as a group of petitioners for such an election have been declared. Before that official declaration, management can easily find another excuse for firing someone they suspect of trying to organize a union.

The writer saw two cases not too long ago where a union shop was successfully organized and where it fell through. In the case where a union was voted in, management had long had a reputation among broadcast employees in the state as being difficult to work for. Even other managers in neighboring towns could see the flaws. In this case, the employees' grievances were practically identical. Since they were in agreement on their grievances and demands, and since they constituted a clear majority of the employees, they won. At the other station, somebody suggested that they have a union and passed a petition around. They got enough signatures to hold an election, but each one had a different view of what his grievances and demands were. Not in agreement with one another, they wavered at election time and fell short of a majority. Most of the pro-union employees left the station shortly thereafter.

Everybody has gripes about the boss at one time or another. If your gripes do not exactly match those of the others, you would do well to handle the situation yourself. Maybe tomorrow will be a better day, or maybe it is time to look for a better job elsewhere. At the organizing stage, you need not only a majority but a clear-cut case. If management is so insensitive, incompetent, inefficient, or even all of these things as to not realize that there is widespread and perhaps unanimous dissatisfaction among employees, then perhaps an attempt at organizing is advisable. If the scope of the problem is less than that, take a second look.

---

*NLRB, National Labor Relations Board.

Photo by Chip Hires.

# Chapter 11

# A Word From Your Sponsor, the Outfit That Signs Your Paycheck

It's New Year's Eve, and you have made reservations to go out tonight when you get home from work. Only trouble is, the guy who is supposed to work the night shift did not show up. You call the boss and he tells you there is not much he can do about it. You will just have to stay there until you are relieved, "for the good of the station." You do, and for some reason nobody notices it. That is, nobody but the wife who was all set to go out with you. There is nothing extra in your next paycheck, not even thanks.

Suppose it is a Sunday afternoon. You have a houseful of guests. You have been working a six-day week, so you are really enjoying your one day off when suddenly the phone rings. It's the station: "Get down to Route 7, there's been a big accident." You hate to leave, but you excuse yourself and hop in the car. About twenty minutes later, you arrive at the scene but there is no one there.

After searching around for another twenty minutes, you find someone who tells you, "Oh yes, there was a little fender-bender but they exchanged license information and drove away."

When you get home, most of your guests have left. No extra pay, no thanks.

These incidents and hundreds of others like them are true. Ask anyone who has worked as a beginner at a small-market station if he has ever been "hung up" like this and you will hear some pretty good stories.

## PROTECTING YOURSELF

At some of the larger stations, a union contract foresees some of these problems and provides for overtime pay and other things to protect employees from many situations that would otherwise constantly inconvenience them. At smaller stations, though, they can give you an "executive" title (like News Director) and a "salary" (like $130 a week) and because you are such a highly paid executive you are exempt from minimum wage laws.

How do you protect yourself? For one thing, start asking questions *in advance.* The time to ask them is during your interview for the job. The time *not* to ask them is when one of these emergencies arises, you are on the phone with the boss, and one of you is going to get "stuck." The boss may squirm a bit when you ask all these things at the interview, but if his answers are evasive or uncertain, or if he says, "Well, we'll take that up when we get to such a situation," those are your danger signals right there. It is better to seek straight answers when both of you are calm and you still have the chance to ask yourself if you really want the job badly enough to accept some of the risks.

Pay careful attention to the questions which follow in this chapter. Memorize as many as possible, so you will not be "stuck" during an interview, and so you will know what to listen for as your prospective employer tells his side of the story.

## SOME QUESTIONS TO ASK BEFORE YOU START WORKING

Every station will have its own policies and procedures for meeting FCC regulations, state employment and labor laws, safety requirements imposed by insurance companies and local authorities, etc. To help you find out what the policies are in "your" station—meaning the one you are presumably working for or applying to work for—here are some questions you'll want answers to before you start.

Some space has been left between the questions. If this copy is owned by a particular station or News Director, you may even find the answers to them written in. If this is your own copy of the book, this is where you can jot down the answers to the questions as you come across them.

## (1) Getting Paid

a) What application-for-employment forms must be filled out and to whom must I submit them?

b) What tax and withholding forms must be submitted? To whom?

c) How do I account for my time: Is there a time card, a punch clock, or what? When are the cards turned in, and how?

d) How do I account for "overtime"? Is there a special authorization needed? From whom? Is it submitted with the time card?

e) I presume that overtime is at least time-and-a-half after 40 hours in one week and after 8 hours in one day. Is this so? If not, why not?

f) Do we work a five-day week, six-day week, or what?

g) Is there at least a 12-hour "turn-around" period between the time we leave work one day and return the next? If not, why?

h) Do we get double pay for being held over or called in early if it goes into this 12-hour turn-around? If not, what *do* we get?

i) Is there double-pay involved for being called in to work on one's day off or during one's vacation? If not, why not?

j) What is the usual practice when you need substitutes for vacations or absences due to illness: Do you have a list of outside people who are called in to substitute or do other employees have to work extra hours to make up for the missing person?

k) If regular employees fill-in during each other's absences, do they get paid according to the time-and-a-half for overtime and double-time for "short turn-around" concepts, or what?

l) I believe state labor laws allow an employee to refuse to work certain overtime shifts, such as substituting for others during vacations and other nonemergency periods. Is this not so? If I were to decline the opportunity to work such extra shifts, it would not count against me, would it?

m) Are my duties confined strictly to news, or will I be playing records, taking care of transmitters, recording commercials, and other things? Under what circumstances will I be asked to perform duties outside the scope of "news"? Will I be paid extra for these nonnews duties? If not, why?

n) Am I to work a "straight shift" (all my hours at once) or a "split shift" (work a few hours, take some time off, then return to work for a few more hours)?

o) If it is a "split shift," what is the status of those hours between the parts of my shift: Am I on "standby"? Will I be paid time-and-a-half for having to perform extra duties during that layover period? If not, why not?

p) (If you have been told that as News Director or some other executive-sounding title that overtime does not apply because you are getting a "salary"):

According to the Federal Wage and Hour law, sir, work such as giving station identification and time signals, announcing the names of programs, and similar routine work is not exempt from overtime provisions, so I would get paid overtime if I did any of these things beyond my normal working hours, right?

The reporting of news, the rewriting of stories from various sources, the routine collection of facts about news events by investigation, interview, or personal observation, and the writing of stories for broadcast is not exempt from overtime provisions (of the Federal Fair Labor Standards Act). I would be paid overtime for performing any of these duties beyond my normal working hours, right?

Covering an outside "news beat" or an assigned story for broadcast is not exempt from Federal overtime regulations either, so I would get paid overtime for that, right?

**(2) News Schedule and Format**

a) When do we have our newscasts? How long are they? Is there a network involved, or are they all locally originated?

b) Are commercials inserted into the newscasts? How and when?

c) Is there a special theme or format used to introduce and/ or close the newscast? How does it work?

d) Do all newscasts follow the same format, or do they differ according to length and time of day?

e) Is there any special way of handling weather forecasts?

f) What is our policy on sports in the news?

g) Are there any particular hard-to-pronounce or unusual names of places, people, and things in the area that I should watch out for? Do you have a list of them somewhere?

h) What is the policy on school-closing announcements? Do just newsmen handle them, or is someone else authorized to do so? What if I doubt someone who calls with such an announcement: What do I tell him and how can I check on it?

i) What is the "disaster plan" for train derailments, plane crashes, and the like?

j) Am I to assume that I am automatically on overtime, pay and all, if I am held over to take care of such an emergency? If not, what are the alternatives and why?

k) Am I authorized to call in extra help in the event of a disaster? If so, who can be called? Is there a list posted with phone numbers? Are these people all aware that they are eligible to be called, or will they question my authority to call them? If I am *not* authorized to call in extra help, what do I do instead?

l) What are the most controversial issues in town, and what are the station's policies for handling them?

m) Who are the most persistent extremists, critics, pests, and other people to watch out for—and why?

n) When I am confronted with something that looks a little too controversial, slanted, or otherwise inappropriate for broadcast, should I refer the sender to someone else? Should I confer with someone else on the side while delaying an answer to the party concerned?

o) What is our coverage area, and how do we treat it? What towns do we cover, what counties, what Congressional Districts? Is it safe to just say "the city council" or must we distinguish between several towns? What about the state government: Can we just talk about a state agency or official without mentioning which state, or are we close enough to a state line that it might become confused?

**(3) The Facilities**

a) What wire service or services do we have?

b) What are their phone numbers to file stories, report machine trouble, report wire trouble?

c) What is our policy on filing stories with wire services?

d) The world and national material is usually pretty good on the wire services, but in some areas the state-and-local "splits" leave something to be desired. What are the major problems we have had with the state wire copy, if any?

e) What about paper, ribbons, etc., for the wire service machine(s)?

f) What are the telephone facilities like? Is there a special way of handling "beeper" calls? What about long-distance calls? Is there a "hotline" number?

g) Do we have any stringers from whom we should accept calls? What is the policy on accepting their calls? Are some of them paid? Do we "swap" stories with stations in other towns? What is the policy?

# Glossary of Broadcast News Terms

This glossary will not insult you by telling you that a *newsdesk* is "a desk where the news is made up," which is found in some glossaries. What you will find here are some of the terms the writer did not stop to explain in the text, such as "daytimer" and "beeper," because it does not occur to many broadcasters to stop and explain words like that; they are just part of the language you hear in newsrooms. If you do not find the term you want here, try the index; chances are that some of the terms you are looking for were discussed earlier in the text.

**"A" wire**—A teletypewriter service offered by AP and UPI wire service organizations. Most radio and TV newsrooms have what is called the "broadcast" wire or "radio" wire; afternoon papers have a "p.m." wire and morning newspapers have an "a.m." wire, and all of them are worded to suit their clients' needs, but the wire where the stories appear *first* and are then rewritten for the other versions is the "A" wire.

**accredited spokesman**—An individual who has the proper credentials and authority to speak for a certain organization, such as a hospital, a police department, a government office, etc., as compared with an individual within one of these organizations who does *not* have permission to speak for publication or broadcast as the official spokesman of that organization.

**accuracy**—A state of precision and exactness; freedom from error as the result of special care and conformity to truth and to particular standards.

**accurate**—*(adj.)* The degree of accuracy achieved.

**actuality; actualities**—An on-the-scene recording of the actual sounds of an event as it occurred, especially the voices of persons involved in the event, as opposed to merely a report or other reconstruction of such an event. (*See also* raw sound.)

**ad-lib interpretation**—A spoken description or narration of an event given by a reporter who is speaking extemporaneously without the benefit of a written text. (*See also* voice-over.)

**advance material**—News copy written about an anticipated event before such an event takes place, usually bearing instructions for release by news media at a prescribed time or upon confirmation that the event is actually taking place or has occurred.

**advance reports**—News reports filed by a reporter covering a story before the story itself is complete. Advance reports usually concentrate on the agenda of scheduled events or upon the status of a story which is in progress, and are subject to revision in later reports.

**advancement-oriented**—As used in this text, stories about minority persons in the news which concentrate on their advancement in education, employment, or other areas of achievement, as opposed to stories which focus on negative information about such people.

**Afghanistanism**—The practice of selecting stories which have little or no relation to current issues in the local area. This is occasionally done by news reporters who wish to avoid controversial situations locally.

**air-check**—A tape recording or videotape recording made of a broadcast program as it actually occurs on the air.

**allegedly**—An important "disclaimer" term used in writing news stories to indicate that all declarations, assertions, descriptions, etc., in a given story or portion of a story are those of someone else, not of the newscaster or the station. Usually these involve charges or accusations made by police, and the newscaster who uses the term by saying that a person in a story "allegedly" committed a crime means, in effect, "according to police."

**alligator clips**—A wire attachment device used by individuals who carry portable tape recorders to enable them to connect a recorder to amplifiers, telephones, or other sound-carrying facilities for purposes of recording or transmitting sounds. At one end of the wire is a plug which properly fits the tape recorder; at the other is a pair of clamps whose jaws open much like those of an alligator in order to connect with equipment of various sizes.

**ambient noise**—The "atmosphere" background of sound which normally accompanies almost all recordings (except those made under the very quietest and most carefully controlled studio situations). (*See also* atmosphere, background.)

**anchor man**—The leading newscaster on a team assigned to a particular newscast. Example: Walter Cronkite on CBS-TV.

**angle**—1. A technique or approach in writing and/or delivering a news story which takes into account the reporter's point of view. 2. A camera angle, the position of a video or film camera in relation to the particular subject.

**AOPA Airport Directory**—An annual directory of public and private airports issued by the Aircraft Owners and Pilots Association.

**AP**—The Associated Press; a wire service used by many broadcast newsrooms as well as by newspapers throughout the U.S.

**arson** (vs. "set" fire)—The act of *deliberately* setting a fire for criminal purposes. Some fires can be deliberately set, but it might just be out of carelessness that they spread farther than intended. Only use the term "arson" for news purposes when quoting a properly accredited fire official who states for the record that their investigation shows the fire was *not* accidentally set and that criminal motives are apparent.

**atmosphere**—The "background" of ambient noise at a given location which may enhance the recording of an event so as to give it some authenticity and to give listeners (and/or viewers) a sense of participation. (*See also* ambient noise.)

**attribution**—The naming of the person or other source whose quote or information is being used in a news story.

**audio cuts**—Separately recorded bands or excerpts of sound on tape or disc. In news, individual reports or actualities on tape for use in newscasts.

**audio hotlines**—Telephone lines to which automatic tape recorders have been attached. When radio stations call the telephone numbers assigned to these tape recorders (usually toll-free), they are automatically "fed" with audio cuts from the organization which is sponsoring the hotline. Some hotlines are not just tape recorders, but are answered by persons on duty at all times, providing news reporters with immediate access to a spokesman for the organization which is sponsoring the line.

**audition**—*(verb)* To listen to something in advance of intended use for the purpose of determining its quality and how it shall be prepared for use.

**audition**—*(noun)* A qualifying test given to those who apply for jobs in the broadcast industry. Usually the individual being given the audition is asked to read some news or commercial copy and to show other skills suitable for the job in mind.

**authoritative vs. authorized sources**—The ability to distinguish between these two types of news sources is vital to good journalism. Authoritative sources are those who assert, claim, or try to give the impression that they have the proper authority to make certain statements, whether they have such authority or not. Authorized sources are those who have actually been given the permission and authority to speak on behalf of a particular person or group.

**background**—1. In news conferences and other news-gathering situations: implied or explicit rules under which reporters are committed to report only certain information released in a limited or controlled manner by a source who is not to be directly quoted or named. Acceptance of an invitation to a "background" news conference implies acceptance of such a rule. 2. In sound recording, see *ambient noise* and *atmosphere.*

**back-timing**—"Counting backwards" on the clock to determine when to start a final portion of a program. For example, if you have a five-minute interview program and your closing remarks will take about 30 seconds, back-timing will tell you that you must complete the interview and turn to your closing remarks no later than 4½ minutes into the program.

**balance**—Proper distribution of items in a newscast so that there is not too much of one particular kind of thing. For example, balance among world, national, and local items; or, on TV, balance between stories with film and those without film so that they are not bunched together in one part of the newscast.

**bar association**—Professional association of lawyers and judges. Most major cities have a local bar association, all states have a state-wide bar association, and at the national level there is the American Bar Association.

**beat**—1. The route regularly followed by a particular reporter in routine gathering of the news. 2. Also, scoring a "beat" is the act of getting a good story on the air before your competitor can do so.

**beeper**—A report which is recorded or even directly broadcast from a telephone line. Originally, such reports had to have a "beep" tone every 15 seconds, but FCC regulations have since been relaxed to allow persons who knew in advance that they were being recorded or broadcast (especially news reporters) to proceed without the beep.

**billboard**—A table of contents for a series of audio cuts, telling the speaker, topic, location, and length of time, along with the "outcue" or last words in each cut. The billboard is either in spoken form at the beginning of a reel of tape which contains the audio cuts, or is issued by AP, UPI, and other news services on their teletypewriter machines just before they send the cuts by way of a separate audio line.

**break**—*(noun)* Station break; time-out to identify the station or to insert a commercial in a newscast. *(verb)* To broadcast a story for the first time, as to "break" the news that something has happened.

**brutality**—A sensitive term among law enforcement groups: It may denote official charges against a particular policeman which may be cause for disciplinary action, claiming that the accused officer savagely beat someone. Check carefully before using it on the air in your area.

**bulletin**—Term used by wire services to convey to newsrooms that a particular story is quite urgent and may deserve such attention as to warrant an interruption in normal programming. Items which the wire service feels are almost as important as bulletins are labelled "urgent," while earth-shaking developments for which practically all broadcast stations in the country would interrupt their programming are labelled "flash."

**bulletinitis**—The name given to the practice of putting too many bulletins on the air; constantly interrupting regular programming with sensationalized presentations of the news.

**bulk-erase**—To "wipe" a reel of tape (or a cassette or cartridge) with an electromagnet which erases all of the audio and/or video on the entire reel.

**bystander** (as opposed to "qualified observer")—One who is standing near an event but who most likely is *not* taking part in it; therefore, one whose remarks to newsmen may have little or no value compared to those of a qualified observer who knows what is going on (such as another news reporter). See Chapter 2, "On the Scene."

**CAB**—Civil Aeronautics Board.

**Canons of Ethics**—The rules which govern the behavior of lawyers and judges. Violation of these rules can lead to "disbarment" or suspension from the privilege of practicing law.

**cartridge; cassette**—Self-contained systems of recording tape encapsulated in plastic containers. The shape of the container is designed for quick insertion into a tape recorder or tape-playback machine. Cartridges contain a single continuous loop of tape on a single reel, while cassettes are reel-to-reel systems which have been encased (and often miniaturized) for easy handling. The terms cartridge and cassette are used for videotape as well as for audio recording tape.

**CATV (cable television)**—A system of wired television originally based on a master antenna feeding TV signals to areas where reception was otherwise poor. (The initials stood for "**C**ommunity

Antenna TV.") This has evolved into an industry which distributes TV signals to subscribers in towns throughout the country whether broadcast reception of such signals is poor or not. The enclosed system can distribute many more channels than are available from broadcast sources in a given area, and may even originate programs of its own.

**caucus**—A closed meeting of leaders in a political party to determine policy, strategy, or candidates.

**censorship**—Orders, usually from an official government source, which forbid the broadcast or publication of material prior to its intended release. Such a practice has been found unconstitutional in the U.S., as it directly violates the First Amendment "freedom of the press."

**change of venue**—An order to change the location of a trial when it has been concluded by judicial authorities that a fair trial is not possible in the geographic area where the defendent was originally to be tried.

**chronological**—An account of events in the same order as they occurred in time (as opposed to other approaches such as order of importance or those which cost the most or which aroused the greatest opposition or controversy).

**civil disorder**—A term slightly stronger than merely "disturbance" for describing disruptive behavior by a number of persons. It is still much safer to use than the word "riot," which implies a tumultuous, wild, or violent disturbance by a large number of persons. ("Riot" should only be used if officially released by police as *their* description of the event.)

**clearance**—Authorization; permission.

**cold**—Description of the approach to a newscast, commercial, or other material which must be read or performed without having been seen beforehand.

**combination disc jockey; "combo" man**—One who performs several functions at a time, such as one who is responsible for the station's transmitter and other engineering duties while playing records as a disc jockey. Sometimes the combination of duties also includes newscasting as well as disc jockey and engineering tasks, but the news is usually of the "rip-and-read" variety.

**comment**—A statement which adds opinion, criticism, or one's point of view to material which may previously have been just a straight presentation of facts.

**commercial policies**—The policies which specify when a particular advertiser's commercials should and should *not* be run, and under what conditions. (In this book, the examples used concern the restriction or complete withdrawal of airline advertising when there has been a plane crash in the news.)

**competence**—Sufficient skill, fitness, and ability to meet the requirements of the job.

**condescending**—Sometimes used to denote a manner of "talking down" to someone in a patronizing manner, as though addressing a child; acting as though he is doing you the favor of lowering himself to your level.

**contempt (of court)**—An act seen by court authorities as obstructing, hindering, or embarrassing the court in its ability to administer justice. "Direct" contempt is that which occurs right in the courtroom; "indirect" contempt includes the refusal to obey subpoenas and other lawful court orders.

**copy**—*(noun)* Typed or printed text of news prepared for broadcast or publication, such as: "Do you have enough copy for a five-minute newscast," or "Hand me that piece of wire copy."

**correspondent**—A journalist reporting from a particular geographical or other specialized area who has expert knowledge of that area, as opposed to a stringer or ordinary reporter who has been sent to an area or who may be located there but who does not necessarily have expert knowledge of that area.

**credentials**—Cards or certificates (such as "Press Cards") carried by persons to show that they are entitled to acquire access to certain locations or sources of information.

**credibility gap**—A term coined by news reporters during the Vietnam War when they did not want to say outright that government officials (particularly President Lyndon B. Johnson) were lying, but that statements made by these officials were hard to believe.

**cue**—*(noun)* A signal to start; usually written into the script, given by a voice or hand-signal command, or occurring as a key phrase in a program already underway. *(verb)* To set up a tape, film, or record in a position ready for playback, so that a simple starting motion will cause the recorded material to play. Also, the giving of the hand or spoken signal as in the noun definition above.

**cut**—One of several separately recorded bands of music, news, or other material on a tape or disc.

**daytimer; daytime radio station**—An AM radio station licensed by the Federal Communications Commission to operate only during certain specified daylight hours.

**deep background**—One of a number of "ground rules" for certain types of news conferences where only limited information may be released for broadcast or publication. Under the "deep background" situation, the source of the story can neither be named nor quoted, and even the time and place of the story's origin must somehow be disguised or withheld in order to protect the source. *(See also* off the record, background.)

**defamation of character**—An attack upon someone's reputation, tending to expose that person to ridicule or contempt. *(See also* libel.)

**degauss**—To erase or "wipe" recorded signals from a tape or videotape with an electromagnet or bulk-eraser for reuse. *(See also* erase, bulk-erase.)

**demonstration**—A public show of feeling or opinion, usually expressed through a parade or mass meeting; the word by itself does *not* imply violence, and should be used in place of other more inflammatory words unless violence has definitely been confilmed. *(See also* disturbance, civil disorder, riot, incident.)

**disturbance**—A commotion or disorder. This term is used by news media when they wish to avoid stronger terms (such as "riot") until it can be accurately determined just how many people are involved and how much actual violence has occurred. *(See also* civil disorder, demonstration, incident, riot.)

**D.O.A.**—Dead on arrival, usually at a hospital or morgue.

**documentary**—A program or movie, usually of considerable length, which shows social conditions or which summarizes and/or analyzes related news events.

**double-track**—A recording situation in which a tape carries two separately recorded programs (also referred to by some as "half-track") with each program occupying about 40 percent of the upper or lower half of the tape. This can be used for recording in stereo or for placing twice as much material on a given reel of tape, but the tape cannot be played back on machines which do not have the proper playback heads to pick up each separate track.

**dubbing**—Making a copy of a tape or record upon another tape or disc. Also, mixing and combining various live and recorded sounds onto a new recording which then has a combination of all the previously separate sounds.

**edit**—To revise news stories or recordings, usually taking out unnecessary, distracting, or inaccurate portions.

**editorial**—Opinion, as opposed to just straight facts, intended to influence the audience; usually done by the station management and presented as the "official" view of the station itself as an organization.

**embargo**—A rule which forbids the release of a story until the word has been given to do so. Usually this is done by a wire service or other news agency which releases certain news stories in advance, asking that broadcast stations and others who receive them hold them until a specified time of release or until a signal has been given. *(See also* hold for release.)

**emergency contacts**—People or organizations whom you may contact for information when an emergency occurs; a list of names and phone numbers *prepared in advance* in case news reporters should need to reach them quickly.

**emergency landing** (airplane)—One in which the safety of the aircraft is seriously threatened and in which the plane may crash if the flight is continued. (Examples: control problems, structural failure, engine fires.) This term is *not* to be used in situations where "precautionary" or "unscheduled" landings take place (see those terms) and only to be broadcast when a properly authorized spokesman can be quoted by name as having officially termed it an "emergency," using that word.

**emergency mobilization chart**—A list of names and phone numbers of all personnel who can serve as reporters and in other related jobs when a news emergency occurs, along with a plan for quickly reaching them and assigning them to specific tasks and schedules.

**event-oriented**—A type of news story for which something must "happen," as one in which an auto must crash or a brick must be thrown through a window, compared with stories based on surveys, trends, comparisons, historical or other "inquiry" approaches not tied to a particular event.

**extremist; extremism**—Persons who hold radical and severe views, usually noted for their "hate" tactics against others with whom they disagree. Extremism: the practice of holding such views.

**FAA**—Federal Aviation Agency; the government body which regulates aviation in the U.S., and which sometimes assists the National Transportation Safety Board in investigating nonfatal airplane accidents, especially those accidents involving smaller privately owned aircraft.

**FCC**—Federal Communications Commission; the government body which regulates radio and TV broadcasting in the U.S., along with other areas involving use of radio and/or electronic transmissions.

**FCC Regulations**—As applied to radio and TV broadcasting, those rules under which all radio and TV stations in the U.S. must operate, and which may be enforced as though they were actually laws by authority of the U.S. Congress granted to the FCC.

**fender-benders**—Insignificant automobile accidents in which no one has been injured and little or no damage has been done; usually not considered newsworthy.

**fifty-thousand watts**—The largest amount of radiated power at which AM stations may operate within the U.S. Stations which may broadcast at this power are normally located in large cities and their signals cover wide areas of the country. *(See also* kilowatt.)

**file**—*(verb)* To "file" a story is to submit it in written or spoken form to a newsroom or other agency which then prepares it for publication or broadcast.

**filler**—Small news item, usually of less importance than the major stories in a newscast, used to fill the remaining time allotted to the newscast.

**First-Class License**—Top-ranking license or "permit" granted by the Federal Communications Commission to individuals who are then authorized to operate and to make adjustments to radio or television transmitters in the U.S. *(See also* Third-Class Permit.)

**first reading**—The practice of reading proposed bills in various city, county, and state legislative bodies so that all who wish to support or oppose such bills will have a chance to become aware of the proposals and to prepare their arguments.

**flash**—The interruption of all other activity to present a news story of momentous, earth-shaking importance. Stronger than the term "bulletin," the word "flash" is saved for such events as the attack on Pearl Harbor or a Presidential assassination.

**format**—The manner in which a program is arranged so as to build identity with its desired audience, including themes and "sounders" used to introduce the program, placement of commercials, writing and delivery styles, etc. Stations also use the word "format" to describe their overall programming styles, such as "rock," "middle-of-the-road," "country," "all-news," etc.

**free-lance**—One who is not employed by the station or other agency receiving his work, but who is selling his services to any buyer. For example, a reporter covering a news story as an individual, not employed by those to whom he sells his coverage.

**futures file**—A datebook or file of events and other possibilities for news story coverage. *Futures releases:* Advance notices of events scheduled by organizations who are inviting coverage of these events as news stories.

**handout**—Written, taped, or filmed material supplied free by the organization which would like to have it published or broadcast.

**hard news**—Straight, factual news of some importance to the general public, as opposed to comment, analysis, background, or items which would be of interest only to a specialized audience.

**Hippocratic Oath**—Pledge made by medical doctors as they are admitted to practice as licensed physicians. Essential to newsmen is the part which states that anything told by a patient to a doctor may be kept secret—something which many newsmen would like to have in their own profession to enable them to protect confidential news sources, but which for journalists has been the source of some controversy.

**hold for release**—Instructions accompanying a news story which state that it not be used until a specified time or until further instructions to release it have been given. *(See also* embargo.)

**hotlines**—*See* audio hotlines.

**incident**—Simply an event or occurrence; a useful term when news reporters wish to avoid the implications of "disturbance" or of any kind of violence. *(See also* disturbance, civil disorder, demonstration, riot, etc.)

**I.D.**—Station identification.

**induction coil (induction ring)**—A term borrowed by newsmen with some modification from its original use in electrical engineering. In broadcast news, a wire device which plugs into a tape recorder at one end and in which the other end is a loop or ring which fits snugly over the mouthpiece of a telephone. News reporters filing tape-recorded actualities by phone use this device in locations where telephone mouthpieces will not unscrew to permit the use of alligator clips.

**inflammatory**—That which is likely to arouse excitement, anger, or violence.

**influentials**—Persons whose positions within a particular community enable them to persuade and to easily communicate with others, not necessarily as the result of force or authority, but as accepted leaders of opinion within the group.

**insert**—*(noun)* An insert is material which has been prepared so that it can be included within a larger body of programming, such as a small paragraph inserted into a larger news story or a tape-recorded excerpt inserted into a "wraparound" narration.

**investigative**—A type of news story compiled by following up or conducting research through careful inquiry and observation, as opposed to a news story which is based upon a happening or event. *(See also* event-oriented.)

**issues file**—A list of the major issues which are sources of public discussion or controversy in the community, ready for follow-up use whenever there are opportunities for investigative stories. *(See also* futures file.)

**jargon**—The technical or semisecret "inside" vocabulary used by members of a profession, trade, or other special group, especially when they are talking with other members of the same group.

**jocks**—Short for "disc jockeys" or "D.J.'s"; those who conduct recorded music shows on radio.

**kill**—An order to stop using certain material immediately, such as to stop using a certain story when an error has been discovered, or to immediately turn off a tape or videotape if the technical quality is too poor to broadcast.

**kilowatt**—A unit of electrical power: one thousand watts. A one-kilowatt (1-kW) AM radio station is usually one licensed to serve a small community within a radius of 25 to 30 miles, as compared with a station of higher power (up to 50,000 watts) licensed to serve large metropolitan or regional areas.

**lead**—The first or main story in a newscast, or sometimes the first or main sentence within a particular story. Also, a reporter who follows a "lead" is thoroughly checking a promising line of inquiry.

**leak**—To allow certain information to become known as if by accident; a practice often employed by those who do not wish to be identified as sources for the stories or information they are releasing in this manner.

**libel**—Any publication or broadcast which tends to expose a person to public ridicule or contempt; essentially the same as slander or defamation of character *except* that when slanderous statements are actually *broadcast* or *published* they are then classified as libelous.

**market**—In advertising, a defined community or area in which opportunities for trade can be identified by population, commercial activity, and other economic indicators. Normally the name of the nearest large city is used, but it implies the surrounding area to which an advertiser would address his message.

**minority**—A group which differs in nationality, political beliefs, religion, or racial characteristics and which is smaller than the controlling or predominant group in a particular society or community. (Examples: Negroes, Orientals, and American Indians are racial minorities within the U.S.; Jews are a significant religious minority.)

**minority coverage list**—A list of agencies and persons within a particular minority group in a station's coverage area who can be called upon to communicate effectively with news reporters when information is needed about these groups.

**minority-oriented news**—News stories about minority groups or their members.

**mistrial**—A trial which must be cancelled because of some legal error, such as improper selection of jurors or disruptive behavior which may influence jurors in a manner not acceptable under court rules.

**monitor**—A loudspeaker or TV screen which enables the listener to check a certain program source. An "on-the-air" monitor enables an engineer to determine whether the station is transmitting properly, a "cue" monitor allows a disc jockey to hear the beginning notes on a record while cueing it up, and a "network" monitor enables control-room personnel to hear the countdown and other cue signals so as to know when to throw the switch which broadcasts the network program. Also to "monitor" something is to pay attention or listen to it.

**mobile units**—In broadcasting, portable two-way communications systems, especially two-way radios mounted in cars, but the term is applied to everything from a walkie-talkie or a portable TV camera to an entire van or mobile studio filled with broadcasting equipment. Varies with each local situation.

**N.A.B.**—National Association of Broadcasters.

**narration**—*See* voice-over.

**net, network**—A system of linking a number of stations together so that they may all broadcast the same program simultaneously if desired.

**network monitor**—*See* monitor.

**neutral observers**—As opposed to merely "bystanders," neutral observers are those persons present at a news event who are likely to have worthwhile information to offer. Such people may include other news reporters or even policemen, depending upon the occasion.

**neutralize racial overtones**—To remove all hints or implications from a news story which may suggest that racial aspects had any connection whatsoever with any of the problems mentioned. For example, instead of saying that a fire occurred in a "predominantly black" neighborhood, say that it was at a certain address, leaving out any mention of "black" unless the fire has officially been described by authorities as caused by racial conflict. *(See also* racial tags.)

**objectivity**—The ability and practice of reporting upon only those characteristics of a person, thing, or situation using only terms with which almost no one would disagree, and without putting any of the reporter's own opinions into the description.

**off the record**—When certain remarks or other activities at a news conference or other news-gathering event are declared "off the record," it is understood that reporters will not publish or broadcast them. It is an arrangement which saves having to ask all reporters to leave the room or to take other hidden or inconvenient measures to avoid publicity. It is usually done *before* such remarks or actions take place, as many reporters will not agree to such a rule *after* something has happened. *(See also* background, deep background.)

**on-the-air monitor**—*See* monitor.

**out of control**—A term describing the nature of a fire which is *not* to be used on the air unless it comes from a fire official who is authorized to make such a judgment. Using this term when it is offered by eyewitnesses or others who are not qualified to draw such a conclusion can lead to trouble.

**outbreak of violence**—A potentially inflammatory term which can lead to trouble if not used properly on the air. Check to see if words like "incident" or "disturbance" would do just as well, and save words like "violence" or "riot" for use only when proper police authorities can be quoted as having made such a judgment.

**outcue**—The last few words in an actuality, a commercial, a news story, or some other section of a program. These few words are used as a signal to stop that portion and to begin the next item in the broadcast.

**patch cords**—Short lengths of flexible audio and/or video cable with plugs at each end, enabling broadcasters to connect various sources of sound (and/or picture), such as tape recorders, phones, network lines, etc., to any other electronic component, such as a control room console, another tape recorder, etc., for purposes of mixing, recording, or broadcasting.

**Photofax™ and Unifax™ machines**—Automatic printers which receive black-and-white still photographs over a wire for use in newspapers or on television. Associated Press calls its machine "Photofax," while United Press International uses the trademark "Unifax" for its receiver.

**police brutality**—*See* brutality.

**pooling**—The selection of just one reporter to cover a story on behalf of several others in cases where they cannot all be accommodated. Also, the selection of a small *group* (including cameramen and technicians) to provide coverage for their colleagues where a much larger group cannot do so or may not wish to do so for economic or other reasons.

**prior censorship**—*See* censorship.

**problem-oriented**—A type of news stories in which a great deal of attention is focused upon the problems of a particular group, as opposed to stories which describe the culture or advancement of that group, especially of a minority racial or religious group.

**promo**—An announcement inviting the audience to tune in to a particular program, as compared with **commercial announcements,** which sell goods or services, or with **public service announcements,** which are broadcast free on behalf of civic or charitable organizations.

**precautionary landing** (airplane)—A landing in which the pilot decides that quick repairs for a mechanical difficulty *(not* an emergency) would be preferable to continuing the flight. For example: loss of some oil pressure or hydraulic pressure, failure of one of the plane's several engines, etc. *(See also* emergency *and* unscheduled landings.)

**prefiled**—Advance stories which are filed with a newsroom but held for release until facts are confirmed or until a certain scheduled time or signal arrives.

**provocative**—Annoying; irritating; that which is likely to stir someone to anger. *(See also* inflammatory.)

**pseudo-events**—Not "real" events, but those which most likely have been staged or contrived so as to gain the attention of the news media. Also, routine operations of groups (such as a government office) where nothing of real news value actually happens but where reporters put a great deal of effort into writing about insignificant details in order to justify their efforts in having attempted to get a story.

**P.I.O., Public Information Officer**—The official in a government agency or large industry (for example, the CAB as it investigates a plane crash) whose job it is to talk with news reporters. This person is provided in situations where it is desirable to keep reporters out of the way of those who may be performing duties of an emergency, dangerous, or confidential nature.

**Pulitzer Prizes**—Annual awards for distinguished journalism, established in the early 1900's by Joseph Pulitzer.

**racial "tags"**—"Labels" attached verbally to persons, places or situations in a news story—usually by use of certain adjectives—which tend to suggest or even to emphasize racial aspects. The use of such tags is considered improper when used in ways that tend to discredit minorities when race is not a legitimate factor in a story. (For example, see "neutralize racial overtones.")

**radio wire**—The wire-service teletypewriter machines (especially of AP and UPI) on which the stories arrive written in a style for broadcast delivery rather than for newspaper or print media.

**ratings**—Measurements of a station's audience compared with those of its competitors during a given period, taken by statistical sampling methods.

**raw sound**—The actual sound of an event, *without* spoken words. Examples: band music, flames crackling, gunfire, sirens, crowds, etc. Similar to actualities, but with no reports, interviews, or speeches involved.

**release**—*(noun)* A report issued by an individual or organization which is seeking, or at least permitting, broadcast or publication of the information contained therein. Also, the time at which the issuing person or organization will allow the broadcast or publication to take place. *(verb)* The act of issuing a "release," as described above.

**remote lines**—Specialized lines installed by a telephone company to receive audio and/or video broadcast material from a location outside the studio.

**reverb sound**—Sound which is electronically "reflected" or reverberated to give the impression of an echo; used by some stations to create the impression that the person speaking is in a large auditorium or hall.

**riding gain**—Controlling the volume of sound by observing a meter (a "V.U." or Volume Unit meter) which measures its loudness, and by making suitable adjustments with a volume control knob or "pot."

**riot**—A term which should *not* be broadcast as the description of a disturbance unless authorized police officials using it can be quoted by name. A riot is a wild, violent public disturbance in which lives and property are endangered. *(See also* disturbance, incident, demonstration, civil disorder.)

**rip and call**—The practice of constantly taking stories from a wire-service machine and calling people who are named in those stories in order to get their voices on tape. Often this serves only to embellish the story but adds little or no new information to the wire-service version. It is done by some stations to create the impression that they, not the wire service, originated the story.

**rip and read**—To take material directly from the wire-service teletypewriters and to read it on the air with little or no attempt at editing, rewriting, or checking facts.

**RTNDA**—Radio-TV News Directors Association.

**running story**—A story which has been in the news for some time, and upon which new developments are reported in the form of "updates," "new tops," or "new leads," as the wire services call them.

**seal-off**—When a civil disturbance is in progress, an order to seal the area off is one given by police to surround that area in order to contain the violence. Persons are not allowed to enter or leave the sealed-off area except under specific police-enforced conditions.

**sensationalism**—The use of certain style, language, subject matter, or other tactics of expression with the intention of shocking, startling, exciting, thrilling, or otherwise arousing the audience. Such tactics used in newscasting may occasionally raise a station's audience ratings for a short period, but in the long run it is believed by many that stations using such practices risk gaining reputations as irresponsible and untrustworthy media.

**sequestration**—The practice of "locking up" a jury so that its members will not hear or read news reports about the alleged crime, about the defendant, or about the trial itself.

**signal strength**—The strength of a radio station or television station as received at a given distance.

**single track**—A monaural tape recording, in which only one track of sound is present on the recording tape.

**Sixth Amendment**—The Sixth Amendment to the United States Constitution, which guarantees a fair trial. Often, in the view of journalists, this conflicts with the First Amendment's "freedom of the press" guarantee.

**slant, slanting**—An opinion or point of view injected into a story in a somewhat "hidden" manner, as compared with "editorializing," in which the views are outspoken.

**snipers sniping,**—Persons firing weapons at others from *hidden* positions, with intent to kill. (Do not use "sniper" to describe persons who are carrying weapons out in the open.)

**source**—A person from whom information is or may be obtained.

**spot**—A commercial or public service announcement on radio or TV.

**staged events**—News events which apparently would not have occurred naturally, but which are "put on" or at least embellished for the benefit of the news media.

**standby**—Substitute or back-up version of a story, usually written without film or tape involved, which can be read to the audience in case a film or tape fails to play on the air.

**stand-up report, "standupper"**—TV news report in which the reporter is seen facing the camera with the scene of the event itself in the background. It may be live, filmed, or videotaped.

**stigmatized**—Way of describing or characterizing which tends to cause disgrace or embarrassment. *(See also* racial "tags.")

**stringer**—A part-time reporter who usually works outside the studio and who often is paid on a "free-lance" basis for the material he submits rather than on a salaried or hourly basis.

**subpoena**—A court document which legally orders a person to appear and to testify.

**tag**—A short phrase or sentence which is added to recorded material, such as in a commercial. Example: "They're open tonight 'til nine."

**tap**—In on-the-scene broadcast reporting, to make a temporary connection to existing amplification facilities, such as hooking up alligator clips to an auditorium P.A. system, in order to obtain a sourch of actualities for recording or broadcast purposes.

**teletype**™, **teletypewriter**—Teletype™ is a trademark for a kind of teletypewriter machine similar to those used by AP and UPI wire services, although the one bearing the trademark is probably most commonly found in the form of the "TWX" machine, upon which there is a keyboard for use in returning messages. The ordinary newsroom teletypewriter looks very much like a covered typewriter, but receives electrical impulses which have been sent over a telephone or telegraph line by the news organization which is supplying the stories.

**Third-Class FCC License**—Officially called a "Third-Class Broadcast Operator Permit" by the FCC, it allows the holder to operate the transmitters of certain AM and FM stations, provided he has passed an examination on basic law, operating practice, and broadcast regulations. *(See also* First-Class License.)

**tight**—1. Well-produced with no noticeable pauses and with smooth transition between the various elements of the program. 2. Also with practically all of the available time filled, so that it would be difficult to add any further material.

**trade-out**—In broadcasting, the purchase of equipment or services in exchange for commercials on the station, not for cash. Example: buying a car for the news department and paying for it by running a certain number of commercials for the auto dealer

**unbiased**—As fair and objective as humanly possible; without purposely selecting or leaving out just certain facts or issues so as to convey an opinion. *(See also* objectivity.)

**Unifax™ machine**—*See* Photofax.

**unscheduled landing** (airplane)—A landing involving a situation in which there is nothing wrong with the airplane itself. Examples: sick passenger, birth of a baby, even hijacking. Do *not* use the term "emergency" landing to describe these situations. *(See also* emergency *and* precautionary landings.)

**UPI**—United Press International; a wire-service news organization used by many broadcast newsrooms in the U.S.

**verbatim**—Word for word, without making any changes.

**verification**—The process of checking, investigating, or confirming information to be certain that it is true.

**vested interest**—An established connection or commitment toward something so as to have a special interest in protecting it.

**video**—The electronic picture which is transmitted or received in television, *not* including audio, which is the electronic sound transmitted or received in both radio and television.

**videotape**—Magnetic tape upon which both video (picture) and audio (sound) can be recorded for playback on television. Also used as a verb: "The report was videotaped for playback during the newscast."

**voicer, voice report**—A packaged description of a news event by a reporter, delivered in that reporter's voice. It may be done "live" or on tape, and it may be "ad-libbed" from memory or direct observation, or it may be read from a written script.

**voice-over, V.O.**—A voice report, as above, plus the raw sound of the event which is being described presented as a background for the voicer. The raw sound behind the voice report may be the event itself in progress, or it may be a tape of that event played in the background to fit a reconstructed or rewritten description.

**voir dire examination**—Questions asked by lawyers for both the prosecution and defense (and sometimes by the judge) to determine whether a person is fit to serve on a jury. As applied to the "Free Press versus Fair Trial" issue, the questions may be specifically to determine whether or not the person has already made up his mind about the case because of having heard or read news reports about it.

**VTR**—Video Tape Recorder (the machine), and Video Tape Recording (the tape, or material played back from a videotape).

**wall-to-wall music**—A style of music format used by some radio stations in which mostly instrumental music is played continuously, often as a background, with very few interruptions for commercials, news, or spoken comments.

**WATS line**—A term used by telephone companies to describe a billing arrangement for long-distance calls. The user of such a line pays a one-time flat fee instead of paying for the long-distance charges on each individual call. The letters stand for "Wide Area Toll System."

**whip antenna**—A large radio antenna which sticks up into the air from a car or other object upon which it is mounted, and which resembles a whip in appearance.

**wire service**—A news organization which transmits its copy by means of a teletypewriter and other machines over wires leased from the telephone company.

**wraparounds**—Voice descriptions of news events which include the insertion of an actuality. The actuality is usually a statement made by someone involved in the story.

**wrapup**—A summary or concluding item in a newscast which will bring the program to its close; the term may also be used by some stations as a synonym for "roundup," which is an entire program in which a number of news stories have been packaged together as a news summary.

# Bibliography

Aircraft Owners and Pilots Association. *AOPA Airport Directory 19—* Washington, D.C.: AOPA, annual.

American Bar Association Project on Minimum Standards for Criminal Justice, Paul C. Reardon, Chmn. *Standards Relating to Fair Trial and Free Press.* New York: A.B.A., 1968.

Associated Press. *The Associated Press Radio-Television News Style Book.* New York: A.P., 1962 and 1973.

Association of the Bar of the City of New York, Harold R. Medina, Chmn. *Freedom of the Press and Fair Trial.* New York: Columbia University Press, 1967.

Aviation/Space Writers Association. *The Newsman and Air Accidents.* Sarasota, Fla.: A.W.A., 1966.

Barrett, Lawrence I., and Eisen, Gail. "Covering Watergate: Success and Backlash," *Time* magazine, July 8, 1974.

Barrett, Marvin, ed. *The Alfred I. DuPont–Columbia University Survey of Broadcast Journalism 1968-1969.* New York: Grosset and Dunlap, 1969.

Bernstein, Carl, and Woodward, Bob. *All the President's Men.* New York: Simon & Schuster, 1974.

Bernstein, Theodore M. *Watch Your Language.* New York: Simon & Schuster, 1965.

Broadcasting Publication, Inc. *Broadcasting* magazine. Washington, D.C.: various issues, published weekly.

Broadcasting Publication, Inc. *Broadcasting Yearbook.* Washington, D.C.: published annually.

Brown, Claude. *Manchild in the Promised Land.* New York: Macmillan, 1965.

Brownson, Charles B., ed. *Congressional Staff Directory.* Washington, D.C.: The Congressional Staff Directory, Inc., published annually since 1959.

Bush, Chilton R. *Newswriting and Reporting Public Affairs.* 2nd ed., Philadelphia: Chilton, 1970.

CBS News. *Television News Reporting.* New York: McGraw-Hill, 1958.

Chaffee, Zechariah. *Government and Mass Communication.* Chicago: University of Chicago Press, 1947.

Cohen, Richard M., and Whitcover, Jules. *A Heartbeat Away: The Investigation and Resignation of Vice President Spiro T. Agnew.* Washington, D.C.: The Washington Post Co., 1974.

Coleman, Howard W. *Case Studies in Broadcast Management.* New York: Hastings House, 1970.

"Columbia Survey of Broadcast Journalism." (*See* Barrett, Marvin, ed.)

Dary, David A. *How to Write News for Broadcast and Print Media.* Blue Ridge Summit, Pa.: TAB Books, 1973.

Dary, David A. *Radio News Handbook.* Blue Ridge Summit, Pa.: TAB Books, 1970.

Dary, David A. *Television News Handbook.* Blue Ridge Summit, Pa.: TAB Books, 1971.

Effron, Edith. *The News Twisters.* New York: Manor Books, Inc., 1972.

Emery, Michael C., and Smythe, Ted Curtis. *Readings in Mass Communication: Concepts and Issues in the Mass Media.* Dubuque, Iowa: Wm. C. Brown Co., 1972.

Epstein, Benjamin R., and Forster, Arnold. *"Some of My Best Friends . . ."* New York: Farrar, Straus and Cudahy, 1962.

Epstein, Benjamin R., and Forster, Arnold. *The Radical Right: Report on the John Birch Society and its Allies.* New York, Random House, 1967; and Vintage Books, 1967.

Famous Writers School. *Famous Writers Course: Nonfiction Writing Volume IV.* Westport, Conn.: Famous Writers School, Inc., 1960.

Federal Communication Commission. *Third-Class Broadcast Operator Permit Study Guide.* Washington, D.C.: U.S. Government Printing Office, 1974.

Franklin, O. Thomas. *Broadcasting the News.* New York: Pageant Press, Inc., 1954.

Freed, Donald. *Agony in New Haven.* New York: Simon & Schuster, 1973.

Freedom of Information Center, University of Missouri. *Fair Trial and Press: A Dialogue.* Columbia, Missouri: University of Missouri, 1967.

Freedom of Information Committee, National Association of Broadcasters. *Broadcasting the News: an Operational Guide.* Washington, D.C.: N.A.B., 1958.

Friendly, Alfred, and Goldfarb, Ronald L. *Crime and Publicity: The Impact of News on the Administration of Justice.* New York: Twentieth Century, 1967.

Friendly, Fred W. *Due to Circumstances Beyond Our Control.* New York: Random House, 1967; and Vintage Books, 1967.

Frost, Richard H. *The Mooney Case.* Stanford, California: Stanford University Press, 1968.

Gillmor, Donald M. *Free Press and Fair Trial.* Washington, D.C.: Public Affairs Press, 1966.

Gillmor, Donald M. and Barron, Jerome A. *Mass Communication Law: Cases and Comment.* St. Paul, Minn.: West Publishing Co., 1969.

Green, Maury. *Television News: Anatomy and Process.* Belmont, Calif.: Wadsworth, 1969.

Grunwald, Henry. "Don't Love the Press, But Understand It: Time Essay," *Time* magazine, July 8, 1974.

Hayakawa, S. I. *Language in Thought and Action.* 3rd ed., New York: Harcourt Brace Jovanovich, 1972.

Hilliard, Robert. *Writing for Television and Radio.* 2nd ed. New York: Hastings House, 1967.

Hohenberg, John. *The Professional Journalist.* 3rd ed. New York: Holt, Rinehart and Winston, 1973.

Holmes, Paul Allen. *The Candy Murder Case.* New York: Bantam Books, 1966.

Kaplan, John, and Waltz, Jon R. *The Trial of Jack Ruby.* New York: Macmillan, 1965.

Kendrick, Alexander. *Prime Time: The Life of Edward R. Murrow.* Boston: Little-Brown, 1969.

Lippman, Walter. *Public Opinion.* New York: Free Press. 1965.

Lofton, John. *Justice and the Press.* Boston: Beacon, 1966.

Mayer, Martin. "The Challengers," 3-part series in *TV Guide,* Vol. 21, Nos. 5, 6, 7 (February, 1973). Radnor, Pa.: Triangle Publications, 1973.

Mayo, John B., Jr. *Bulletin From Dallas: The President Is Dead.* New York: Exposition Press, 1967.

McGinniss, Joe. *The Selling of the President, 1968.* New York: Trident Press, 1969; Pocket Books, 1972.

Medina Report. (*See* Association of the Bar of the City of New York.)

Nadelson, Regina. *Who is Angela Davis? The Biography of a Revolutionary.* New York: P. H. Wyden, 1972.

National Advisory Commission on Civil Disorders ("Kerner Commission") *Report of the National Advisory Commission on Civil Disorders.* New York: Bantam Books, 1968.

National Association of Broadcasters. *Careers in Radio.* Washington, D.C.: N.A.B., 1965.

National Association of Broadcasters. *Careers in Television.* Washington, D.C.: N.A.B., 1965.

National Commission on the Causes and Prevention of Violence ("Walker Report"). *Rights in Conflict.* New York: New American Library, 1968.

Nelson, Harold L., and Teeter, Dwight L., Jr. *Law of Mass Communications: Freedom and Control of Broadcast and Print Media.* Mineola, New York: Foundation Press, Inc., 1973.

Newman, Edwin. "Fit to Print: A Treasury of Journalism's Hack Phrases and Labored Points," *Atlantic Monthly,* October 1974.

New York Federal Executive Board Public Information Committee. *A Directory of Public Information Representatives in the Federal Establishment: Greater New York Area.* New York: N. Y. Federal Executive Board, c/o U.S. Atomic Energy Commission, published periodically.

Nisbett, Alec. *The Techniques of the Sound Studio for Radio, Television and Film.* 3rd ed., rev. New York: Hastings House, 1972.

Office of Collective Bargaining (New York City), Edward J. Silverfarb, ed. *Directory of New York City Public Employee Organizations.* New York: Office of Collective Bargaining, published annually.

Oringel, Robert S. *Audio Control Handbook for Radio and Television.* 4th ed., rev. New York: Hastings House, 1972.

Peterson, Wilbur. "Helps for Radio Station News Correspondents," (leaflet). Iowa City: University of Iowa, 1964.

Price, Monroe, and Wicklein, John. *Cable Television: A Guide for Citizen Action.* Philadelphia: Pilgrim Press, 1972.

Public Relations Officers Society of New York. *Directory of Public Relations Contacts in Government Agencies in New York City.* New York: PROS, published annually.

Quaal, Ward A., and Martin, Leo A. *Broadcast Management.* New York: Hastings House, 1968.

Reardon Report. (*See* American Bar Association.)

Reinsch, J. Leonard, and Ellis, E. I. *Radio Station Management.* 2nd rev. ed. New York: Harper & Row, 1960.

Rivers, William L.; Peterson, Theodore; and Jensen, Jay W. *The Mass Media and Modern Society.* San Francisco: Rinehart Press, 1971.

Rivers, William L., and Schramm, Wilbur. *Responsibility in Mass Communication.* rev. ed. New York: Harper & Row, 1969.

Roe, Yale, ed. *Television Station Management: The Business of Broadcasting.* New York: Hastings House, 1964.

Schramm, Wilbur. *Men, Messages and Media: A Look at Human Communication.* New York: Harper & Row, 1973.

Seng, R. A., and Gilmour, G. V. *Brink's—The Money Movers.* Chicago: Lakeside Press, 1959.

Siegenthaler, John, and Ritter, Frank. *A Search for Justice.* Nashville: Aurora, 1971.

Strunk, William, Jr., and White, E. B. *The Elements of Style.* 2nd ed. New York: Macmillan, 1972.

United Press International. *United Press International Broadcast Stylebook.* New York: UPI, 1966 and 1969.

University of Missouri, Freedom of Information Center. *Race and the News Media* (symposium). Columbia: University of Missouri, 1968.

White, Paul W. *News On the Air.* New York: Harcourt-Brace, 1947.

Wood, William. *Electronic Journalism.* New York: Columbia University Press, 1967.

# index

# Index*

*Page numbers in italics refer to investigative projects.